Rhododendrons and Azaleas

*R.* 'Lady Rosebery'

# Rhododendrons and Azaleas

⫸⫸⫸⫸⫸⫸⫸⫸⫸⫸⫸⫸⫸⫷⫷⫷⫷⫷⫷⫷⫷⫷⫷⫷⫷⫷⫷

JUDITH BERRISFORD

FABER AND FABER
LONDON

*First published in 1964*
*This New and Revised Edition*
*Published 1973*
*by Faber and Faber Limited*
*3 Queen Square London WC1*
*Printed in Great Britain by*
*Butler & Tanner Ltd., Frome and London*

ISBN 0 571 04798 X

To the memory of Mr. and Mrs. A. T. Johnson,
who, by giving me the freedom of their garden, widened
the gate to rhododendron bliss

# Acknowledgements

❯❯❯❯❯❯❯❯❯❮❮❮❮❮❮❮❮❮

One of the most pleasant things about rhododendrons is the way in which other addicts are always ready to come to one's aid. In the writing of this book my thanks are especially due to Mr. Charles Puddle, V.M.H., Superintendent of Bodnant Gardens, who patiently read through my manuscript and, from the depth of his boundless knowledge and very kind heart, made many helpful suggestions and amendments; to Dr. Henry Tod of the Edinburgh School of Agriculture, for answering the many questions arising from a non-scientist's research into the problems of growing rhododendrons and azaleas on limy soils, and for so kindly checking the relevant chapters; to Mr. David Leach of U.S.A., author of *Rhododendrons of the World*, for going to much trouble to explain to me the probable evolution of the azalea series and for giving me permission to quote from his work; to Mr. A. Sigston Thompson, Honorary Director of the Northern Horticultural Society's Gardens at Harlow Car, Yorkshire, who greatly helped by reporting his findings on the hardiness of various species and hybrids under exposed conditions; to Lord Aberconway, President of the R.H.S., for so generously allowing me to visit the gardens at Bodnant during the winter and early spring when they are not normally open but when many rewarding rhododendrons are in flower; to the Librarian and staff of the Lindley Library of the R.H.S.; and to all those owners of lovely rhododendrons and azalea plantings who have welcomed me into their gardens.

7

# Acknowledgements

I am grateful, too, to Mr. Richard de la Mare for giving me the chance to write about my favourite genus, to Mr. Lawrence Hills from whom the scheme for this book originated, to Mr. Downward, Mr. Woodland, and to Mr. Graham Thomas, my valued friend and adviser, for allowing me to use their excellent photographs.

Mr. Roy Lancaster of Hilliers Nurseries, Winchester, has been kind enough to check through the nomenclature and bring it up to date and in line with the latest rulings, for this new and revised edition, and I am most grateful for his help in this rather troubled field!

J. M. B.

# Contents

꽈꽈꽈꽈꽈

## Part One

## Part Two

9

# Illustrations

⫸⫸⫸⫸⫸⫷⫷⫷⫷⫷

## COLOUR PLATES

## MONOCHROME PLATES

Acknowledgement is made to the following photographers: Dennis Woodland for the cover illustration, frontispiece and plate

## *Illustrations*

I; J. E. Downward for plates II and III, in colour, and black and white plates 1, 9, 10, 11, 12, 13, 16, 18, 19, 20, 21, 22, 26, 27, 28, 29, 30, 31, 32, 33; G. S. Thomas for plates 2, 3, 4, 5, 6, 7, 8, 14, 15, 17, 23, 24, 25.

# PART I

꙳꙳꙳꙳꙳꙳꙳

CHAPTER 1

# Rhododendrons in the Wild

Older than time and, like the camellias, descended from the giant tree magnolias, the rhododendrons comprise an exotic genus of primitive plants. Many millions of years ago the race had its beginnings in the Sino-Himalaya—the eastern region of the Himalayas, its extension into North Burma and into the Yunnan and Szechuan provinces of South-West China. From this cradle, where even today the flux of evolution continues and as many as three hundred and twenty species may be found in one small area, the rhododendrons spilled outwards—their prodigious quantities of seeds borne on every chance current of air. Aided by the changing contours of the cooling earth's crust, they spread across Asia to Europe by way of the Black Sea and the Caucasus, southwards to Indonesia and the Philippines, establishing their outpost in Northern Australia, and east and north through China, across the land bridge that then existed north of the Bering Strait into America, thence down along the Rockies to Florida and south-east Texas.

Fifty-million-year-old fossils show that the rhododendrons originally found in America were of the same type as those growing in China today. The present-day American rhododendron species, *catawbiense*, *albiflorum* and *carolinianum*, as well as those of the North American azaleas have evolved through the ages from the more primitive Sino-Himalayan types. In Europe and Asia Minor, one may suppose a similar evolution has given rise to *Rhododendron caucasicum* and *ponticum*, that eastern escapee that has settled itself within our islands and overrun so many British woodlands, making them its home.

Ranging from the large-leaved giants of the monsoon rain forests, through the smaller species and undershrubs of the pine forests and mountain scrub, to the spreading dwarfs that carpet the moorlands, rhododendrons show more variation within their family than any other genus. Basically similar, the blossoms and leaves vary in scale to the size of the plant. The bright and airy little trusses of the members of the moorland Lapponicum series resist the full force of winds that would instantly tatter and brown the papery flower-delicacy of the forest-reared *R. diaprepes*. As the rhododendrons climb above the tree line so the leaves, too, decrease in size, offering less surface for the winds to sear and dry, until at one end of the scale we have the little lavender-blue *R. intricatum* of the Lapponicum series with leaves under half-an-inch long while, down in the steamy moisture of the rain forests, the giant *R. sinogrande* may have leaves three feet or more in length.

The question of leaf size is bound up with the moisture need of the plants. Small-leaved species inhabit the drier, colder regions of the mountains and need but little water from the atmosphere. Yet even they have their roots in the well-drained but spongy, moisture-retaining peat. Others hug the rocks but their fine, fibrous roots probe beneath the boulders and into the cliff crevices to catch and use any available moisture. In winter, when icy breezes sweep across the moors and mountain tops, the little rhododendrons crouch together, each protecting the other in mats and carpets of solid growth. Farther down the mountain the medium-leaved species furl their leaves into quills, reducing their leaf area and at the same time shielding the stomata, through which excess moisture transpires, from the drying cold. At the same time many species hang their leaves to shed the snow and to shield their vulnerable trunks and bark from the frost. Many species have scales, devised to prevent excessive moisture-loss on the under surface of the leaves. Shaped like tiny cups with flat covers, these scales are so small as to be only just perceptible. The naked human eye sees them only as dark dots. In some species, the scales are carried on short stalks, leaving an area into which excess water vapour may be given off during the over-wet rainy season. Overlapping to form a sheath, they shield the underside of the leaf and so protect the stomata from the drying winds of the cold season. At the same time they prevent the heavy rain of the wet season from covering the under surface of the leaves and sealing the stomata so that necessary transpiration is prevented.

In the monsoon regions, where most of the nine-hundred-and-ninety-odd known species are found and from which all the rhododendrons of the world have come, there are three main seasons. The cold dry winter begins in November to be followed by two warm months in April and May, during which most of the rhododendrons flower, and a rainy season from June to October when the vegetation steams beneath the heavy downpour of the monsoon. The rhododendrons therefore have to be able to adapt themselves to each of these conditions—to lift their leaves to catch and take advantage of sudden warm showers in times of drought or to curl up and hang dispirited, protecting themselves from the effects of cold. Not all rhododendrons have scales. In the elepidote (without scales) section, the scales are replaced by hairs or papillae—closely spaced waxy pegs off which the water runs. When papillae are present the under surface of the leaves is always dry and so water cannot seal the stomata and prevent transpiration.

In some hairy-leaved species the hairs are close enough to form a woolly indumentum. This sheds water and also acts as a blanket allowing a sheltered air-space into which the water vapour can continuously be given off. In some species the hairs themselves give off water to aid transpiration when the atmosphere is over-humid.

Altitude as such plays a great part in the distribution of rhododendrons. Comparatively few come from the really hot equatorial and tropical regions. Those that do, live in the mountains where altitude reduces the temperature. There the epiphytic species grow upon trees, perched like orchids in the forks of the branches or rooting into cracks in the bark where an accumulation of spongy moss, fallen leaves and other debris provides nourishment and a congenial root-hold. Here, too, they are nearer the light and air and their scented pale blossoms shine through the green jungle gloom and lure pollinating insects and birds to their nectaries. Such species are to be found in Malaysia, Indonesia and the Philippines. In cultivation they must be grown in hothouses.

Epiphytic species are to be found also in the forests of Burma, in Sikkim and Bhutan, at a height of about 4,000 feet. At such comparatively low altitude the rhododendrons are small, scattered and few. They are unused to frost and in Britain the species from these areas will grow and thrive out of doors only in those parts of Cornwall, the Western Isles of Scotland and the west and southwest of Ireland that are most influenced by the warm Gulf Stream current. Elsewhere they need to be in a cool greenhouse.

In their natural home, as the altitude increases so the rhododendron population increases in size and numbers until at 7,000 feet in the Assam Himalayas, as that great plant hunter, Frank Kingdom Ward wrote, 'one climbs through thickets of *triflorum*, *souliei* and *taliense*' into forests of the large-leaved *grande*, the bristly-haired scarlet *barbatum*, glowing crimson *thomsonii* and *lacteum* to emerge at 11,000 feet into the alpine region where there are 'seas of sulphur, carmine and rose-pink. Rivers of purple *lapponicum* flow into lakes of brick-red, lemon and snow-white *anthopogon*; strains of cherry-brandy *glaucum*, clumps of merry little pouting *campylogynum*, pink and plum purple, are plastered like swallows' nests against the grey cliffs, and pools of canary yellow *trichocladum* glow from the brown grass slopes. Along the snow-fed streams the twin flowers of a royal purple *saluenense* nod in rising spate!'

Rhododendrons are mainly plants of the monsoon forests, the mountain valleys, and moorlands where the rainfall is high and the temperature too low for the fallen leaves to rot down quickly. The humus decays so slowly that it builds up in layers of acid peat, the nutriment content of which is so limited that the plants living there have had to adapt their nourishment needs accordingly. This somewhat limits the competition for space and, combined with their extremely free-seeding and colonizing habit, results in the dominant and ever increasing hold that rhododendrons have upon the vegetation of south-west China and the eastern Himalayas.

Even more astonishing than their numbers is their extreme variety. This is no doubt due to the great age of the genus. As mentioned at the beginning of this chapter, rhododendrons have been growing, blooming and regenerating in the wild over many millions of years; so naturally there are many variations. For not only do the members of the species breed and rebreed within themselves but, although various opinions have been expressed to the contrary, there is no doubt that they cross also with nearly allied species. For instance, in the Thomsonii series the two species *stewartianum* and *eclecteum* are found in south-east Tibet, Yunnan, north-eastern Upper Burma and Assam growing in rhododendron thickets, mixed scrub and on the open mountainside. These species resemble each other closely but a reliable guide to identity lies in the length of leaf-petiole which is much greater in *stewartianum*. Other differences concern the colour and texture of the under-surface of the leaves—light, grey-green and hairy in *stewartianum*, dark green and glabrous in *eclecteum*. The territories of these two species overlap and, as might be expected, hybridization has given rise to several intermediate forms of leaf and to colours ranging from white through yellow and champagne to many shades of pink, to rose and even scarlet often with a band of one of the contrasting colours rimming the bells. Other series in which hybridization is apparent are the Triflorum and the Lapponicum.

Colour variation at least may also be accounted for by the presence of albinos which occur in rhododendron species as in most other wild flowers, viz.: the white Herb Robert and white campion of this country. The albinos cross with the type, and seedlings of intermediate colour result. In rhododendrons this is easily shown by reference to the species *arboreum* where besides the lovely blood-red of the type, a white form is often found together with various pink forms that are obviously the offspring of the red and the white.

Variations between the species are influenced by the physical habitats in which they grow. For instance, the east and west sides of the same valley may have entirely different rhododendron populations. The species change, merging one into the other, as conditions change. Some are so nearly alike that it is easy to see how they have adapted themselves to more sheltered or more exposed habitats, to shade or to sun. The low-growing *forrestii* var. *repens* with its blood-red bells and rock-hugging, mounded growth is found on exposed cliffs. In sheltered crannies and gullies, where the snow lies longer, it is replaced by its sub-species *chamaedoxa* and *chamaethauma* which, though still having the same blood-red bells to attract pollinating insects across the vast mountain spaces, are taller and slightly less hard in leaf. Protected longer by their blanket of snow and sheltered by the cliffs, they have not the same need to cower close to the rock to dodge the force of the elements. In the same way the quaint, little, thimble-flowered *campylogynum* varies in height from two inches to two feet or more, according to the degree of exposure or shelter in which it is found. In sunnier places it is replaced by the duller-flowered *tsangpoense* (which although placed by the botanists in a different series—Glaucophyllum—does in fact resemble it closely). Dark of blossom, *tsangpoense* relies upon the aromatic scent of its sun-warmed foliage to attract the insects that pollinate it.

Perhaps more than in the case of any other genus, the rhododendrons are, in shape, flower colour or scent, form of leaf, root system, and dietary needs entirely the product of their natural environment. It is, therefore, by a close study of their habitat in the wild that we get the most reliable clues to their needs in cultivation.

Dwellers as they are in forests or on mountains, in the garden they enjoy cool, moist peaty or woodsy soil. They like a loose, coarse, rooting medium than ensures aeration at their roots but which does not induce drought. Even the dwarf members of the Lapponicum, Saluenense and Anthopogon series which grow above the tree line with full exposure to the mountain sun and wind have always moist peaty conditions at their roots just as have the heath and ling on the mountains and moorlands of our own country. Like the heaths, the dwarf rhododendron species grow close together forming solid mats and carpets of plants, sheltering each other and reducing their exposure to wind, and at the same time blanketing the ground and so keeping down the rate of moisture-evaporation from the soil. This gives some indication as to the way in which the dwarf rhododendrons should be grown in our gardens.

The rhododendron regions of the world are places of copious moisture—often of tropical heat tempered by altitude or shade, and by rain. On the exposed moorlands and mountains the dwarfs are sheltered from the drying cold in winter by a blanket of snow. They emerge to enjoy a warm spring amid the moisture of the melting snows followed by a wet summer. In the rain forests below, however, frost is seldom known and the large-leaved members of the Grande and Falconeri series are often the dominant trees with an undergrowth of dwarf bamboo. Although they grow at a height of perhaps only 8,000 or 8,500 feet in the hot districts, the heat is tempered by the forest shade, by summer fogs and by the monsoon rains. The large-leaved rhododendrons need a great deal of moisture and a humid atmosphere. For this reason they succeed best in the moister west and south-west of the British Isles. Wherever they are grown, their big, heavy leaves must have wind shelter. In dry gardens they succeed only by water—in well-drained soil at the edge of a stream or pool, and they are particularly subject to frost damage. A specimen of *Rhododendron falconeri* at Bodnant,* in the dell which at times does seem to hold the frost, in the winter of 1961–2 was almost defoliated by icy winds and although it later recovered the plant had received a severe check and shock which if repeated often might cause its death.

Rhododendrons of more moderate size such as *griersonianum* and *stewartianum* cluster together in rhododendron thickets and forest clearings at higher elevations, clearly showing their need

---

* This plant was again badly frosted in 1962–3 but by January 1964 had made fair new growth and seemed as if it would again recover well. Other plants in the same garden with better air drainage near the upper reaches of a stream and planted very close to the water survived both winters untouched.

for wind shelter and the association of other plants. In the provinces of Hupeh and parts of Szechuan, tall rhododendrons of the fairly large-leaved Fortunei series such as *sutchuenense* and *fargesii* are found in the woodlands. Flowering early, in February and March, when grown in this country they need at least an approximation of woodland shelter.

In cultivation, rhododendrons fall into two distinct types, the more vigorous growers between twelve and forty feet with medium to large leaves which need moisture, wind shelter and shade, and the dwarfs which, given enough moisture at their roots and some shade in the south, will stand full exposure to wind and weather. In between are species such as *dichroanthum* and *haematodes* which grow as low bushes on the lower mountain slopes or dwell in the open Alpine meadows where lilies and meconopses are also found. These are fairly easy to accommodate in the garden although too much shade will make them leggy.

Because of the very acid soils in which they grow in the wild, rhododendrons have adapted themselves to exist on such elements as are found therein (iron, manganese, magnesium, etc.). In calcareous limestone and chalky regions these foods are often locked in the soil and so rhododendrons starve, their leaves turn yellow and they die. Sometimes, however, plant collectors have reported finding various rhododendron species growing actually upon limestone formations. Often the limestone has been magnesian limestone; occasionally it has been calcareous. One or two species, notably *hirsutum*, the hairy-leaved form of the European *alpenrose*, are found on formations of calcareous limestone while in cultivation magnesian limestone offers little difficulty to successful rhododendron growing because the magnesium cancels out the calcium, leaving the essential elements available to the plant.

Calcareous limestone and chalk, however, present a problem. This will be dealt with fully in the chapter on rhododendrons and lime. Here it is enough to say that the areas of calcareous limestone on which rhododendrons of calcifuge species were found growing in the wild were in districts of heavy rainfall and excellent drainage where existed a top layer of acid peat deposits while the calcium was leached away by rain. In such areas in this country, especially on the calcareous limestone hills around Colwyn Bay in North Wales, rhododendrons of various kinds grow happily and without chemical help.

# CHAPTER 2

# Garden Rhododendrons

Older than history the rhododendron race may be, but it was not until 1656 that we hear of a rhododendron in cultivation in Britain—the dwarf *R. hirsutum* that is found growing on calcareous limestone in the European Alps, with its neat, hairy evergreen leaves and small but showy racemose heads of funnel-shaped, rosy-red flowers. Its fellow, the similar but acid-soil dwelling, non-hairy *R. ferrugineum* (the second of the two species known as *alpenrosen*) did not reach Britain until 1752.

Yet charming and attractive though these two species are, their coming did little to affect the future of the rhododendron race. More important to present-day gardeners was the introduction of the tall white North American *R. maximum* in 1736 followed by the common mauve *R. ponticum* in 1763. The winter-flowering, rosy-purple azalea-like *R. dauricum* arrived in 1780 followed by the magnificent blood-red Himalayan, *R. arboreum* in 1796. *R. caucasicum* reached us in 1803 and the ultra-hardy, often crudely coloured American *R. catawbiense* in 1809. *R. campanulatum* arrived from the Himalayas in 1825 but its worth was not at once recognized and the first hybrids raised by enthusiastic nurserymen, who realized the garden value of these colourful evergreen shrubs, were bred mainly from *R. maximum*, the glamorous *R. arboreum* into which it was hoped to infuse hardier blood, the tough, neat-habited little *R. caucasicum*, the rather

26

straggly, slightly less hardy *R. ponticum*, and *R. catawbiense* (in its varying forms of magenta, purple and white) which was used to give hardiness and a late-flowering habit by which it was hoped to dodge the May frosts.

Among the hybrids so raised between 1820 and 1850 was *R. (maximum × arboreum)* 'Lady Eleanor Cathcart'—a plant the beauty of whose peachy-pink flowers has now been surpassed but which had the asset of unassailable hardiness and which is still worth growing as a foliage plant for the elegance of its long strap-like leaves. Other hybrids were the valuable winter-flowering *R. (caucasicum × arboreum)* 'Nobleanum' group and the now-surpassed 'Prince Camille de Rohan' and 'Cunningham's White'. At the same time appeared the still good 'Cunningham's Sulphur' which was probably a yellow-flowered *caucasicum* clone, whose full potential in hybridizing has yet to be realized, and the pleasant double-flowered lavender 'Fastuosum Flore Pleno' which many think to be a double-flowered clone of *R. catawbiense*.

The years from 1850 to 1860 were occupied by the crossing and recrossing of these early hybrids back to the basic species with the object of stabilizing a late-flowering habit and to give greater hardiness combined with improved flower colour and trusses. This second crop of hybrids included such well-known ironclads as 'Cynthia', 'Doncaster', 'Lady Clementine Mitford' and the dark-blotched, white 'Sappho'.

So far rhododendron hybridizing was carried out mainly by nurserymen wishing to improve their wares. However, in 1847 Sir Joseph Hooker visited the Sikkim Himalayas where he discovered forty-five new rhododendron species and brought back seed which he distributed to those of his friends and acquaintances who had large gardens in favourable climates. Among other gardens, seed reached Carclew and Penjerrick in Cornwall, Leonardslee in Sussex, Culzean Castle and Logan in south-west Scotland and Stonefield in Argyll.

Private garden owners in this country were taking an interest in plant breeding and introduction. Sir Joseph Hooker's Himalayan expedition caught and fired their imagination, and at about the same time Robert Fortune, who had been sent to China to collect plants for the Royal Horticultural Society, began to send back rhododendron descriptions and seed.

Perhaps the greatest stir was caused by the introduction from the Himalayas of the scented, pale pink *R. griffithianum* with its large, glamorous flowers. *R. griffithianum* was too tender for all but the very mildest British gardens and so the nurserymen and private enthusiasts began to cross it in the hope of combining its great beauty with the hardiness of the original hybrids. Mated to the old *catawbiense* hybrids, *R. griffithianum* produced among others 'George Hardy' the parent of the famous but overrated 'Pink Pearl', 'Manglesii', the still good 'Beauty of Littleworth' and 'Loder's White'.

From China, Robert Fortune sent back *R. fortunei*, a member of the same series as *R. griffithianum*. Its sweet-scented, blush-pink flowers were smaller than those of its sister species but it was bone hardy. It was crossed at Kew with the beautiful, tender *griffithianum* to give the reasonably hardy 'Kewense' which, however, lacked the quality that its auspicious parentage should have ensured. This cross was made again at Leonardslee, using better clones of each species and resulted in the magnificent 'Loderi', some forms of which bore ten or more, scented, seven-inch, pale flowers in each truss, yet as the late Mrs. Nora Johnson of Bulkeley Mill used to point out, 'never carrying so many trusses at a time as to be vulgar'.

In the last quarter of the nineteenth century, gardeners were greatly helped by the interest shown in plants by the French Catholic missionaries who, often stationed in lonely and mountainous parts of western China and in Yunnan and Szechuan on the Tibetan border, devoted their spare time to collecting plants. From such men as Farges, Delavay and David, a constant stream of seeds came back to Europe. At the same time Dr. Augustine Henry made extensive journeys to China and Formosa and discovered among others the lovely, lavender-blue member of the Triflorum series, *R. augustinii*, which bears his name.

From Sir Joseph Hooker's expeditions, seeds flooded into Britain. In addition to the coveted *R. griffithianum* he sent back, among others, seed of the yellow *campylocarpum*, the handsome-leaved *wightii*, the blood-red *thomsonii, falconeri* and *grande*, two of the great tree rhododendrons, the scented, tender *maddenii, fulgens, niveum, hodgsonii, wallichii, lanatum*, the pretty, aromatic-leaved, dwarf *glaucophyllum, lepidotum, edgworthii* and the brilliant scarlet *barbatum*.

In the early nineteen-hundreds, a wealth of exciting and beautiful new rhododendron species was beginning to flower in British gardens and enthusiasm among the garden owners was high. All over Britain the band of rhododendron fanciers grew and many hybrids were made between the new species. At Coombe Royal in Devon, Mr. Luscombe had crossed *R. fortunei* with *R. thomsonii* of Sir Joseph Hooker's introduction and raised the large-flowered 'Luscombe's Scarlet' therefrom. At Penjerrick in Cornwall a clever and discriminating head-gardener named Smith crossed the tender and beautiful *R. griffithianum* with Hooker's new yellow *R. campylocarpum*, to give the great 'Penjerrick'—a reasonably hardy hybrid with a better truss and enlarged reproduction of *campylocarpum's* open, bell-shaped flowers. Some of the progeny echoed *griffithianum's* pale pink while others inherited the yellow of *campylocarpum* muted to a soft and lovely cream, enhanced by black anthers within. The strawberry-red 'Cornish Cross' was another of Smith's fine hybrids—a first cross between the blood-red *thomsonii* and *griffithianum*.

In colder Berkshire, Mr. Tom Lowinsky crossed a particularly fine clone of *griffithianum* with such hardy hybrids as 'Doncaster', 'White Pearl' and 'Corona', raising among other seedlings 'The Don' and 'Mrs. Tom Lowinsky'. Again in Cornwall *R. griffithianum* was used to cross with a tender blood-red clone of the magnificent *arboreum*. The flowers of the progeny varied in colour from the rose-red 'Gill's Triumph' and 'Glory of Penjerrick' to the white-feathered, pink 'Beauty of Tremough'. However, as might be expected from their parentage these were hardy only in south-western gardens. At Leonardslee in Sussex, too, Sir Edmund Loder was flowering further seedlings of his wonderful 'Loderi', while at Caerhays and Lanarth in Cornwall the cousins J. C. and P. D. Williams were exchanging plants and enthusiasm.

In 1905 *R. discolor*, *R. leutescens*, *R. orbiculare* and *R. souliei* had reached Britain to be followed in 1906 by *R. dichroanthum* and in 1908 by *R. Williamsianum*. So with more and more rhododendron species coming into Britain and more and more exciting hybrid seedlings flowering it was small wonder that the rhododendron growers' interest should reach an all-absorbing pitch. In 1914, the year in which the first world war broke out, Mr. Charles Eley wrote to Mr. P. D. Williams of Lanarth suggesting the formation of a Rhododendron Society and in 1915 the first meeting was held. The object of the society was to exchange information about rhododendrons between members and to carry out research. A series of yearly notes was to be published and to these each member was expected to contribute; thus came into being the *Notes of the Rhododendron Society*, copies of which are still in existence and of great value to the intending hybridist today.

Membership of the Rhododendron Society was always exclusive; at first the numbers were to be limited to thirteen, but included in addition to the keen owners of large rhododendron gardens, collectors such as Ernest Wilson, who knew the plants in the wild, and botanists such as Professor Isaac Bayley Balfour of the Royal Botanic Gardens, Edinburgh and W. J. Bean of Kew whose work and observations were of great help to the society in accomplishing their proposed study of the genus. Later the membership was further extended and, under the leadership of J. C. Williams of Caerhays, shares were taken in George Forrest's plant-hunting expeditions. Williams even paid Forrest a bonus for each new rhododendron introduced and so the seeds of more and yet more new species reached Britain to be distributed and grown in the gardens of the members of the Rhododendron Society.

From Forrest's expeditions came back *R. arizelum*, *chaetomallum*, the scented white *diaprepes*, the majestic *sinogrande*, *fictolacteum* and *giganteum*, the brilliant *griersonianum*, *neriiflorum*, *fulvum* and *didymum*, the yellow *croceum*, forerunner of *wardii*, temperamental *lacteum*, the delightful *oreotrephes* and *tephropeplum*, the charming early *eclecteum* and the useful little rock-garden species, *radican*, *repens*, *russatum*, the dwarf form of *racemosum*, and *impeditum*.

As soon as the new species flowered, enthusiasts used them to raise still more hybrids. Lacking an understanding of scientific breeding principles, the hybridizers enthusiastically crossed each new species with everything in sight and too many indifferent offspring were retained and named. However, of the species which emerged as first-class parents with a high proportion of really good progeny were *campylocarpum*, *williamsianum*, *neriiflorum*, *dichroanthum*, *barbatum*, *orbiculare* and the orange-scarlet *griersonianum* which tops the list with upwards of two hundred and eighty hybrids listed in Part Two of the Royal Horticultural Society's Rhododendron Handbook, the rhododendron stud book, as it were.

A nurseryman, Mr. Walter Slocock of Goldsworth Nursery, Surrey, became interested in breeding hardy yellows, using *campylocarpum* as one of the parents. Many of these were cream rather than true yellow, but among outstanding hybrids to come from his nursery were 'Unique', 'Souvenir de W. C. Slocock' and 'Goldsworth Yellow', the only one whose complete parentage we know, a *campylocarpum* × *caucasicum* hybrid, a cross made to take advantage of the dwarf neat habit, hardiness and inherent yellow in the Caucasian species. Unfortunately 'Goldsworth Yellow' is apt to be leggy in growth and should perhaps be crossed back to *caucasicum* to improve its habit.

Private garden owners, too, were interested in the yellow potential. In particular Mr. Lionel de Rothschild of Exbury was breeding yellows, using the Midas touch of *campylocarpum* with the larger-flowered, stronger-growing *discolor* to give 'Lady Bessborough' and then crossing 'Lady Bessborough' to another yellow, *wardii*, to gain the winning 'Hawk' grex.

A first cross between suitable species can usually be relied upon to give a fairly high percentage of good offspring. Crosses between hybrids are more uncertain in their results. They may yield three hundred indifferent plants to one chance hybrid of really good quality, and three hundred rhododendron seedlings are a lot to raise in order to find perhaps one good plant. However, if one breeds a first-cross seedling back to the parent or another species with the characteristics it is desired to impart, a large proportion of good plants should result and one or two of the progeny will have every chance of being outstanding.

Lionel de Rothschild used this principle in breeding the beautiful *cinnabarinum* hybrids 'Lady Rosebery' and 'Lady Chamberlain' with their hanging, lapageria-like bells. He mated the lovely but tender 'Royal Flush'—the offspring of *cinnabarinum* crossed with the very tender *maddenii* back to *cinnabarinum* var. *roylei* to gain the desired hardiness of that species. He used the pink form of 'Royal Flush' to give 'Lady Rosebery' and the orange form for 'Lady Chamberlain'.

From Exbury came some first-class pink and red-flowered hybrids too. 'Naomi', 'Grosclaude' and 'Goblin' together with the hardy late-flowered pale, scented (*discolor* × 'Loderi') 'Albatross' and the *discolor* × *griffithianum* hybrid, 'Angelo', along with some splendid late reds are some of the plants by which we shall remember a great rhododendron lover.

In another fabulous garden, this time in North Wales, at Bodnant in the Conway Valley, the Hon. H. D. McLaren later, as Lord Aberconway, to be President of the Royal Horticultural Society for very many years, was breeding red and orange rhododendrons, using the fiery *griersonianum* with the orange *dichroanthum* to give 'Fabia' in its several forms, one of the finest and best known modern hybrids. With the shy-flowering but beautiful scarlet-crimson *forrestii* var. *repens* he again used *griersonianum* and the resultant 'Elizabeth' is one of the freest-flowering and hardiest, compact, scarlet hybrids for the small garden. Again, with the early, hairy-stemmed *strigillosum* he used *griersonianum* to raise the blood-red, waxy-flowered 'Matador'.

With his inspired head-gardener, the late F. C. Puddle, a successful hybridizer of orchids—and father of Mr. Charles Puddle who presides over Bodnant Gardens today, and with the present Lord Aberconway continues the tradition—the late Lord Aberconway achieved success after success.

1. *R. sinogrande* from above showing formation of truss and pattern of very large, leathery leaves

2. The Glade at Bulkeley Mill, Conway, the garden of the late Mr. and Mrs. A. T. Johnson, showing rhododendrons used with other shrubs and trees to make an informal glade planting

3. *R. albrechtii*, a brightly-coloured rose-pink species of the azalea series,
delightful in an informal planting

4. *R. orbiculare*, a fine form of one of the most distinctive species with its sage green orbicular leaves and tubby pink bells

## Garden Rhododendrons

Unlike some of the Exbury hybrids, those raised at Bodnant are seldom line-bred. Instead red was put to red for more intense red. Early-flowering yellows, too, were bred and always the combined instincts of master and gardener for the right parents triumphed.

In Cornwall, meanwhile, Mr. J. C. Williams was hybridizing and from his garden 'Blue Tit', the neat-foliaged, dwarf, blue offspring of the great but slightly tender *augustinii* and the tough, little *impeditum* set the fashion that resulted in different raisers producing a whole series of dwarf blues that were suitable for all gardens.

In *williamsianum*, also, the hybridizers sensed a winning strain and the mounded, small-growing rhododendron with the pretty rounded leaves was crossed with the crimson *haematodes*, the yellow *wardii*, the rose *orbiculare* and with good pink hybrids such as 'Corona' and 'Dawn's Delight' to give a race of rounded-leaved semi-dwarfs, often with the same neat growth and sometimes with the fine bronzy young leaves of *williamsianum* and with flowers in cherry, crimson, yellow, and varying shades of pink and rose.

In line with the private garden owners, Mr. Walter Slocock of Goldsworth Nurseries was still hybridizing and from Knap Hill and Sunningdale nurseries also, came some good plants.

Many of the new hybrids looked quite unlike the old hardy hybrids of the 1820's. In some, the tight, rounded truss had been replaced by a looser inflorescence. Some, like (*neriiflorum* × *dichroanthum*) 'Nereid' and (*griersonianum* × *dichroanthum*) 'Roman Pottery' of the 'Fabia' grex had drooping almost lily-like bells. 'Lady Chamberlain', 'Lady Rosebery' and 'Lady Berry' had the lovely, lapageria-type of flower. 'Blue Tit', 'Blue Diamond', 'Augfast', and the rest, did not, to the uninitiated, look like rhododendrons at all with their neat, tiny leaves and flowers like small blue azaleas. And so, somehow, the legend grew up that the new hybrids were not for all gardens. Nurseries listed them as 'woodland hybrids' and some nurserymen declared that these lovely new plants were hardy only in the great estates of the south and west and that the only rhododendrons the average gardener could hope to grow successfully were the old 1820 iron-clads of which the nurserymen had large stocks, a statement that is reasonably true with regard to the colder and drier parts of the United States and to much of central Europe but certainly does not apply to the greater part of the sea-girt British Isles with its twin blessings, for the rhododendron-lover, of atmospheric moisture and comparatively mild winters.

Another factor that inhibited the spread of the new hybrids to the gardens of all but the cognoscenti was the custom among some of the nurserymen of buying from Holland bulk lots of Dutch-grown plants. Now the climate of Holland is much colder than that of Britain—even 'Pink Pearl' needs winter protection there—and so the Dutch nurserymen grow only the very toughest hybrids. Sooner than go to the expense of buying stock plants of the scarce new hybrids and raising their own plants therefrom, a lengthy and expensive business, many of the less devoted rhodo-dendron addicts among the nurserymen preferred to go on buying Dutch plants to retail to their customers to raising their own, so they fobbed off inquiries for the newer hybrids by decrying their hardiness without fair trial. Much of this was done in good faith. Perhaps some of the nurserymen did not *want* to know just how adaptable and hardy were some of the amateur-raised hybrids.

Some of the newer rhododendrons need shade and shelter it is true, but these are requirements that can be met outside the wood-lands that their catalogue designation induces one to believe necessary. Even in quite small gardens, shade and shelter can be found on the north or west of a hedge or wall. An overhead branch canopy can be provided by a Japanese cherry or sorbus species. Apart from that, many of the newer hybrids are as hardy as the old ironclads themselves. 'Elizabeth', the scarlet 'May Day', 'Hawk', 'Fabia', 'Unique' and the late-flowering, scented, blush-pink 'Avocet' are among those that are hardy in this country wherever rhododendrons can reasonably be expected to grow.

In the past many rhododendrons have been officially rated less hardy than they really are. Some of the ratings may have been decided without due knowledge of the behaviour of the rhododendrons concerned in other than optimum conditions. *Rhododendron griersonianum* is known to be a touchy species. Yet it withstands in Scotland more severe frosts than those that cut it in southern England. Nevertheless, its hardiness is suspect, so when the hardiness ratings of the *griersonianum* hybrids were under consideration it was natural that they should be given B or C ratings without due allowance being made for the fact that hybrids, as a general rule, are hardier than their species parents and that in many cases the second parent was unassailably hardy. Thus the tough little 'Elizabeth' had for one parent *R. forrestii* var. *repens*, which can withstand most frosts, to counteract any tenderness on the side of *griersonianum*. In 'Fabia', too, the *griersonianum* strain is offset by *dichroanthum* which is generally acknowledged to be a Category A, 'hardy anywhere in the British Isles', rhododendron. The hardiness of individual clones may vary, too, as the parent species may have been bred from seed collected at different exposures or different altitudes. Thus one might say that the Bodnant 'Fabia' is perhaps hardier than the Exbury form possibly because at Exbury a more tender form of *griersonianum* was used.

In 1931 the Rhododendron Society was absorbed into the much larger Rhododendron Association which had been formed to give scope to the increasing number of enthusiasts, some with quite small gardens, which the older society could not accommodate. In turn the Rhododendron Association later became the Rhododendron Group of the Royal Horticultural Society holding its shows and competitions within the framework of the R.H.S. and publishing (now in amalgamation with the Camellia Group) the extremely useful and reasonably priced Year Book which has replaced both the Rhododendron Society's 'Notes' and the handbook of the Rhododendron Association. In addition a *Rhododendron Handbook* is published, and from time to time revised, Part I containing a review of the species within their series of associated groups and Part II being a stud book and list of rhododendron and azalea hybrids with their raisers, hardiness and quality ratings.

Since the second world war, rhododendron breeding has been

seriously taken up by the Wisley Gardens of the R.H.S. and also by the Crown Commissioners in the gardens in Windsor Great Park.

The late Francis Hanger who, as a former head-gardener at Exbury, had shared with Mr. Lionel de Rothschild the planning and crossing of the Exbury rhododendrons and azaleas, became curator of the gardens at Wisley and began to hybridize there. One of his objects was to breed a good yellow, really hardy rhododendron. This resulted in the Moonshine grex of which 'Moonshine Bright', 'Moonshine Crescent' and 'Moonshine Supreme' are fine clones of compact growth and with pleasant, deep-green foliage.

Other Hanger hybrids are the reds 'Beefeater' and 'Rosenkavalier' and the primrose 'Tosca', while the latest development in rhododendron breeding both at Wisley and elsewhere is the production of a race of hardy, compact semi-dwarf hybrids for small gardens by using the ultra-hardy *R. yakushimanum* as one of the parents. *R. yakushimanum* itself has fine foliage and an interesting truss of apple-blossom pink flowers and never exceeds three feet in height. It is hoped that its hybrids will retain the dwarf habit and splendid foliage but give a wider range of flower colour and shape.

Good though the new race of *yakushimanum* hybrids may be, it would be unfortunate if its members were to be regarded as the only hybrids for the average small garden in the way that the old 'ironclads' used to be regarded as the only hydrids for the average villa garden of more spacious days. The *yakushimanum* hybrids are no hardier than 'Elizabeth' or 'Ethel', 'Blue Diamond' or 'Bow Bells'. A wider choice of delightful rhododendrons—both species and hybrids—is available to the present-day gardener. It is in its variety that the main charm of the race lies. Uniformity leads to monotony, so the garden owner should select as many different rhododendrons as he can, choosing some to flower early, some late, some for flower colour and some for foliage effect, some that are low and mounded in shape, others of light and airy growth—only in this way can the maximum garden effect be achieved.

I. *R.* '*Emasculum*', Savill Gardens, Windsor Great Park,
with *Narcissus cyclamineus*

# Garden Rhododendrons

At the time of writing rhododendron interest in this country is high. The steady flow of new and good hybrids continues not only, as has already been indicated, from the R.H.S. gardens at Wisley and from the Crown Commissioners at Windsor Great Park but from the nurserymen—Messrs. W. C. Slocock & Co., Mr. Michael Haworth-Booth, Messrs. Hilliers of Winchester, Messrs. Waterer Son & Crisp, Mr. James Russell of Sunningdale—and from private gardeners, among them Sir James Horlick of Gigha.* Formerly the Scottish gardens were noted for their rhododendron species rather than hybrids. Many of even the more difficult species did so well there that there seemed no need for the garden owners to interest themselves in hybrids. From Sir James, however, has recently come a succession of new and interesting hybrids, the fruit of his hybridizing programme in the 1930 era and now to be propagated by the National Trust for Scotland for distribution through the Trust's gardens. In addition the late J. B. and Roza Stevenson collected together at Tower Court, Ascot, one of the finest and most complete collections of species and bred several good hybrids. When this collection was sold it was bought to form the basis of the now famous Windsor Great Park collection.

*Note: Since revising the above, I am sad to have to report that Sir James Horlick has recently died. It is good to know that he has a fitting memorial in the hybrids distributed through Scottish gardens.

# CHAPTER 3

# Azaleas in the Wild and in the Garden

⪼⪼⪼⪼⪼⪼⪼⪼⪼⪼⪼⪼⪼⪼⪼⪼⪼⪻⪻⪻⪻⪻⪻⪻⪻⪻⪻⪻⪻⪻⪻⪻⪻⪻

The azaleas, though now botanically existent only as a series within the genus rhododendron, are for most of us entirely distinct. They may be evergreen, semi-evergreen or deciduous—so may rhododendrons. Their stamens number from five to ten—and many rhododendron species have ten stamens. Azaleas never have scales but always a particular kind of stiff, strigose hair. Yet the deciduous rhododendrons nearest to them in appearance—*mucronulatum* and *dauricum*—have leaf scales. As we have seen, however, both scales and hairs fulfil the same purpose in conserving moisture and preventing excessive transpiration. What then is the truth? Are azaleas merely a type of rhododendron—a series within a great genus? Or are they distinct? Modern botanical thought has it that azaleas are descended from certain primitive rhododendrons. They are eighty million years or so removed in evolution from the large-leafed rain-forest giants—the most primitive species. The deciduous rhododendrons—*dauricum* and *mucronulatum*—are still in their transitional state, halfway between the rhododendron and the azalea. So, to a lesser degree are the semi-deciduous Triflorum and the Trichocladum series, which, with their hairy leaves, more nearly resemble the evergreen azaleas of Japan although they themselves are deciduous or semi-deciduous in habit.

Mr. David G. Leach, a leading American authority and author of the thoughtful and comprehensive *Rhododendrons of the World*, wrote to me that in his opinion 'the evidence indicates that the Ovatum series of rhododendron split off from the main line of evolutionary development in a primitive phase of the development of the genus, probably before the precursors of the large-leaved rhododendrons evolved into the Falconeri series. The Ovatum series, then, gave rise to the *albiflorum* type of rhododendron and this in turn to the azalea series as we know it today.'

The Ovatum series come from eastern China and are in fact closely linked with *R. albiflorum* from western North America. *R. ovatum* itself is an azalea-like rhododendron, growing to six feet or more in height with small ovate leaves and inch-wide flowers, flat and open in shape—white or pink in colour with some spotting on the upper lobes—and borne singly from axillary buds at the end of the branches. A significant point is that it has only five stamens and crosses easily with azaleas of the Obtusum series.

*Rhododendron albiflorum* is an erect shrub growing five to six feet high and, as stated above, is a native of the Rockies. It is a pretty and uncommon little rhododendron with thin, narrowly oval leaves and dark hairs on the young stem. Its small creamy flowers are shaped like open bells and borne along the shoots of the previous year's growth.

Mr. Leach continues: 'Within the azalea series, the Canadense sub-series appears to be the most primitive, giving rise to the Obtusum sub-series which evolved into the Luteum sub-series. Luteum, Tashiroi and Schlippenbachii sub-series appear to be on the same rung of the evolutionary ladder.'

So the deciduous azaleas (apart from the Canadense series which comprises the lovely little grey-leaved 'rhodora' and the butterfly-flowered *vaseyi*, *albrechtii* and *pentaphyllum*) are the most highly developed azaleas, having sprung from the slightly more primitive evergreen azaleas.

Mr. Leach concludes: 'Thus the azaleas represent a culmination of an evolutionary line which developed concurrently with the "true" rhododendrons from a common ancestor.'

As, therefore, the rhododendrons were changing and new

## Azaleas in the Wild and in the Garden

species were being evolved as they spread from their cradle in the Sino-Himalayas, so we may assume it was with the azaleas. The Ovatum series of rhododendrons probably gave rise to *R. albiflorum* before this latter crossed the Bering Strait and spread down through Canada and the Rockies to Oregon in eastern U.S.A. to produce *canadense, vaseyi* and *albrechtii*. On the way, pockets of its distribution changed to *pentaphyllum* which in turn gave way to the Japanese evergreen azaleas, from which evolved the *schlippenbachii* azaleas of Asia, *luteum* of the pontic area of the Black Sea and the Caucasus and the whole race of North American deciduous azaleas—*calendulaceum, roseum, arborescens* and their kin.

Does not then the azalea merit generic status? The rhododendrons, and camellias likewise, are descended from magnolias, yet no one suggests that they should be reduced to mere series within the genus magnolia. They have generic rank. The azaleas are as distinct from rhododendrons as are the moltkias from the lithospermums, at least, and for the gardener they are forever separate. Why, for once, should not botanical science be the tool of the gardener and not his master? For the purpose of this book at any rate I shall consider the azaleas as distinct from and of equal dignity and status with the rhododendron. For in the garden at any rate their uses are distinct—the azalea in general being more tolerant to lime, rather less subject to drought and in many ways more accommodating than the rhododendron.

Azaleas in the garden are older than time. Before there were gardens in England or villas in Rome, the Japanese had taken the evergreen azaleas from their native hills and trained them into their traditional shapes. By 1692 there were in Japan over a hundred and sixty cultivated varieties of the dwarf evergreen *Azalea macrantha*, for tortuous botanical reasons now officially known as *Rhododendron indicum* even though it is a Japanese species.

It was as greenhouse plants that the mis-named 'Indian' azaleas first came to England from Holland to which country they had been imported as early as 1680 in the gallant merchantmen of the Dutch East India Company. Yet the true *Rhododendron indicum*

## Azaleas in the Wild and in the Garden

needed no greenhouse and is in fact hardy over much of the country. Only now is it taking its place as a late-flowering outdoor azalea. It flowers in June and into July in such varieties as the double salmon 'Balsaminiflorum', the white 'Hakatashiro' and the carmine 'Crispiflorum'. Later the more tender *simsii* azaleas came to Britain. In the seventeenth century there were in Japan only fifteen different hybrids from the hardier *obtusum* which grows like heather on its native mountains. But in the eighteen-twenties a cult arose among the feudal gentlemen of Japan and the dwarf evergreen azaleas were bred privately as an interest and competition among friends in much the same way that the gardening landowners of Britain have introduced and hybridized rhododendrons from the mid-nineteenth century until the present day. Thus arose the two-hundred-and-fifty-odd known varieties of Kurume azaleas, so called from the town of Kurume where they were later discovered.

In 1844 the plant collector Robert Fortune sent *Azalea obtusum* home to England where it was not realized that it was a hardy outdoor plant and where as it was already outclassed for greenhouse purposes by the *indicum* and *simsii* hybrids, its worth was not fully appreciated until much later when the azaleas took their rightful place in the outdoor garden and, indeed, the popular pink 'Hinomayo' was one of the first to reach Europe, and by its fresh beauty and accommodating nature, to help to set the new trend.

Later, in 1914, E. H. Wilson, famous for his plant collecting journeys in China, went to Japan and, at a nursery a few miles north of Tokyo, saw in flower thousands of the dwarf evergreen Kurumes which with their tiered habit and soft brilliant colours he thought 'the lovelist of all azaleas'. In 1918 he selected the famous 'Wilson Fifty' which he shipped to the Arnold Arboretum in the United States whence a complete set eventually reached Britain. Not all the fifty proved reliably hardy here but the survivors are to be seen on Battleston Hill at Wisley and in the Kurume Punchbowl in Windsor Great Park as well as in many private gardens.

41

## Azaleas in the Wild and in the Garden

Between the wars many more varieties of dwarf evergreen azaleas poured into the British Isles, some of them introduced from Japan by the Dutch nursery firm of C. B. Van Nes and widely taken up by the Boskoop nurserymen who then sold them in bulk to nurseries in this country. Other nurseries and garden owners imported plants direct from Japan. My memory turns at once to Mr. A. T. Johnson's Bulkeley Mill garden and a bed of the June-flowering *simsii eriocarpum* Gumpos with their crisply frilly, double blossoms in white and pink which Mr. Johnson used to point out as having been imported by himself *via* the Trans-Siberian railway, as romantic a history as their beauty undoubtedly deserved.

As the dwarf azaleas grew in popularity so the possibilities of hybridizing became apparent and the taller, deciduous flame-coloured Japanese azalea *kaempferi* was used to add extra hardiness. The resulting hybrids have larger flowers than the Kurumes but their colours are less resistant to sunlight and semi-shade is necessary for many varieties to prevent bleaching. Later the Dutch-bred Malvaticum hybrids brought in the blood of the *mollis* azaleas and gave yet larger flowers and a still wider colour range; and since the war an ultra-hardy race from America—the Glenn Dale hybrids—have begun to arrive in Britain. The Glenn Dales incorporate the blood of the hardy flame-coloured *kaempferi* azaleas, the white or lilac, large-flowered *mucronatum*, some of the original Kurume varieties and the late-flowering *indicums*. Some also contain the more tender *simsii* strain and others the blood of *yedoense* var. *poukhanense*, an ultra-hardy azalea of the Obtusum sub-series. The result is a race of large-flowered and usually extremely hardy evergreen azaleas flowering a little later than the Kurumes. A few have been planted at the R.H.S. gardens at Wisley where they have proved undeniably hardy but the most interesting promise for their future lies at Bodnant and at Windsor, where Sir Eric Savill, creator of the beautiful Savill gardens, made a collection of three hundred plants raised from cuttings to form a permanent planting.

So much for the evergreen azaleas. The first deciduous azalea, the yellow *luteum* which used to be known as *ponticum*—the most

## Azaleas in the Wild and in the Garden

familiar azalea of all—reached Britain in 1793 and was practically ignored by gardeners. Meanwhile, however, European travellers had discovered the beautiful, deciduous American azalea species and brought some of them back to Europe. Nine years later, in 1806, *calendulaceum*, the fiery-orange 'Sky Paint Flower' of the Cherokee Indians bloomed, for the first time in Europe, in Belgium where its beauty was to endow the famous race of the bone-hardy deciduous azaleas that were to be given to the world by the genius of Monsieur Mortier, a baker of Ghent, the town which they have immortalized by name. By forcing the American species *calendulaceum* and *viscosum*, M. Mortier was able to make their flowering time coincide with that of *luteum* and so raise hybrids from the three species. He worked from 1804 to 1834, using also *nudiflorum* and *roseum*. The resulting hybrids gave rise to the forerunners of the race of Ghent azaleas that we know today with scented flowers like large honeysuckle blooms in vivid shades of orange, pink, red and yellow, and with vivid autumn leaf tints.

Meanwhile, in England, J. R. Gowen, gardener to the Earl of Caernarvon at Highclere was crossing *calendulaceum* and *luteum* also *viscosum* and *luteum* to yield a similar hybrid group.

These two groups were later used by other hybridists who recrossed them to give rise to the Ghent hybrids we know today.

At about the same time that M. Mortier and J. R. Gowen were breeding their azaleas, a young German doctor, von Siebold—working as a medical officer in Japan in the service of the Dutch East India Company—developed a passion for flowers. In his spare time he journeyed up and down the country collecting plants until he was deported for possessing maps—a serious offence in Japan at that time—and was sent back to Holland whence he took many of the plants he had collected, including the orange-flowered *Rhododendron japonicum*, formerly known as *Azalea mollis*, one of the parents of another popular race of garden azaleas—the mollis hybrids.

In 1843 the yellow *R. molle* (*Azalea sinensis*) was collected by Robert Fortune. This was the plant that was thought to be the other parent of the Mollis azaleas. In fact, however, it is hopelessly

43

tender and has had little effect on the race. It is more than likely that most of the Mollises are not true hybrids but seedling forms of *japonicum*, mentioned above. These seedlings were freely inter-bred and, among the varieties raised at this time, were 'Comte de Gomer', 'Comte de Papadopoli', 'Consul Pecheur', 'Comte de Quincey' and 'C. B. Van Nes'—all popular Mollis azaleas varieties today.

The Mollis azaleas had larger flowers that were more funnel-shaped than those of the Ghents. Their colours ranged from pale pinks and yellows to soft flame and hotter tangerine reds; but they had little scent and the autumn colour of their leaves was not as brilliant as those of the Ghent hybrids. Some of the Ghents had double flowers and these were crossed with the mollises to give the larger-flowered double 'rustica flore pleno' group.

In Britain the hybrid story had begun in the early eighteen-hundreds, when William Thompson, a nurseryman in the Mile End Road, introduced the first azaleodendron—'Odoratum'—the scented, pale-mauve, semi-evergreen cross he had raised between the common purple *R. ponticum* and the pink honey-suckle azalea *R. nudiflorum*. At the time the object was to use the azalea to add scent to the limited variety of evergreen rhodo-dendrons then available and *R.* 'Odoratum' was followed by the yellow-flowered azaleodendrons 'Norbitonense Aureum' and 'Broughtonii Aureum'—both fine plants that are still worth grow-ing today. The first of the yellow rhododendron species had not yet been introduced and these two azaleodendrons, raised by a Mr. William Smith of Norbiton, were an attempt to add yellow to the, so far, limited palette of colours available in the evergreen rhododendrons.

However, in the eighteen-twenties and thirties, in York, Dean Herbert, the 'father of English hybridizers', was interested not only in improving the evergreen rhododendrons by an infusion of azalea blood but also in crossing azalea with azalea to improve the deciduous race. He crossed the vivid orange *R. calendulaceum* with the scented *viscosum* and the little lilac *canadense* with the Euro-pean, yellow, wild azalea *luteum* (*ponticum*).

In the south as well, Standish and Noble of the Sunningdale

Nurseries were working on the American azaleas by crossing and re-crossing them in much the same way that M. Mortier had done in Ghent and producing, among others, the brilliant orange-and-yellow azalea 'Unique'.

Hybrids were also being raised between the Chinese mollis azalea, *R. sinensis* and the American swamp honeysuckle *R. viscosum*, the size of bloom of the mollis type merging with the scent of the honeysuckle-flowered species in 'Daviesii' and the well-known 'Viscosepalum' which has played such a large part in the parentage of many of the more popular azaleas that we grow today.

'Viscosepalum' was raised by Michael Waterer of the famous Knap Hill nursery which was to become one of the greatest centres of British azalea-breeding. In 1855 Michael's great-nephew Anthony Waterer imported a quantity of M. Mortier's Ghent azaleas and began an intensive programme to improve the race, using the so-called Mollis Hybrids to add size and the more recently discovered *occidentale* for its scent. The resulting 'Knap Hill' azaleas seemed to have everything—size, scent, glorious autumn tints and a scheme of flower colours ranging from flame, orange-red, pinks and yellows to pale cream and white with gold or orange blotches.

In Holland, too, *R. occidentale* was being used by Anthony Koster of Boskoop who crossed it with his mollis azaleas to give the later-blooming, pale-flowered, Occidentale Hybrids famous for their scent. The well-known 'Exquisitum', 'Gloriosum', 'Graciosa' and 'Superbum' were of this breeding. These hybrids like the Ghent and Mollis azaleas found their way to England and in time were used by Anthony Waterer to improve his Knap Hill strain.

In 1919 Mr. Lionel de Rothschild began to plant his rhododendron garden at Exbury on the Solent and in 1920 he received among a batch of azaleas from Anthony Waterer's Knap Hill nursery 'George Reynolds', an outstanding azalea in soft yellow and pink with a wavy-petalled flower that sometimes measured six inches across. This prodigy inspired him to wish to perpetuate its good features, so its seed was collected and sown and from the resulting seedlings the best were kept and crossed and re-crossed

45

again by colour. Pink was always crossed with pink, yellow with yellow, and orange with orange in order to get clearer and more intensive colours. Finally in 1937 the Exbury azaleas were introduced to the gardening public at the Chelsea Show—a new strain developed *via* the azalea 'George Reynolds' from the already good Knap Hill azaleas and selected and re-selected until every seedling could be relied upon to give a perfect flower. Hardy and vigorous, with a wide colour range, wonderful scent and fine autumn tints the Exbury strain has the last word in hybrid deciduous azaleas.

So far we have considered the hybrids. In the larger gardens of this country are grown many of the delicate and lovely azalea species most of which are hardy enough and easy enough eventually to find their way into the smaller gardens, too. Azalea hybrids and species do not really mix in the garden scene. The species have in the main smaller flowers but are more finely drawn. To do them justice they should be grouped on their own. The early, butterfly-flowered, pale-pink *vaseyi*, the brighter but still delicate *albrechtii*, the larger-flowered *schlippenbachii*, the extremely lime-sensitive *reticulatum* with its blaze of claret-purple; these look best in informal woodland conditions when grown in a big garden or grouped among ferns and silver birches, with bluebells and foxgloves, to follow in a smaller plot. The modest little 'rhodora'—*canadense* as she should be called—is enchanting by the waterside where her little lilac butterflies can echo the mauve of the ladysmock. Later to flower, such species as *occidentale*, with its wonderful carnation scent and velvet-textured flowers of pink-tinged-white or blush and the July flowering *arborescens* are at their best in cool green shade.

The common yellow *luteum* comes from the Pontic area of the Black Sea. From China and Japan come *albrechtii, schlippenbachii, reticulatum* and the dwarf evergreen azaleas while *vaseyi, canadense* and the honeysuckle-flowered *calendulaceum, viscosum, arborescens, alabamense* and *viscosum* are to be found on the American continent. So have some of the rhododendrons evolved—into the seventy species of the azalea so far known, many of which have yet to be introduced into our gardens.

46

CHAPTER 4

# Plant Associations

No other genera with the possible exception of the rose can compare with the combined glory of the rhododendrons and azaleas in flower power, length of season, foliage value and sheer garden worth. Even if they never bloomed, the magnificent foliaged giants, the very large, leathery-leaved *R. sinogrande*, rusty-felted *fictolacteum*, the *arboreum* hybrid 'Sir Charles Lemon'; the blue-green of the smaller-growing *campanulatum aeruginosum*; and *calophytum* with its striking rosettes of long, graceful leaves, are worth their places as garden-furnishings alone. Associated with bamboos, giant rheums, ferns and the tropical banana-like leaves of *Lysichitum americanum* and the glaucous *L. camtschatcense* (which thrive in the moist, spongy, well-aerated, woodsy soil that the big rhododendrons like best) they make a complete garden picture to which may be added the dwarf *Narcissus cyclamineus*, the American erythroniums and trilliums, candelabra primulas, astilbes and rodgersias, hydrangea species, azaleas for autumn leaf colour, hellebores and snowdrops to give year-round interest and beauty.

And, of course, the big rhododendrons need not rely on foliage effect alone. When they reach maturity they flower, and the shady parts of the woodland are lit by the yellow globes of *R. falconeri*, the blood-scarlet of *arboreum* and *barbatum*, and the scented rose-pink trusses of the best form of *R. fortunei*, 'Mrs. Charles Butler'. The cool scent of 'Loderi' floats on the air to be followed by that of 'Angelo', *R. auriculatum* and 'Polar Bear'.

47

It is important to consider foliage effect and grouping when planting medium-sized rhododendrons also. Here, variety is all. Nothing looks worse than the heavy effect of a bed of the old hardy hybrids lumped together without relief. Such a group is over-garish when in flower. Many rhododendrons are at their best when used alone. Compare the effect of the scarlet *R. (griersonianum × haematodes)* 'May Day' glowing from between the green foliage of two earlier-blooming rhododendrons with that of the same hybrid planted between other reds whose colours do not quite agree. Occasionally two rhododendrons of contrasting colour may be planted together to make a satisfactory grouping. 'May Day' for instance might be associated with the tight trusses of the rich yellow *R. (campylocarpum × 'Gladys')* 'Marcia' or one might plant the smoky-lavender *campanulatum* hybrid 'Susan' with the creamy-yellow *R. ('Naomi' × campylocarpum)* 'Carita', two hybrids which in our garden usually flower at the same time. Their foliage effect, too, is good; the dark green, pointed leaves of 'Susan' complementing the fresh green rounded foliage of 'Carita'.

Great variety in foliage can be obtained by using evergreen and deciduous azaleas along with the rhododendrons, and with allied genera such as kalmia and enkianthus and by grouping together the dwarf rhododendrons with the most distinctive foliage. The little moorland members of the Lapponicum series with their tiny leaves in grey, bronze and emerald make a filigree effect at the front of the larger rhododendrons. Add the rounded leaf-patterns of *R. williamsianum* and *R. orbiculare*, the aromatic grey foliage of *R. glaucophyllum*, the blue young growth of *R. lepidostylum*—its leaves covered in soft hairs—the smooth blue-green of *R. concatenans* and various members of the Cinnabarinum series and there is a picture of considerable interest, containing various degrees of light and shade, of contrasting patterns and colours, even without a single plant of any other genus being used.

Rhododendrons, however good though they may be when planted alone, derive added charm from the varied forms and textures of suitable companions. They are helped by the distinctive leaves and bark of many of the maples, particularly those of

5. *R. lepidostylum*, a dwarf species worth growing for its wonderful blue-green softly hairy foliage

6. *R. sutchuenense*, a delightful early-flowering species for a sheltered position with dark blotched soft lilac flowers and a delicious scent

7. *R.* 'Polar Bear', probably the latest-flowering hybrid, making a tree-like shrub with icy-white, very fragrant flowers in August

8. *R. campylogynum* var. *myrtilloides*, a quaintly flowered dwarf species for the rock-garden or the front of a glade bed

# Plant Associations

the *Acer palmatum* and *A. palmatum* 'Dissectum' class; *A. griseum* with its tattered cinnamon bark; the green-and-white snake-barks; *A. nikoense* with its airy leaves; the elegant stewartias; the beautiful magnolias in their varied forms; and the round-leaved *Cercidiphyllum japonicum* with its autumn tints and scent of ripened strawberries. Conifers with not-too-greedy roots such as the weeping *Juniperus recurva* var. *coxii* with its soft red trunk, *Ginkgo biloba* with leaves like a maidenhair fern, the spreading dwarf blue *Juniperus sabina* var. *tamariscifolia* and *Chamaecyparis pisifera* 'Filifera' with its soft grey-green branchlets—all these will add contrasting but much larger texture and form to a rhododendron and azalea garden.

Underplantings, too, are needed to complement the rhododendrons and azaleas and to build up the flowering and enchanted wood that the garden on suitably acid soil may so delightfully become. Snowdrops, species crocus, hellebores, trilliums, daffodils, primroses, bluebells, erythroniums, heaths, ferns and the charming berry-bearing dwarf gaultherias and pernettyas, with butcher's broom and *Sarcococca humilis*—these are the groundlings that best capture the atmosphere we want. The deciduous trees before mentioned give light shade and add interest and height. *Hamamelis mollis* and *H. japonica* bear their golden, spidery blossoms in January and February to contrast with the purples and pinks and crimsons of the early rhododendrons and winter-flowering heaths. The yellow 'catkin' flowers of *Stachyurus* and *Corylopsis* strike the note of spring to be echoed by the first daffodils and *Rhododendron lutescens*. Other earlies follow with the lily-of-the-valley flowers and scarlet young leaves of *Pieris formosa* var. *forrestii*. In May and June it is best to let the rhododendrons and azaleas dress the stage with the purple-pink blossom of the Judas tree, the pendant waxen bowls, scented with honey and roses, of *Magnolia sieboldii* and *M. wilsonii* and, perhaps, a distant flame of *Embothrium coccineum* muted by surrounding green.

By July only a few of the rhododendrons and azaleas, with the chintzy kalmias, will still be in flower and the support of the hydrangeas will be needed. No other shrubs can compare as can these with the rhododendrons in size and weight of flower.

## Plant Associations

Hydrangea blooms are large and last long. It has been said, to my mind wrongly, that the hydrangeas are too artificial in appearance to fit the mood of woodland and garden glade. I do not agree. Nothing is more fitting, more cooling, amid the ferns and greenery of July and August than the blue globes of the Hortensia hydrangeas. The lace-caps, too, are good. There is 'Veitchii', superb in shade with its large white sterile flowers surrounding the turquoise fertile 'beads'. 'Blue Wave' and 'Blue Bird' one can picture from their names. Finest of all perhaps are the larger 'tree' hydrangeas—*H. sargentiana* with its rich baize-green leaves and enormous heads of lilac and white florets, and *H. aspera* with misty heads of rose and blue. Good and very hardy blues among the Hortensias are 'General Vicomtesse de Vibraye' and 'Mousseline'. For milder areas near the sea, or for gardens which do not suffer severe frosts, one might add the black-stemmed 'Nigra', the purple 'Heinrich Seidel' and 'Altona' with extra large heads of fimbriated-petalled florets that are a cornflower blue in summer turning to a warm crimson and green as they age. Also useful are the white, blue-eyed 'Mme E. Mouilliere' and the tall-growing *H. arborescens* 'Grandiflora', the white, cone-shaped panicles of which make a cool froth in a shady place.

Golden hypericums may be used to associate with the hydrangeas along with tree brooms such as the silvery-leaved *Genista cinerea*, *G. aetnensis* with its yellow veils of scented fireflies and the later *Spartium junceum* with its upright spikes of narcissus-scented gold. Mock-orange blossoms of character are useful and of these *Philadelphus* 'Beauclerc', *P.* × 'Burfordensis' and the grey-leaved *P. incanus* have enough natural grace to keep the woodland note. Deutzias of quality such as 'Magicien' with its large, fringed, pink-petalled flowers, the willow-leaved *D. chunii* and *D. kalmiiflora* are splendid as they all flower freely in shade. Finest of all late-summer subjects, though, are the eucryphias especially *E. glutinosa*, the hybrid 'Rostrevor' which does not grow as tall as 'Nymansay' and 'Nymansay' itself where one is prepared for its ultimate height of perhaps thirty to forty feet. In August and September some of the rhododendrons begin their second flowering. Notable among these are such members of the Lapponicum series as *hippo-*

*phaeoides* and *intricatum* as well as *charitopes* of the Glaucophyllum series and the quaint *campylogynum*. These combine well with drifts of moor-purple ling.

Then, after the flowers, come the berries of which the cotoneasters and stranvaesias may be relied upon to provide the yellow and red. Mountain ashes of various species add orange and pink and white. Spindleberries with their dangling crimson sealingwax cases spilling the orange seeds must not be forgotten. Nor must the more lowly pernettyas, the prickly Chilean heaths, with perhaps the prettiest berries of all, as big as marbles and coloured in all shades of rose and red, mulberry, pale pink and white.

It is in winter, I suppose, that one appreciates most the birches —Chinese and Himalayan, North American, Swedish and the *B. pendula* of our own woods and heaths—when, having shed their golden rain of autumn leaves, their stems gleam in coffee, cream and white. The eucalypti, too, although they do not lose their leaves have the same charm of striped, stippled, peeling bark. Their leaves, rounded when young, achieve a lance-like shape as they mature and like lance-pennants ripple and reflect the light; blue and green and grey they are, with an occasional winter scarlet to strike the season's note. Of them the species that seem hardiest in cultivation are *gunnii, urnigera* and *dalrympleana*.

*Arbutus unedo*, the 'Strawberry Tree' and its pink form, 'Croomei', are at their best in winter when their little urn-like flowers join the previous year's ruby fruit. Better, though, for bark effect are the smooth cinnamon boles of *A.* × *andrachnoides* and *A. menziesii*. Add to these the polished leaves and rosette or bowl-shaped flowers of the camellias, that are co-descended with the rhododendrons and azaleas from the magnolias of primitive times, and the flowering wood is complete.

Such a scheme can be adapted to the small garden as well, as rhododendron lovers can see for themselves if they pay a visit on one of its open days to Tree Tops, Heswall, Cheshire, the garden designed by landscape architect, Mr. Walter Irvine. Tree Tops is a suburban garden planted on the 'close boskage' system of underplanting, and featuring medium and dwarf rhododendrons together with heaths, gaultherias and trees and shrubs of quality. It is a garden of limited size where every plant must earn its place —not merely by beauty of flower but by an additional bonus of autumn colour, berries, or good evergreen foliage. It is this emphasis on quality that has led Mr. Irvine to depend so much on rhododendrons and azaleas in planting the garden and all owners of small gardens who would like to specialize in rhododendrons and azaleas would do well to study his success.

At Tree Tops, dwarf Japanese azaleas are massed with dwarf rhododendrons of the Lapponicum series in front of deciduous azaleas and medium-sized rhododendron hybrids such as 'Naomi' —in several forms, the late scarlet 'Impi', 'May Day', 'Fabia', 'Elizabeth', the Ludlow and Sherriff form of *wardii*; and many of the pretty *williamsianum* hybrids. Rhododendrons with interesting foliage such as *arizelum, wasoni, bureavii, concatenans* with its offspring 'Peace', and *coriaceum* with its young foliage of white kid, play their part and there are magnolias and Japanese maples, too. Most remarkable of all is Mr. Irvine's choice of trees to give height, light shade and a sense of distance to the garden through which stepping-stone paths wind as through woodland glades. June-flowering styraxes and *Halesia carolina*, together with the paper-bark maple and such remarkable snake-barks as *A. davidii* and *pensylvanicum* are used along with the Tibetan cherry, *Prunus serrula* remarkable for its glossy chestnut trunk. Lovely in the autumn, the pink-berried *Sorbus vilmorinii* is particularly suited to the small garden in which it will never outgrow its space. Various cotoneasters, pernettyas and the silvery *Elaeagnus multiflora* are destined to add their berries to the autumn feast.

On yet a smaller scale even a pocket-handkerchief plot can be changed into a garden of discernment. Dwarf azaleas and rhododendrons, chosen to give a succession of colour and interest, may be used to plant miniature shrub belts. *Acer palmatum* and *A. p.* 'Dissectum' in green and bronze as well as purple will give height. Heaths of real distinction such as the Christmas-flowering 'King George', the summer-blooming *Erica tetralix* 'Alba Mollis' and *Erica* × *watsonii* 'Dawn' may be used with fine callunas such as the double lilac 'H. E. Beale', the golden-leaved 'Serlei Aurea' and the woolly-foliaged 'Silver Queen' to extend and bridge the season. All that is necessary is a suitably acid soil and a careful choice of plants. On difficult soil, peat blocks and beds might be used (see Chapters 5 and 8), and dwarf gaultherias, pernettyas and cassiopes added with peat-garden subjects.

For the peat or rock-garden there are numerous dwarf rhododendrons, both species and hybrids from which to choose. It is important, though, to remember that most rhododendrons and azaleas suffer when in contact with excessive lime and the use of limestone for the rhododendron rock-garden is to be avoided. Most dwarf rhododendrons and even azaleas need adequate moisture at the root and many benefit from some shade and so a site should be chosen which will offer shade as well as sun. North or west-facing slopes are useful and the plantings should always be made with a half-buried boulder strategically below the proposed site of the plant to hold moisture and to offer a cool root-run.

Rhododendrons and azaleas associate well with heaths and small conifers, and the combined heath and dwarf rhododendron garden can be a delightful sight. Here could be planted the smaller dwarfs in drifts as one might plant heathers, using the tiny-leaved members of the Lapponicum, Saluenense and Anthopogon series to make pools and rivers of colour as one would see in nature. The deep violet-blue *R. scintillans* might merge into the paler *intricatum* which in turn would give way to a drift of the red-purple *lysolepis* before mingling with the yellow *chryseum* and flowing on to meet the glaucous-leaved, rosy-purple *calostrotum*.

Low-growing heaths such as the mat-forming, winter-flowering *Erica carnea* cultivars should be placed in the foreground while the taller *E.* × *darleyensis* clones, the fine white *Erica mediterranea* 'W. T. Rackliffe', the summer-blooming *E. vagans* and *calluna* cultivars should be given equal status with the rhododendrons, each merging into the other in sheets of foliage of different shades and texture to flush in turn with flowers. Tree heaths such as the white *Erica arborea* 'Alpina', *E. lusitanica*, the rose-purple *E.* *australis* and its white cultivar 'Mr. Robert' and the autumn-flowering *terminalis stricta* should, with the tallest of the dwarf conifers—*Picea glauca* var. *albertiana* 'Conica', *Thuja occidentalis* 'Rheingold' and *Juniperus* × *media* 'Blaauw'—be used in smaller groups or as isolated specimens to give height. Taller rhododendrons of lighter build look at their best arising from a drift of heaths. Good for this purpose are the rosy-purple 'Praecox', the aromatic *charitopes* and *glaucophyllum* and the lovely *aberconwayi* with its beautifully-shaped saucers of white flushed with rose and delicately speckled with purple. Species azaleas, too, are suitable, especially the airy pink *vaseyi* and *albrechtii*, the purple *reticulatum* and the white *atlanticum*. Lowly, cushion-like rhododendrons such as the rosy-mauve *uniflorum*, the yellow *sargentianum* and blue *impeditum* look well as solitary mounds.

Public parks are often associated in the mind with rhododendrons but much thought is needed on the part of the planners if we are to see them looking other than leggy, tattered and distressed such as the specimens we too often find. The open, sun-baked, windswept surround of a playing-field or park is not the place for rhododendrons. Even the toughs look unhappy and the garish 'Cynthia', candy-floss 'Pink Pearl' and the thin-flowered 'Caucasicum Album' and 'Caucasicum Pictum' are not calculated to improve the level of the public's floral taste. Give them the rhododendrons they can see at Kew and Wisley and in the Savill gardens at Windsor and they will appreciate them and treat them with care. To plant the better hybrids in the football-ridden open spaces of the parks, however, is to invite destruction. How many parks would be the better for a woodland corner, perhaps with primulas and suitable associates? That such a scheme would be appreciated is shown by the popularity of the woodland gardens in Stanley Park, Blackpool. It is proof of the ability of such a garden to catch the imagination of the public in a way that ensures the safety and respect of the plants that the rate of vandalism in such a necessarily secluded corner is usually extremely low.

Near the lake, too, the planner of public parks may find a use for the larger and better rhododendrons. Strong growers such as the extremely hardy *discolor* hybrid 'Avocet' with its pale-pink scented trusses in June, forms of the yellow 'Hawk', pink 'Aurora' and the later 'Vanessa' might be planted where they will reflect the water, interspersed with blue hydrangeas to take their place through July and August and often to continue in flower until far into the autumn. With them the larger ferns and the tropical-looking blue-grey and green leaves of the spring-flowering lysichitums would associate well. The effectiveness of such a theme may be judged by the startling beauty of the mill pool at Bodnant in early September when the blue hydrangeas and green foliage are reflected in the calm brown water.

Rock-garden schemes in parks may be stiffened by the use of dwarf rhododendron species, or an enterprising parks department might give the public 'something to look at' by filling even a flat bed with dwarf Kurume and 'Malvaticum' × *kaempferi* azaleas planted in peat and set among a few picturesque rocks. Creeping junipers might be added along with berrying pernettyas and gaultherias to extend the season of interest or, more ambitiously, a peat bank might give a series of beds and peat-block walls in which homes might be found for many dwarf rhododendron species and hybrids along with other treasures such as *Philesia magellanica*, ramondas and haberleas, nomocharis, *Pernettya tasmanica*, *Gaultheria trichophylla* with its hedge-sparrow-blue berries and *G. cuneata* with its large white 'marbles'. Peat-garden construction together with suggestions for planting will be gone into more fully in Chapter 8.

Rhododendrons in the main are long lived. In such woodlands and gardens as those belonging to Carclew in Cornwall and Stonefield and Lochinch in Scotland there are specimens raised from seed brought back from the Hooker expeditions of the eighteen-fifties still in good health. When well-suited, in good rhododendron soil and in the conditions they like, some of the big tree rhododendrons may live a hundred years and more. Many of the medium-sized species and hybrids will outlive their planters. The dwarfs, too, are healthy if conditions are airy. Damp, shut-in, humid valleys spell trouble to the little rhododendrons from the high mountains. In some gardens, as species after species was sent back by the collectors, too many rhododendrons were planted too close to each other and in these old gardens plants may be seen drawn up and straggly and now having either to be removed and replaced or else cut back so drastically that their survival chances are slender. Present planters can avoid this trouble by planting large-growing specimens far enough apart and filling in the spaces with smaller rhododendrons and azaleas which, as the key plants spread, may easily be removed and used to make new plantings elsewhere in the garden.

## CHAPTER 5

# Rhododendrons and Azaleas on Limy Soil

In soils that are acid or neutral most rhododendrons and azaleas will grow without trouble although certain rather 'choosey' species such as *Rhododendron lacteum* and the lovely purple azalea known as *reticulatum* need optimum conditions and a pH of 4·5 if they are to succeed.

As many readers of this book will already know, the pH scale (scientifically a measure of hydrogen *ion* concentration) is used by gardeners to denote the degree of acidity or alkalinity in the soil. At pH 7 the soil is neutral; pH 8 is ten times more alkaline than pH 7. A pH of 8·5 is again five times more alkaline than pH 8 and so on, although in practice it would be most unusual to meet a soil more alkaline than pH 8·5 in the British Isles. Going down the scale from neutral, pH 6 is ten times more acid than pH 7; pH 5 is ten times more acid than pH 6 and so on. The optimum acidity for rhododendrons is reached, as mentioned above, at pH 4·5 and below pH 4 even they have difficulty in making growth. It is often said that rhododendrons become difficult when the pH rises to 6·5 but in fact most of them will do well at even pH 7 provided their humus needs are met by planting them in an acid grade of peat or rotted bracken with spent hops added for nourishment and with a yearly mulch (of spruce needles, rhododendron peat, or bracken) given to provide an acid material into which the roots can thrust up.

Rhododendrons and azaleas with other member of the *Ericaceae* are often referred to as lime-haters. According to recent scientific investigation, however, this description is not strictly accurate. It seems that, like all plants, rhododendrons and azaleas need some calcium, but because they live in nature on acid soils with a low free-calcium content they are adapted to take up all the available calcium. Unfortunately, when they are grown in a more limy soil they are not able to discriminate or to take up only the required amount of calcium. They absorb too much to the exclusion of other necessary elements, particularly iron, manganese and magnesium. Dr. Henry Tod of the Edinburgh School of Agriculture who has done so much valuable work on the problem writes to me that he has proved, as he says, to his own satisfaction, at least, 'that the calcium levels of leaves, etc., of rhododendrons growing on an extremely acid soil, where the calcium level is very low, is of the same order as, say, of black-currents growing in a well-limed garden soil. This seems to show that the real problem with the genus is that it is too efficient in picking up calcium from the soil, for they will grow under conditions where more normal plants would show very severe calcium deficiency *and will build up normal leaf-calcium levels* where other plants would be at very low levels indeed.' Far from being lime haters, therefore, it seems that rhododendrons and azaleas have too great an appetite for lime when they can get it and indulge themselves over-freely to the exclusion of other foods.

In an effort to avoid iron deficiencies in fruit trees, *Sequestrene* 138 *Fe* was evolved. It was known that iron and other elements in limy soils remained locked to the plants that needed them. *Sequestrene* 138 *Fe* was iron (with magnesium and manganese in small quantities) in a form that could be absorbed by any plant even on limy clays, the most obstinate to treat of all alkaline soils. This *Sequestrene* was applied to rhododendrons, azaleas and other *Ericaceae* in the hope that it might overcome the difficulties experienced in growing the family on alkaline soils and so open up the way for the gardener on lime and chalk to enjoy these wayward beauties.

To some extent the experiment has succeeded. Sequestered iron chelates restore to health chlorotic hydrangeas, fruit trees and roses. They also improve yellow and sickly rhododendrons but do not seem to me alone able to effect a permanent cure. The repeated use of such iron chelates can result in an over-accumulation of iron in the soil, and in the alkaline soil of our own garden we found that when sufficient was used to give a really healthy deep leaf-green, symptoms of toxicity began to occur, and at the same time faint yellow mottling and striation remained. It seemed, therefore, that something further was needed.

The reason for this was explained to me by Dr. Henry Tod as follows: 'Iron is not in itself a constituent of the chlorophyll molecule' (as readers are aware, it is chlorophyll that is responsible for the green colour of the leaf). 'Magnesium, however, *is*.' Dr. Tod continues: 'Iron is quite essential in one stage of the formation of chlorophyll, hence no iron, no chlorophyll; but even more, no magnesium, no chlorophyll. You must have both to get the true green of the leaf, so the lack of either can cause chlorosis but I think that when the colour is very severely affected, and even more, when other colours appear, for example, orange and red shades, the trouble is more likely to be magnesium deficiency, though very probably coupled with shortage of iron as well.'

Magnesium is important, too, because it is antagonistic to calcium and if used in a heavy enough dressing tends to crowd out the calcium so that the rhododendrons and azaleas take up more magnesium and less calcium.

In the absence, at the time of writing, of a sequestered iron product that really contains sufficient magnesium, this deficiency can best be met by watering a solution of magnesium sulphate (Epsom salts)—at the rate of two tablespoonsful to two gallons of water—over the root area of each plant. This treatment may be used as a routine measure three or four times a year; spring and autumn seem to be the most effective. Where chlorosis exists, however, an application of *Sequestrene Plus* or *Sequestrene* 138 *Fe* should also be given, preferably in spring, at the rate of a quarter of a teaspoonful to two gallons of water.

Besides magnesium and iron, rhododendrons need manganese and this may best be supplied as a leaf-spray of manganese sulphate —one ounce to two gallons of water—applied in the evening of a dull day.

## Rhododendrons and Azaleas on Limy Soil

So much for the chemical aids that enable one to grow rhododendrons and azaleas in limy soil. The actual physical preparation of the ground is most important. Let me say at once that so far no one has proved it possible to grow the larger rhododendrons on chalk. But in rhododendrons the smaller the leaf, the easier it is to grow the plant in alkaline conditions and so dwarf rhododendrons may be grown quite happily in beds of acid peat retained by peat blocks above the soil level (see Chapter 8). For some reason, limestone seems more accommodating than chalk. On the limestone hills surrounding Colwyn Bay in North Wales, medium-sized rhododendron species and hybrids thrive in many gardens. The same phenomenon may be found in Dorset where, near the late Lord Digby's rhododendron garden at Minterne, Dr. Tod found 'right on the top of the chalk ridge, a hollow with bracken, heather, vaccinium, etc.—the typical acid moor flora—and a few feet away a solid mass of chalk with flints. The soil pH in the hollow was 4·1 and in the surrounding alkaline soil 7·8!!! The area involved represented a fully leached patch where, presumably, the drainage was very much sharper than elsewhere and the considerable rainfall had washed out the calcium, leaving an acid soil. The organic matter gradually gathering in such a spot would become progressively more acid as well. This is why on the west coast of Britain one may find good rhododendron gardens over calcareous rock.'

In cultivation one should aim to help nature by providing acid rooting material, viz, rhododendron peat or rotted bracken, and to add further acid material by yearly or twice yearly mulches of acid peat, spruce needles, rotted bracken, brown bracken, or bracken cut green in June and passed through a chaff cutter to break it down. In our own garden, with an alkaline soil of pH 7·5 and a clay subsoil one spit down, my husband and I grew rhododendrons and azaleas well, over a ten-year period, by digging out individual sites for each plant, improving the drainage by adding stones at the bottom of the hole, lining the hole with flowers of sulphur and filling in with *Eclipse* rhododendron peat and rotted bracken.

Care was taken to mix the peat and rotted bracken well with

the surrounding soil also, so that the questing roots should not suddenly encounter a barrier of hostile soil. After planting we added a six-inch mulch of bracken and pine needles, keeping the mulch away from the actual stems of the plant. The mulch was renewed twice yearly and its success was shown by the way in which the rhododendrons rooted up into the mulch, making solid mats in some cases six or more feet across, thereby avoiding sending down their roots into hostile and limy clay.

In this garden we successfully grew rhododendrons of all sizes from the tree-like *discolor* × *fortunei* hybrid 'Avocet'; hybrids of medium size such as 'Carita', 'Roman Pottery', 'Goblin', 'Nobleanum Venustum' and 'Susan'; the old 'Fastuosum Flore Pleno', 'Lady Eleanor Cathcart' and 'Britannia'; species such as *augustinii* and *lutescens*; *stewartianum*, *dauricum* and the deciduous *mucronulatum* as well as dwarf species and hybrids and evergreen and deciduous azaleas most of which are, like the small-leaved rhododendrons, easier than many to grow in alkaline conditions.

From time to time the medium and larger rhododendrons showed chlorotic symptoms. At no time were these severe and all yielded to the combined treatment with magnesium sulphate, *Sequestrene* 138 *Fe* or *Sequestrene Plus* and manganese. The small-leaved members of the Lapponicum series and hybrids such as 'Blue Tit', 'Blue Diamond', 'Sapphire' and 'Augfast' together with *augustinii*, *lutescens*, 'Yellow Hammer', 'Remo' and 'Praecox', together with the azaleas needed no treatment. Several were dosed experimentally with an iron product but showed their acute resentment by developing toxic symptoms and so treatment was discontinued. None of the untreated plants of this type developed chlorosis. The smallest-leaved rhododendron to show yellowing of the leaf was 'Humming Bird', a hybrid between the dwarf *williamsianum* and *haematodes*. It is interesting to note that *williamsianum* itself grew in the garden without chlorosis but was noticeably slow to get established.

Of the larger rhododendrons, some species and hybrids when growing in limy soil show chlorotic symptoms more markedly than others. Quickest to show such symptoms in our garden were

## Rhododendrons and Azaleas on Limy Soil

R. 'Nobleanum Venustum', 'Britannia' and 'Lady Eleanor Cathcart'. The parentage of 'Nobleanum Venustum' is *caucasicum* × *arboreum*. That of 'Lady Eleanor Cathcart' is *maximum* × *arboreum*. 'Britannia' has been given as a cross between 'Queen Wilhelmina' and 'Stanley Davies'. We know that one parent of 'Queen Wilhelmina' was *griffithianum*. The pedigree of 'Stanley Davies' is unknown to me. Did the noble *arboreum* play some part in its descent or, more probably, in that of 'Queen Wilhelmina'? It is unlikely that 'Queen Wilhelmina' was a straight cross between the species because that would have resulted in too tender an offspring. Could the missing parent of 'Queen Wilhelmina' have been *arboreum* × *caucasicum*—or *catawbiense* × *arboreum* giving us *arboreum* as a common factor between the three lime sensitive hybrids? 'Britannia' has a characteristic light green leaf that might give a clue and it has also the shaggy, reddish bark of *arboreum*.

*Campylocarpum* offspring such as 'Carita' and the poor-foliaged 'Goldfinch' showed few symptoms while the *griersonianum* hybrids 'Goblin' and 'Fabia' seemed to need more manganese than most.

The old *catawbiense* variety 'Fastuosum Flore Pleno' and 'Susan', a *campanulatum* hybrid, showed few symptoms.

The rhododendron and azalea addict whose garden is on limy soil would benefit greatly from the introduction of a new sequestered compound containing much more magnesium and manganese in proportion to the iron. In addition, the environmental needs of the plants must be met by providing shade and shelter where needed and an adequately drained yet moist, acid rooting medium. It is in the provision of this last that one or two additional pitfalls lie. Coarse rhododendron peat is ideal, as stated earlier, yet care must be taken that it really is an *acid* peat that one buys because some horticultural peats have been treated with alkali to reduce their acidity, and some fen peats are alkaline when dug. Peats that have a neutral or even alkaline pH reaction, of course, defeat the main object underlying their use. An excellent grade of acid rhododendron peat may be obtained from the Eclipse Peat Company, Bridgwater, Somerset. Spruce needles and those of other conifers, contrary to a belief held by some, are beneficial to rhododendrons and azaleas both as a feed and as a means of supplying acidity.

Leaf-mould, too, is good, providing that it comes from trees growing in acid soil. In an article published in the *Gardeners' Chronicle* during 1957 Mr. J. P. Fanning, of Glasnevin Botanic Gardens, showed that the leaves of broad-leaved trees growing on calcareous soil may have as much as four times the content of water-soluble calcium as those grown on acid soils. At Glasnevin, in beds made up of leaf-mould from trees grown on limy soil, plants showed extensive chlorosis. Mr. Fanning's investigation showed that as the leaves rotted so the calcium content rose bringing the pH to 7·8. After mixing with peat (four parts) *acid* mountain loam (one part, pH 4·7) and sand (one part pH 6·1) the final pH was 7·1!

Beech, oak and pine absorb less calcium than other trees. Even so it is as well to make sure that one uses only material from trees growing in acid soils. Bracken, too, is sometimes found growing on limestone and so it is wise to use only bracken or bracken peat from known acid ground. Some spent hops, too, have been found to have a high pH value and should not be applied without testing for alkalinity. Old mushroom compost, too, is alkaline.

Freshly dug peat should always be stacked and weathered for at least a year before use.

To recapitulate, the lover of rhododendrons and azaleas can, therefore, hope to succeed in growing his treasures on many alkaline soils provided that due regard is paid to the following points.

1. To grow those members of the family that are least sensitive to lime and less likely greedily to absorb all the available calcium to the exclusion of other foods, i.e. the small-leaved and deciduous rhododendrons and azaleas with only as many of the medium and larger hybrids and species as can be given special treatment.

2. To construct raised beds of acid material to a depth of at least eight inches above the surface of the ground, retaining them with peat blocks, sandstone, or granite, rocks or slate (*not*

limestone). A layer of gravel under the peat helps to prevent limy surface water percolating through the peat. Such raised beds may tend to dry out a little and so due attention should always be paid to watering. Alternatively but less advisably one may take out individual sites for each plant, lining the hole with flowers of sulphur and planting in acid material adding a six-inch mulch of conifer needles, bracken or acid peat into which the plants can send up their roots. (This will work only on slightly alkaline soil (pH 7·5 or so), or in the west. In chalky districts in the south, calcium-rich water from the surrounding soil would probably drain into the site.)

3. Regularly to mulch around the plants in June and November with acid rhododendron peat, chopped or rotted bracken, conifer needles, or oak or beach leaf-mould made with leaves from trees growing on acid ground.

4. At the first signs of chlorosis, to render chemical aid, remembering that magnesium sulphate and sulphate of manganese are *at least as important* as iron compounds and that the small-leaved and deciduous rhododendrons and azaleas are very liable to toxicity when given too much iron. Epsom salts and a spray of sulphate of manganese at the strengths given earlier in this chapter are best for them.

An additional example of the importance of magnesium in maintaining rhododendron health is illustrated by the occurrence of chlorosis in many plants ('Penjerrick', 'Elizabeth', 'Loderi', 'Mahomet' and 'Naomi' were among those affected) on acid soil pH 4·5 at Bulkeley Mill. With the permission of the present owners I obtained leaf samples, some of which were sent by Dr. Aiken and Mrs. M. Bennett of the Geigy Company to Dr. Henry Tod. About this problem Dr. Tod wrote to me as follows: 'I was, in the early stages, severely shaken to find this chlorosis at low pH values, but things have become much clearer with an increased number of samples, for in almost every case it has become evident that the cause on low pH soils is magnesium deficiency.'

In a paper in the *Rhododendron and Camellia Year Book* for 1961 Dr. Tod points out that in nineteen of twenty-three matching

9. *R. leucaspis*, an early-flowering dwarf with milky-white salver flowers, here seen fronting a shrub bed at Nymans

10. *R. davidsonianum*, one of the most attractive species of the Triflorum series with narrow leaves and flowers that in the best forms are warm pink, speckled with brown

11. *R. macabeanum*, a comparatively recent introduction and one of the finest large-leaved species with deep yellow flowers

12. *R. souliei*, a pretty species of the Thomsonii series with pink or white, silky-textured flowers and heart-shaped leaves that when young have a bluey sheen

leaf-samples analysed by him the real cause of the trouble was magnesium deficiency (8 cases), potassium deficiency (2 cases) or combined magnesium and potassium deficiencies (9 cases). Six samples from alkaline soils were also interesting as they showed low magnesium and/or potassium levels as well as manganese deficiency.

Dr. Tod sums up: 'The results would seem to indicate that at neutral alkaline soil reactions, magnesium is as important as manganese, and perhaps more so, and that 'lime-induced chlorosis' may, in rhododendron, be more a manifestation of magnesium deficiency induced by an excess of calcium than a deficiency of other elements such as manganese or iron.'

Apart from interveinal chlorosis, magnesium deficiency some-times shows itself by orange, purple or rose blotchings and spot-tings on the leaves. In our garden this occurred on evergreen azaleas and camellias, while ornamental cherries and roses, as well as rhododendrons, showed interveinal yellowing of the leaves in patterns indicative of deficiencies of both manganese and mag-nesium.

Readers will have noted that Dr. Tod mentions also potassium deficiency. This may be prevented by a mulch of bracken cut green in June and passed through a chaff cutter or chopped with shears. Green bracken is extrmely rich in potassium which as the bracken rots will become available to the rhododendron roots.

Another solution to the problem of accommodating rhododen-drons on limy soils might lie in the breeding of a non-lime-greedy race. *Rhododendron hirsutum*, that near relation of *R. ferrugineum*, grows upon calcareous limestone formations in the Alps. Now, in other genera, hybrids between the so-called 'lime-tolerant' and 'lime-sensitive' species have been found to do well on limy soils. There exists a hybrid between *R. hirsutum* and *R. minus* (a form of the North American *R. carolinianum*) *R.* 'Myrtifolium' which seems quite happy in untreated limy ground. I intend to experi-ment with this with the intention of crossing it with other scaly-leaved species and hybrids (scaly and non-scaly rhododendrons are reluctant to cross) such as *racemosum*, 'Blue Diamond', and

## Rhododendrons and Azaleas on Limy Soil

the members of the Glaucophyllum and Cinnabarinum series in the hope of building up a race that will do well in alkaline soils. It has been suggested to me that the lime-tolerant trait might be weakened in successive generations but I think a second crossing to another species known to do well on lime might strengthen the lime tolerance and so overcome this objection.

*R. calciphilum* of the Saluenense series has been found in Asia growing on calcareous gravel so it may be presumed that this species, too, has potentialities as a parent to produce offspring less sensitive to an excess lime content of the soil and this is the species to which I think the secondary cross should be made.

Dr. Tod has satisfactorily proved that rhododendrons and azaleas grew happily in soils of over pH 8 provided that the high pH was due to a high magnesium content rather than high calcium levels. This may account for the reports of many rhododendron species growing in China on limestone formations. In a paper read before the Rhododendron Society on 20th July 1915, the plant collector, George Forrest, stated: 'Most of the rhododendrons I have collected in the region (west and north-west Yunnan) grow directly in or on pure limestone.' The limestones in question, as far as they have been investigated, have been found to be magnesian limestone with magnesium present in quantities large enough successfully to inhibit the uptake of excess calcium by the plants.

Even though I, or others, may be successful in raising a race of rhododendrons that are less affected by the presence or otherwise of lime in the soil they will still need proper rooting conditions of a moist yet friable and well-drained soil. It seems to me likely that it will be necessary, also, from time to time to add Epsom salts to correct any magnesium deficiency that may arise. On heavy, limy land *Erica carnca* and *E. × darleyensis, both* of which are known to do well on lime and chalk, develop considerable chlorosis due to magnesium deficiency.

Such rhododendron species (*hirsutum, calciphilum* and in some cases *lapponicum*—the species, not any of its fellow members of the series) as grow upon calcareous limestone in the wild presumably differ in their lime intake from those species which grow upon acid soils. The acid-soil dwellers need to abstract *all* the available calcium from their calcium-poor surroundings. The limestone-dwellers have no such need. It is necessary for them to modify their calcium intake in order to take up the other necessary foods. I hope that the lime-dwelling species will pass on this power of discrimination to their offspring just as has the lime-tolerant *Eucryphia cordifolia* to *E*. 'Nymansay' its offspring with the lime-sensitive *E. glutinosa*.

Mycorrhizae, the root fungi that are found in or on the roots of rhododendrons, azaleas and other *ericaceae*, constitute a problem that has long puzzled the botanists. Kingdon Ward, the plant-collector, wrote in his book on the genus: 'It is hard to believe mycorrhiza is found in the coarse, gravelly soil of the Tibetan plateau where some species are found.'

In 1933, the New Jersey Agricultural Experimental Station, U.S.A., grew *R. ponticum* in clean, coarse quartz sand, fed by a constant drip of mono-potassium phosphate, magnesium sulphate, ammonium sulphate, calcium nitrate and a little ferrous sulphate. No root fungi were present and the rhododendrons instead formed root-hairs (normally absent in the genus). As a result of this an American authority, Dr. C. G. Bowers, decided that mycorrhizae must be regarded as fundamentally parasitic and without benefit to rhododendrons.

David G. Leach in his *Rhododendrons of the World* states that he cannot agree with Dr. Bowers's conclusion. 'I have observed,' he writes, 'without exception, that rhododendron seedlings in a variety encompassing scores of species and hybrids which are grown in pure sphagnum moss develop root hairs in the absence of mycorrhizae; but when they are transplanted outdoors into suitable soil, the mycorrhizal fungus invariably soon forms and the new root development is without hairs from that time onward. It seems much more likely that the generation of root hairs under these synthetic conditions of sterile culture in sand and sphagnum moss is just another of the marvellous ways in which rhododendrons adapt themselves to unnatural conditions in order to survive. It is probable that the root fungi play a natural, beneficial role in their nutrition under normal conditions and soil acidity is one of the factors favourable to their development. The others are adequate moisture, and abundant amounts of organic matter in process of decomposition, particularly when it approaches humus.'

Enthusiasts who are growing rhododendrons in an alkaline region may be faced with a problem during dry weather when their supply of stored rain-water runs out. This may be offset during an emergency by using tap-water with a teaspoonful of Epsom Salts (magnesium sulphate) and a teaspoonful of aluminium sulphate or commercial alum added to every gallon to counteract the alkalinity of the water supply.

Dwarf rhododendron species and hybrids may be grown successfully for many years in large plastic bowls with drainage holes punched in the bottom sunk into the garden and stood on sandstone blocks at the bottom of the planting hole so that any tendency to root downward into the alkaline soil is effectively discouraged. Rhododendrons and azaleas, in any case, usually make their roots only just below surface level and if a yearly mulch of rotted bracken or rhododendron peat is added they will tend to root up rather than down and so there will be no problem.

## CHAPTER 6

# Soil, Shelter and Site

The reader who, in spite of gardening upon acid soil, has had the patience to read the last chapter will have some idea of the basic soil requirements of the rhododendron family. For those who have felt that the problems of a limy soil do not concern them we should summarize as follows:

(*a*) Rhododendrons and azaleas do best on an acid soil, pH value 4·5 to 6. Above this level they need the provision of acid rooting material and twice-yearly mulches of similarly acid material.

(*b*) Rhododendrons and azaleas need a moist yet porous rooting medium. They will not tolerate badly drained conditions. Ideally rhododendrons like a woodland soil or a medium, rich acid loam. A heavy loam is better than light, hungry, sandy soil. Open heathlands have acid soils upon which birch and heather thrive yet they are often too dry and hungry for rhododendrons and, before shelter is provided, are also too open and wind-swept. Such soils unless treated often suit azaleas and the small-leaved dwarfs better than the larger-leaved rhododendrons which would grow stunted and sickly without more moisture and food. On the other hand, heavy soils are sticky, cold and often badly drained, offering little encouragement to the fine, fibrous roots of rhododendrons and azaleas. A waterlogged soil will quickly damage their roots.

Rhododendrons and azaleas need a coarse, well-aerated soil to do well. They will thrive at the edge of water providing the land is porous and well-drained. Waterlogging suffocates the roots and kills the plants. In the past it used to be said that rhododendrons needed peat. Certainly a coarsely-grained acid peat suits them well but they will do equally well in an acid fibrous loam.

Most soils are short of humus. Heavy soils need well-rotted organic material to lighten them. Light soils need humus to give them body and to supply plant food to replace that which is too quickly broken down and equally quickly disappears. Really coarse rhododendron peat is valuable to supply bulk. It lasts in the soil for eight to ten years, but it has no food value. Rotted bracken, spruce needles, or spent hops, should be mixed with it to supply the nutriment so desperately needed by plants on hungry light soil.

Clay soils should always be worked in dry weather as wet weather makes them so sticky that one cannot break down the lumps. Heavy clay soils are best rough-dug in autumn and left to the wind and frost to work during the winter so that peat and sand may be more easily added before planting in spring. On heavy soils added nourishment is less important. The urgent need is to improve the drainage. This can be done by placing a layer of stones or gravel at the bottom of the planting holes which are then filled with a suitable rhododendron compost. I plant in pure bracken peat but I live where bracken is plentiful. Where bracken is scarce, Eclipse rhododendron peat mixed with spruce needles makes a good substitute. Coarse sand, too, may be added to improve the soil texture. I hesitate to recommend leaf-mould because it is too quickly absorbed in the soil. In really heavy soils all traces of well-rotted oak leaf-mould will have disappeared by the end of a year. When leaf-mould is used it is important to be sure that it has rotted down completely into a crumbly black mould. If half-rotted material is added to the soil it causes serious nitrogen deficiency and soil-unbalance, because soil nitrogen is used to break it down when the rotting process is completed underground. Leaf-mould from broad-leaved trees on limy ground is a danger as it has a high calcium content. When experimenting to find the best planting medium I did plant one or two rhododendrons in acid leaf-mould and the plants made much slower growth than their neighbours planted in bracken-peat.

Sawdust should never be dug into the soil as, so used, it causes nitrogen deficiency, although it may—with the addition of sulphate of ammonia, as described later—be used as a mulch. I do not consider that garden compost is suitable for rhododendrons.

Instead of preparing single sites for rhododendrons and their companions, it is better where possible to prepare a wide bed, digging it a spit deep and incorporating gravel with the broken-up undersoil before replacing the topsoil well mixed with coarse peat, rotted bracken or conifer needles.

When preparing sites for single plants it is important to mix the bracken peat, rhododendron peat or conifer needles well into the surrounding soil otherwise the plants hesitate to thrust out their roots. They are confined within the narrow space of the planting hole as in a pot. Eventually they starve, become sickly and die. A surface mulch, by encouraging the rhododendrons to send their roots upwards into its well-aerated and suitable texture, helps to counteract some of the dangers inherent in growing rhododendrons on very heavy soil.

As stated in the last chapter, it is not only on limy soils that the characteristic yellowing of the leaves known as chlorosis occurs. In many gardens on acid soil extensive chlorosis sometimes occurs. The late Mr. A. T. Johnson's garden at Bulkeley Mill is an ideal rhododendron garden with a moist, well-drained, woodsy acid soil of pH 4·5 to 5. Yet a considerable interveinal yellowing showed itself in the leaves of a dozen or more plants. I have noticed similar symptoms, too, in dry and rather windswept gardens on sandy, acid soil, Dr. Tod of Edinburgh has given the explanation (see the foregoing chapter). It seems that such deficiency symptoms on acid soils are caused by a shortage of magnesium. It is probable that in the soil of China and the Himalayas more magnesium exists than in many acid soils in this country. We remember again how most of Forrest's rhododendrons were found on magnesian limestone. On acid as on alkaline soils, chlorosis due to magnesium deficiency may be cured by a dosage of Epsom salts (magnesium sulphate) administered in solution (two tablespoonsful of Epsom salts to two gallons of water) and applied over the roots of each affected plant. On a larger scale the rate of administration would be six pounds to a hundred gallons or, if applied dry as a soil dressing, ten pounds per thousand square feet.

A shortage of potassium also induces chlorosis and this can be corrected by yearly mulching with chopped green bracken, cut fresh in June, or by a dressing of potassium sulphate which leaves an acid residue. Potassium nitrate is to be avoided.

Occasionally, and rather surprisingly, very acid soils may be short of calcium, a certain amount of which rhododendrons (as we saw in the last chapter) have a definite need. When there is a shortage of sufficient calcium in over-acid soils, yellowing occurs between the veins of new leaves followed by a burning and blackening of the tip (this also occurs when plants growing in alkaline soils have been over-dosed with iron sequestrenes). As the yellowing progresses, the terminal leaves become twisted and the end buds are killed. Scorching affects the older leaves and die-back of the shoots may sometimes occur. Some growers have experimented by treating affected plants in over-acid ground with applications of limestone but this is a risky business and the missing calcium is best supplied by adding gypsum which while curing the trouble will not reduce soil acidity.

Chlorosis, or sometimes leaf-dropping and even death of the affected plants, may be caused by too-deep planting which prevents air getting to the roots and so stops them functioning and taking in their proper nourishment from the soil. I have also known leaves yellow and drop from root-suffocation caused by a mulch of too fine a peat or too close-textured a leaf-mould which when watered by flooding, instead of by an overhead spray, washed close against the stem of the plant and matted densely, denying all air to the roots. Lifting and planting again at the proper depth with only a light covering of *coarse* peat above the root ball is a speedy and reliable cure. Over-watering, or the waterlogging of badly drained soil, is another cause of trouble.

Good rhododendron soils are moist (but well-drained) and rich and on these there is little need for plant foods other than those supplied by the natural leaf-fall of the rhododendrons themselves and an occasional mulch of bracken. On light, hungry soils it is a different matter and extra food must be supplied. Well-rotted cow manure, of course, is excellent but in these days cow-manure is not always easily come by. Spent hops, however, make a good substitute and may be applied as a mulch when mixed with coarse rhododendron peat or rotted bracken. A couple of bucketsful, too, added when planting will pay dividends in good growth over the years. A word of caution must be added here, however, because some treated hop-manures have been neutralized with lime. This might not have very much effect on plants in very acid soils but at pH values above 5·5 it might cause trouble, so it is safer to use only those hop-manures with an acid reaction.

Bone-meal is sometimes advised but although it may not cause apparent damage on very acid sandy soils it is not to be recommended on account of its high calcium content. Hoof and horn, on the other hand, is perfectly safe. In some areas fish-manure and guano are used but these, like bone-meal and superphosphate, have too high a lime content to be safe for lime-sensitive plants except on some extremely acid soils where heavy rainfall or extreme porosity results in the rapid leaching away of the lime.

Mulching plays an important part in the cultivation of rhododendrons and azaleas and should be carried out twice yearly—in May or June when the soil has warmed up but is still moist, and in November before the ground is too cold. The function of the mulch is threefold. (1) It acts as a blanket, keeping the soil warm in winter and helping to retain the moisture through the summer months. (2) It rots down to add humus to the soil. (3) An ideal mulch also supplies plant food. In addition, on inhospitable limy or heavy clay soils, the mulch should provide a congenial material into which the rhododendrons can thrust up their roots.

Bracken, cut from acid ground, is one of the best of all mulching substances for rhododendrons and azaleas. It is rich in potash and other plant foods and makes a loose, non-clogging mulch, rotting down to a rich, black, peaty tilth. For the early summer mulch, bracken should be cut green in June, chopped to lengths of a foot or less and applied when the ground is moist after heavy rain or after a thorough, deep watering. In November one may cut and use the rust-brown fronds or one may scoop the already rotted, crumbly brown residue from under the clumps. Coarsely chopped fronds may be applied in a mulch a foot deep around large rhododendrons. For the dwarfs the rotted deposit is probably best and a four-inch depth of this will suffice. Some of the small Lapponicum type rhododendrons like the hybrid 'Blue Tit' like to have the mulch heaped over their branches at ground level and will respond by rooting along the stems and providing new plants. It is sometimes said that low mounded rhododendrons of the *forrestii* var. *repens* type must have their centres kept clear of leaves or they will die back. I think, rather, that a certain amount of die-back is natural to some of these creeping species and that working the top-dressing well in to the centre helps to stimulate new roots and to keep the plants going. *Forrestii* var. *repens* and also the little creeping *radicans* and others of the Saluenense series need the provision of a suitable rooting medium on their perimeter to encourage them to keep spreading and rooting as they grow in a healthy manner.

Conifer needles are an excellent mulching material which may be used either in conjunction with or to replace the bracken. I like to use both, sometimes mixed, and sometimes alternately. On limy soils I think that the needles are an even better corrective of alkalinity than is the bracken.

A coarse grade of acid rhododendron peat fulfils the mechanical requirements of mulching well. Its only shortcoming is its lack of plant food content. On good rhododendron soils this does not matter. On poor, hungry soils, or where the pH is 6 or above, the peat should be supplemented by spent hops of an acid reaction or cow-manure at the rate of half a bucketful per large plant. If one digs one's own peat, however, it is important to allow the blocks to weather for a year before breaking up for use.

Garden compost may be limy, due to the high calcium content of cabbage stalks and leaves, eggshells, etc., or because an alkaline activator has been used. Also it is apt to clog and mat, and seems to attract slugs. I would never use it as a mulch for rhododendrons or azaleas.

Leaf-mould is not as good as bracken or spruce needles and it, too, is apt to clog or to have a high calcium content if made from the leaves of hardwood trees growing on limy ground. When the leaves have been taken from trees on acid soil, however, it does have a certain food value. Beech or oak leaf-mould is best.

Grass clippings are definitely harmful as they mat and prevent the aeration of the soil.

Some growers have used sawdust as a mulch but this is not always successful. It may, as it rots, use up nitrogen from the soil and so induce a nitrogen deficiency. To counteract this, sulphate of ammonia should be mixed with the sawdust at the rate of a pound per bushel or else applied in spring over the root area at the rate of a handful per plant, well watered in. Care should be taken to keep the sulphate of ammonia away from the rhododendron stems and indeed all mulching material should be kept well clear of the stems or trunks.

When cow-manure is obtainable it may be applied at the rate of a forkful or so per plant around the outer part of the root area in spring. Many experts stipulate well-rotted cow-manure but I have applied cow pats fresh from the fields with only beneficial effect.

Two handfuls of hoof-and-horn per plant mixed with a mulching material will also prove of help.

Tea leaves and cold tea which would otherwise be thrown away is a splendid tonic for rhododendrons and azaleas. It has been said that their use applies only to a small garden where the owner can readily empty the contents of the pot over each plant in turn but this need not be the case. In larger establishments a receptacle should be provided within easy reach of the kitchen and bothy, or potting shed. This will quickly be filled and the contents can be emptied over any plant that seems in need of a stimulant. I have brought rhododendrons back almost from the dead solely by regular dosing with cold tea. Tea leaves are rich in nitrogen and are of course acid into the bargain.

Natural leaf-fall, both from the rhododendrons themselves and from nearby trees and shrubs, is of course beneficial. Fallen leaves should never be collected or burned and when ivy happens to cover the ground it should be left, as it not only acts as a living mulch but helps to trap and retain falling leaves and so add to the humus and nourishment content of the soil.

Some wind shelter is a *must* with many rhododendrons. Generally speaking, the larger the leaf the greater the protection needed, although some members of the fairly large-leaved Fortunei series are remarkably wind-hardy and provide an exception to prove the rule. The dwarf species and hybrids, on the other hand, do not mind some wind and do better when exposed to it than in an enclosed, stuffy part of the garden or in a humid glen. Wind damage to the leaves of even the 'ironclad' hybrids is unsightly and so where a rhododendron with even medium-sized leaves is grown on its merits as a plant of attractive appearance it should be planted out of the wind. Some medium and quite large rhododendrons are virtually indestructible and may be grown to provide shelter for more sensitive types. In this case, foliage appearance is of secondary consideration. Such species as *rubiginosum* (a species which is to some degree insensitive to lime), *desquamatum, fortunei* and the Kingdon Ward forms of *decorum* are useful to provide shelter as are the big old hardy hybrids (which could well be transplanted from choicer parts of many gardens to fulfil just this purpose) and some of the *discolor* hybrids as well as *ponticum* which is particularly useful for stopping draughts at ground level but is apt to be a nuisance on account of its seeding propensity.

Other evergreens which are useful to provide shelter include thuja, chamaecyparis, junipers, holly, *Osmanthus heterophyllus*, the fragrant × *Osmarea burkwoodii, Elaeagnus pungens* and × *ebbingei*, the glossy-green, unspotted form of aucuba, and near the sea, or in milder climates, escallonia, nothofagus, and the strong-growing *Olearia macrodonta* with its greyish, holly-like leaves and daisy flowers, the remarkably strong scent of which mingles headily with that of the azaleas in the warmth of the early summer sun. Shelter should always be planted to break the force of the prevailing wind and to cut off cold winds from the north and east.

Those planting in old gardens or woodland are lucky to have shelter ready-made. In new gardens it may be necessary to provide temporary windbreaks of wattle hurdles or fine-mesh rabbit-netting until the living shelter becomes established. The most-quickly grown of living shelter-belt subjects is undoubtedly × *Cupressocyparis leylandii*, a bi-generic hybrid between the fast-growing but fickle *Cupressus macrocarpa* and the ultra-hardy *Chamaecyparis nootkatensis*. The cupressocyparis is even quicker growing than *Cupressus macrocarpa* and does not suffer from wind-rock or frost damage. Planted from pots, in eight years it will top ten feet and should be planted as a screen four feet apart.

Belts of Sitka spruce in dotted lines of three make a good outer windbreak in very exposed places. By the sea, where winds are often devastating, they may be supplemented by inner belts of griselinia, senecio and escallonia.

Where established shelter belts have suffered a 'blow-through' and trees have fallen during severe gales, effective temporary 'stop-gaps' may be made from coir fibre netting mounted on six-foot frames of wood, or on aluminium or tubular iron supports of the type used for supporting the netting around tennis courts. I have seen this successfully used at Brodick and other west-coast gardens that are exposed to the full fury of off-the-sea gales.

Even in an established garden it is sometimes necessary to protect newly-planted rhododendrons from cold, drying winds in spring. A temporary shelter of hessian firmly nailed to four stakes and placed so as to enclose the plant on three sides, leaving it open to the south, is generally the answer. Syringing with water also helps to offset the destructive drying force of the wind. 'Cages' of branches and bracken may be used to protect tender plants against frost.

Frost is an old enemy in rhododendron gardens, and frost hollows are to be avoided when planting all but the hardiest rhododendrons. It is important to watch air-drainage and when planting on a slope to avoid blocking the downward flow of frost by belts of evergreens or by walls. Where such exist, gaps should be cut at the lowest points to allow the frost to seep away. Valleys and glens can be dangerous, too, when the lower ends are blocked by buildings or thick shrub plantings.

The north side of a building or large evergreen offers early-flowering rhododendrons the best hope of surviving frost with their blossoms unscathed. In my own garden I grow *mucronulatum*, the similar but evergreen *dauricum* and the February-blooming *moupinense* on the north side of a tall, beech hedge.

An overhead canopy formed by the branches of deciduous trees also helps to protect rhododendron flowers from frost. Another dodge is to plant such small early rhododendrons as *moupinense* and *leucaspis* in rather exposed sites where the sun can ripen their wood in summer and where the winter cold will retard their flowers until the worst frosts are past. Often it is the May frosts which do the damage, reducing to browned pulp the flowers of many rhododendrons and cutting back the young shoots of plants which make their growth early. Apart from avoiding frost-hollows and planting in shelter from icy winds, there is little one can do about spring frosts. In gardens that are badly affected every year by April or early May frosts one might decide to plant only the earlier-flowering rhododendrons (which often seem to miss being cut in just those gardens) and later-blooming species and hybrids. This is a counsel of despair. It is rarely the same plants which are cut year after year and I would always be willing to sacrifice the scented, glorious flowers of, say, 'Loderi' after a couple of days if I had enjoyed them in perfection for the first forty-eight hours.

For smaller plants, polythene offers the perfect solution to the problem. Plant one's early beauties near to the house and then it is easy to slip out in the still, cloudless dusk that foretells frost to envelop any plants in bloom with polythene bags of the type sold for storing blankets or eiderdowns. Several thicknesses of newspaper laid flat on the top of a dwarf species will also afford protection and I know of two gardens, at least, which regularly resemble white-sheeted ghosts under the frosty stars of April and May!

Tender rhododendrons pose a different question. Only the warmth of a south or west wall will enable most of the gardeners in Britain to grow many of the members of the Maddenii series or the fragrant greenhouse hybrids out of doors. In frosty inland gardens the plants rated Category C in the second part of this book will also need the shelter of a wall or hedge, and when planting in such positions even more careful attention than usual must be paid to soil preparation. All traces of limy rubble should be removed, any encroaching roots should be cut back to give the plants a start, and plenty of moisture-holding peat (well-damped before use) together with cow-manure or spent hops and hoof-and-horn should be incorporated. Care must also be taken to prevent the plants drying out during the summer months.

CHAPTER 7

# Shade, Planting, Watering and Cultivation

>>>>>>>>>>>>>>>>>>>>>>>><<<<<<<<<<<<<<<<<<<<<<<<

Shade is less important in Scotland and the north of England than in the south. However, light, dappled shade should be arranged for all but the dwarfs, most of which are better without it. Apart from helping to cut down excessive transpiration in hot, dry weather, shade also helps to prevent the flowers wilting and preserves their colour. This last factor is particularly important with regard to many of the evergreen azaleas. The flowers of the little Kurumes are remarkably sun-fast but the Kaempferi hybrids and others are very apt to fade—the orange and flame colours being particularly bad and giving an ugly mottled effect.

In new gardens where little shade exists it will be necessary to plant fairly quick-growing—yet not too greedy—trees to provide the chequered shade and branch canopy that most rhododendrons need. Particularly suitable are the maples—seed-raised *Acer palmatum* saplings are often an economic proposition—the paper-barked *Acer griseum* with its lovely cinnamon trunk, *Acer rufinerve*, *A. circinnatum*, *A. nikoense* and the striped snake-barks *A. hersii*, *davidii* and *capillipes*. Also good are the snowdrop-trees, *Styrax japonica* and *hemsleyana*, *Halesia carolina* and *monticola*; the stewartias, beautiful in habit, bark, leaf, flower and autumn-colour; *Pterostyrax hispida*; cherries such as *Prunus subhirtella* 'Autumnalis', 'Beni Higan' and *sargentii* with their frothy clouds of small flowers, the pale pink *yedoensis*, and such larger-flowered varieties as 'Ukon', pale creamy yellow, the fine white 'Tai Haku' and 'Shim-

13. *R. discolor*, one of the fine, scented species of the Fortunei series

14. The barn garden at Bulkeley Mill showing some of the many pretty dwarf rhododendrons

15. *R. hanceanum* 'Nanum', the dwarf form of this yellow-flowered species of the Triflorum series is much finer than its large relative

16. *R. oleifolium*, an attractive deep-pink early-flowered relation of the well-known *racemosum*

idsu', and such pinks as 'Fugenzo', 'Pink Perfection' and 'Mikuruma-gaeshi'. The pinks should, I think, be kept away from rhododendrons of a hot red—the cooling yellow of 'Ukon' suits the red rhododendrons best—while blue rhododendrons such as *augustinii*, 'Susan', and the dwarfer 'Blue Diamond' and 'Sapphire' group look delightful in association with the white 'Shirofugen' which usually blooms at about the same time.

Sorbus species such as *vilmorinii*, *decora*, *cashmiriana* and *hupehensis* are useful to provide just the right degree of shade as well as the interest of autumn-colour and berries when few rhododendrons are in flower.

Birch roots are said to compete with the rhododendrons for nourishment and perhaps the birches are better planted in conjunction with the dwarfs rather than the bigger species and hybrids which need correspondingly more moisture and nourishment. *Betula ermanni*, the rare *jacquemontii*, *Albo-sinensis septentrionalis pendula* 'Dalecarlica' and *nigra* are all worthy of places where their beauty of bark can be seen to perfection. Other useful trees to provide light shade are the arbutuses and amelanchiers and cornus species.

On the other hand, shade can be too dense and in many of the older rhododendron gardens more light needs to be let in by removing some of the overhanging branch canopy and occasionally cutting down a conifer or two. This has to be very carefully done, with due regard to preserving windbreaks and frost protection. It is so easy to let in light where dense shade has resulted in straggly, drawn-up growth and at the same time to create a wind-funnel in which the poor, spindly trunks are exposed to icy bark-splitting blasts.

Where rhododendrons have been drawn-up by shade one has to consider carefully whether or not to cut them back severely so that they will make decent, compact growth. Many rhododendrons respond well to being cut back although some of the species and hybrids may take a little time to recover and build up their growth before flowering freely again. In my opinion, a year or two without flower is a small price to pay for a shapely, well-clothed plant. On the other hand, smooth-barked rhododendrons should never be cut back as they seldom make satisfactory new growth. One has, therefore, to decide whether one prefers to keep one's old, spindly *thomsonii*—a tuft or two of leaves and a few trusses of glorious, blood-red bells on top of nine or ten feet of beautifully dappled but naked bark—or to uproot and burn the plant and start again with an eighteen-inch youngster which will take a number of years to flower satisfactorily. As a compromise one might keep the *thomsonii* and transplant a three- or four-foot species from elsewhere in the garden to cover the worst of its legginess.

Where pruning is decided upon, it should be carried out at the end of March or after flowering. A close watch should be kept on grafted plants after pruning as the cutting-back stimulates the root-stock and makes it throw up suckers.

What size of plants to buy is a vexed question. With an eighteen-inch plant, of a species that may take another five years or so to flower, costing perhaps £1·75, one is tempted to be rash and buy a two-and-a-half to three-foot plant at two or three pounds. But when one is buying two or three dozen plants at a time the price difference may make one think. When it comes to planting in hundreds, of course, the price probably does not matter anyway. For myself, when buying species that take a long time to flower, I would—from sheer impatience—buy the larger plant. Specimens above three feet in height, however, I would hesitate to purchase because they are so much more difficult to establish, so much more sensitive to drought and wind and frost. Within one's own garden rhododendrons of almost any size are highly portable—provided one keeps intact the root ball, they even seem to benefit from the change—but plants bought-in from a nursery undergo a severe shock. They are apt to dry out. They are sometimes half-suffocated by their wrappings or they travel with their foliage unwrapped (which is preferable) but are left about in icy draughts on railway stations. Large specimens take a long time to get over this and to adjust themselves to a change of climate, so, while I would often recommend buying the second or third size plant, beyond this I would not go.

With dwarfs and species that flower at an early age I usually buy smaller plants which seem to get away quickly and to do well.

A question that often arises is whether or not to buy grafted plants. I would never buy a grafted rhododendron if I could buy one on its own roots, even at a much higher price, and I would not have a grafted azalea within the garden.

Unless the plants are root-grafted, suckers of the understock always arise. When one grows more than half a dozen or so plants it is a nuisance always to have to be on the look-out for them. Moreover, they are not always easy to distinguish or to remove satisfactorily and already too many gardens are full of *ponticum* rhododendron and *luteum* azaleas that have overthrown and often starved to death the choicer hybrids which were grafted upon them. For this reason it is always preferable to deal with a reputable nursery and to state that you will accept only those plants which are on their own roots. From the better rhododendron nurseries and from the gardens attached to private estates such plants (raised from cuttings, or as layers) can readily be obtained. Nor are they always more costly and even if they were, to be sure that one is forever free of the suckering nuisance makes them cheap at the price. It is amazing how many people will pay a hundred or two hundred pounds for a carpet or to have furniture recovered and yet quibble when it comes to buying plants that will give a lifetime-and-a-half of beauty.

In these days of mist propagation and improved rooting methods, there is little excuse for grafting rhododendrons except perhaps for the odd plant of the handsome-leaved, yellow-flowered *lacteum* which when on its own roots is so difficult to grow in anything but the optimum conditions. Even then I would prefer to content myself instead with the easier *wightii* or the good and easy *macabeanum*. Another excuse made for grafting is that it may result in reducing the flowering age of the bigger species and of some of the first-cross hybrids which, like 'Loderi', take a number of years to bloom. Even in the face of this argument I think that I prefer to be patient. While one is waiting for the plants to flower, one has their beauty of leaf and bark—the lift of their leaves to a warm shower, their quilling and drooping to protect themselves from cold, and the gradual assuming of a happier port when spring is near. Moreover, in the end the grafted plant usually proves shorter-lived than the one on its own roots. Think of the rhododendron woods and old gardens that one knows where grafted plants were used. How many of the grafted varieties remain as against the forest of ponticum? Think again of woods and gardens in the west where the old Hooker species were grown from seed and planted out. Today there remain giant specimens of the Arboreum series, *arboreum* hybrids, and the *niveum, rex falconeri, hodgsoni* and *grande* species. Many of them are in good health today and thriving more than a century after planting! I should like to see a hundred-years-old grafted plant that would compare with them.

It is usually best to plant rhododendrons and azaleas at the same depth as that at which they were previously growing. This will easily be seen by a glance at the stem. In case of doubt, the top of the root ball should be covered by no more than an inch of peat, bracken or pine needles. It is important that the part of the root ball near the stem of the plant is covered by only the lightest and most porous material so as to allow air to reach the roots.

On dry sandy soils, the plants should be set a little deeper than normal, leaving a shallow depression above the root ball and around the stem. This 'saucer' should be perhaps eighteen inches across and will serve to collect rainwater which, in such a dry soil, will quickly percolate to the roots. On heavy soils this practice would be dangerous as stagnant water would lie in the 'saucer' and cause suffocation and death of the roots.

On really heavy soils it is advisable to plant at a shallower depth than usual, leaving the top inch or two of the root ball above ground, and topping off with a ten-inch mulch of coarse peat, pine needles or rotted bracken. As stated earlier the plant will eventually root into the mulch and so avoid contact with the wet, cold clay.

Planting in a suitable medium that will remain moist and yet provide proper drainage together with the provision of the right amount of shade are among the most important factors for success with rhododendrons. Nothing is sadder than the sight of rhododendrons in dry soil and without shade, their leaves rolled in a desperate attempt to prevent dehydration by their last remaining moisture being drawn off by transpiration.

Many woodland gardens have steep slopes that present a planting problem. The danger is that the drainage will prove too sharp and that the rainwater will run downhill without penetrating to the roots of rhododendrons and azaleas growing on the slope. To offset this it helps to cut a step or shelf out of the bank and to set the rhododendron or azalea on this, mounding the excavated earth at the front to form a shallow rim to trap the water which will then drain down to the plant's roots rather than running away down the slope. This was the method that Mr. A. T. Johnson successfully used at Bulkeley Mill and which enabled him to grow even such large-leaved species as *falconeri* on a steep woodland bank with a gradient of 1 in 3. The planting depressions serve another useful purpose in catching falling leaves and retaining them to rot down into humus and plant food.

Some trees are exceptionally greedy and it is unwise to set and plant rhododendrons within fifteen feet of Scots pine, birch, poplars, sycamores, or beeches. Old oaks and alders are more hospitable as are many of the magnolias and crab-apples while one can safely plant up to a few feet of cherries, the smaller maples and others which are recommended earlier in this chapter as shade-trees.

Half-buried stones and boulders are useful to conserve moisture and may be placed over the roots of dwarf rhododendrons and azaleas growing in sunny places. They are also useful when planting on a slope and many plants on sun-baked rock-gardens owe their survival to being planted above a large stone, under which their roots can find moisture and coolness.

Watering is all too necessary in many rhododendron and azalea gardens during the summer months and it is not at all unusual for rhododendrons to die of drought. Indeed, over much of the country more losses are often due to drought than frost. Some means of watering should therefore be available and in these days of plastic pipes and automatic sprays it should be possible to arrange a permanent watering system in all but the biggest gardens. However, in many areas, the public water supply is often restricted just at the time when the rhododendrons need it most. The keen rhododendron grower, therefore, must devise alternate and independent supplies. Rainwater tanks or barrels can be used to catch the drips from every roof and it is even more satisfactory if such catchment can flow into an underground reservoir tank or container from which water can be pumped at will to supply the garden. It is important, however, that a plastic or metal container is used, or if one resorts to concrete to see that it is treated with the appropriate paint to prevent it giving off lime and other harmful substances which might pollute the water supply.

In an acid-soiled garden where the tap water is limy I do not think one need have too much heart-searching over using it when no other water supply is available. In North Staffordshire where, until 1950, we grew rhododendrons for many years, we often used the hard water supply of the district to water plants in time of drought. Our soil, however, was sand and gravel and very acid. I never saw any suspicion of chlorosis as a result. On neutral or limy soils, however, using water from an alkaline source might well be the last factor in a losing battle and in such areas one really must use rainwater or else be resigned not to water at all.

Advice to 'keep the hoe going' is, of course, disastrous where rhododendrons and azaleas are grown, as such mechanical interference would harm their fibrous, shallow roots. A deep mulch of suitable material is a far better conserver of moisture than any dust-bowl tilth that the hoe ever induced!

Much of a rhododendron's strength goes into the setting of unwanted seed. Its health and future flowering prospects are best protected by the removal of the dead flower-trusses as soon as flowering is over. The base of the truss should be grasped between the finger and thumb and broken-off by a sharp twist of the wrist. At the same time care must be taken not to damage the growth buds at the bottom of the stalk. The trick is quickly learned and with practice one can dead-head a sizeable *fargesii* (a prodigious flowerer with which this operation is an absolute *must*) in ten to twelve minutes flat. With azaleas, dead-heading seems to be not nearly so necessary and indeed the growth buds are so vulnerably situated that I usually decide to leave well alone.

The biennial flowering of certain rhododendrons is an uncomfortable fact that sometimes causes their devotees frustration. Many rhododendrons, including most of the dwarfs, the willowy-leaved members of the Triflorum series, many of the *griersonianum* hybrids and some species flower madly year after year. Others such as some of the *discolor* hybrids, 'Britannia', 'Carita', many species, and even the old 'Lady Eleanor Cathcart', frequently miss a year or even two. There is absolutely nothing we can do about it. Feeding and dead-heading help a little, that is all. In the wild, many rhododendrons do not flower every year. They have a glorious burst of blossom, regenerate themselves by seed, and for the next year or two sit back and build up their strength for the next burst of flowering.

Some rhododendrons—*griersonianum*, and some of its hybrids, comes at once to mind—have a straggly habit of growth. This can be counteracted if one hardens one's heart and for the first season or two removes the flower buds to encourage side shoots. A desirable, mounded habit will result with the plant well-furnished with foliage to the ground.

Happily, weeds do not grow easily under established rhododendrons. Also a thick mulch discourages all such growth. It also makes it difficult to use herbaceous plants as ground cover beneath them. I think it best to restrict one's immediate underplanting to bulbs such as lilies, daffodils, the American dog's-tooth violets, trilliums, hardy orchis and endymions (*Scilla hispanica*) which will spear-up through the mulch, and to restrict one's *Cornus canadensis*, gaultherias, pulmonarias, geranium species (the delightful *endressii*, *alpinum* and *nodosum* are among the best) and other woodland treasures to form a living mulch beneath the rose species, deutzias, philadelphus, stachyurus and the other shrubby companions which one may choose as associates for one's rhododendrons and azaleas.

87

# CHAPTER 8

# Rhododendrons
# and Azaleas in the Rock- and Peat - Garden

⫸⫸⫸⫸⫸⫸⫸⫸⫸⫸⫸⫸⫸⫸⫸⫸⫸⫸⫸⫸⫸⫷⫷⫷⫷⫷⫷⫷⫷⫷⫷⫷⫷⫷⫷⫷⫷⫷⫷⫷⫷

Rhododendrons and azaleas are not plants for the ordinary, sun-baked, limestone rockery. In such places they die lingering deaths from too much sun, drought and chlorosis. In a well-constructed rock-garden it is usually possible to find a north-facing slope or the shady side of a big boulder where there is a pocket wide and deep enough to fill with the peat or rotted bracken and pine-needle mixture that rhododendrons and azaleas love. It is possible, too, to counteract any seepage of calcium from the limestone by watering with two tablespoonsful (one ounce) of Epsom salts (magnesium sulphate) to two gallons of water at the first sight of chlorosis. Rhododendrons and azaleas, however, look more at home and do better among sandstone rocks or peat blocks and it is worth constructing a separate rock- or peat-garden for them where they can either dwell aloof or associate with plant-companions that enjoy similar conditions.

If possible, the rhododendron rock- or peat-garden should face north or west. Sloping ground is the most satisfactory, but if one's garden is level, a series of low peat walls might be built to accommodate such plants as lewisias and lithospermums on their sunnier faces with, to the north or west, peat-terraces supported by single or double rows of peat blocks. Dwarf rhododendrons such as the foot-high lavender-blue *impeditum*, the little yellow *hanceanum* 'Nanum', *campylogynum* with its plum-coloured 'thimbles', and others would then grow happily on the low terrace in the shade of the taller, north- or west-facing peat walls.

Many of the peat blocks sold for fuel are too small, hard and crumbly and are, therefore, useless to form the walls which are the basis of such a peat-garden. Local sources of supply will often yield larger blocks containing heather roots which help to bind the peat and so are much to be preferred if one can get them. One must beware, though, of blocks containing bracken roots as these are more likely to grow again and a bracken-infested peat garden could only be a source of annoyance and despair. Peat blocks for wall-building should not be less than a foot long by eight or nine inches wide and six inches deep. However, if one can get them bigger than this, so much the better. The blocks should of course have weathered for at least a year before planting.

Peat walls of a height greater than three feet are seldom satisfactory. Where it is desired to use a bank of greater height as the foundation of a peat garden it is advisable to carve out shelves and build in a series of terraces using sandstone where it is necessary to make steps.

Just as when dealing with stone or brick, retaining walls built of peat blocks should always have a slight backwards 'batter'. It helps also to drive stakes vertically through the blocks at four- or five-foot intervals to bind the wall. Acid-soil ferns, and heaths— whether moorland or garden varieties—will root deeply into the peat of the wall-face and serve also to hold the wall. They should be used at frequent intervals, planted in holes cut into the blocks and rammed home with loose peat.

Before starting to build, one must ensure that the peat blocks are moist. If they seem at all dry they must be thoroughly moistened by standing them in a tub of water for six or seven hours. A wall of large blocks, moistened in this way, is unlikely to dry out, particularly if sited in shade.

Once building starts, one proceeds as with building a brick retaining wall, using peat debris and leaf-mould as mortar, and occasionally setting a block the wrong-way-on, projecting back into the bank to help hold the wall. The terraces should slope slightly backwards to retain as much moisture as possible and should be filled in with loose peat and rotten bracken or pine needles to form peat-beds.

Lower peat-beds, just a foot or so above the surface of the soil, may be held by split tree trunks (pine would look the most picturesque) and would make an attractive feature for park planting or exhibition when set out with drifts of rhododendrons and azaleas interspersed with patches of a really good double-flowered ling such as the new *Calluna* 'Joan Sparkes', *C.* 'H. E. Beale', *C.* 'J. H. Hamilton' or *C.* 'Serlei', with gaultherias and pernettyas to follow for autumn and winter berries. Such methods are not expensive when contrasted with the cost of cutting and transporting 'best water-worn' Westmorland limestone halfway across England to build a conventional rock-garden for lime-loving plants.

Where sandstone or granite are readily obtainable one may use these to make a shady rock-garden for lime-sensitive plants, either filling the pockets with peat or rotted bracken and pine needles. One can also use granite and sandstone rock with peat blocks to give greater support to a peat wall.

The size of the peat- or rock-garden naturally determines the scale of one's planting. For the big garden, with sizeable paths leading through outcrops of stone, or for extensive peat terracing such rhododendrons as the pinky-mauve, airy-flowered 'Praecox' and the creamy-yellow 'Butterfly' would not be too big while for a rock- or peat-bed a few square feet, the smallest members of the Lapponicum series, the true Kurume azaleas and the more compact members of the Saluenense and Uniflorum series best set the scale.

The flowers of the true Kurume azaleas do not fade in the sun as do those of the bigger 'Malvaticum' × *kaempferi* hybrids. They should be reserved for the sunniest places on the rock-garden together with such rhododendron species as the rosy-purple *calostrotum* of which the slightly paler *calciphilum* is the dwarfest type, the mounded *keleticum*, and the carpet-forming *radicans* with its mossy little leaves and large red-lilac salvers-flowers. The rich, plummy-magenta flowered *prostratum*, however, is better in the shade of a boulder.

Other dwarfs that withstand full sun provided there is enough moisture at their roots are the February-flowering *leucaspis* with its silvery, black-anthered flowers that need the protection of a cloche when frost is threatened, *imperator* with its funnel-shaped flowers of light purple and the very free-flowering *uniflorum* with its lavender-pink blooms.

For sun or shade, the early-blooming *racemosum* is among the best of all dwarf rhododendrons. Forrest's dwarf form 19404 with its bright pink, widely funnel-shaped flowers with their tufts of white stamens is the best for the small garden. For larger rock-gardens I like the tall deep-pink form offered by Mr. E. H. M. and Mr. P. A. Cox of Glendoick. This is an excellent plant, too, to form a neat hedge which should be clipped if it shows signs of becoming leggy. Even more attractive for the larger garden is *virgatum*, with lavender-pink flowers that are carried in the axils of its handsome olive-green leaves and appear freely all along the branches. Unfortunately this is not a reliably hardy rhododendron. It is safe enough for North Wales and the south coast but for cold midland or northern gardens it often proves bud tender as unfortunately does its hybrid with *ciliatum*— 'Multiflorum'. For really cold districts in Scotland and elsewhere, where zero Fahrenheit temperatures and below are expected during most winters, the hardiest dwarf rhododendrons—and indeed, frequently the only ones to survive—are those small enough often to be protected by the snow-blanket from the more prolonged frosts. This rules out most of those above eighteen inches in height.

Some dwarf early-flowering rhododendrons like *leucaspis*, the pretty *moupinense* and the well-known 'Praecox' may have their flowering delayed by being planted in full exposure, and in cold areas this often prevents their being tempted into precocious flower by the deceitful February sun only to have their blossoms browned by a sharp night frost.

In favourable climates, the rhododendron season for the rock- and peat- garden may start in January with the rosy-purple butterflies borne on *mucronulatum's* bare branches. However, this species is a sturdy grower quickly reaching three feet and eventually making a bush of five or six feet or more. For the small rock-garden there is a semi-evergreen type of the similar-flowered *dauricum* known as 'Wada's dwarf form'. I have grown both this and *mucronulatum* (which species has now received a First Class Certificate from the R.H.S. in recognition of its merit) for a number of years and have found the flowers resistant to several degrees of frost. They should be planted with a north exposure. In severe winters in North Wales the precocious young growth of our plants was severely snubbed but new shoots quickly replaced those frosted, and flowering buds appeared in good time for the next winter.

Next to flower of the species is the six-inch *leucaspis* mentioned above with the larger *moupinense* with dark-anthered, azalea-like flowers in milky-white or pink. Making a full and rather bulky two feet in time this is perhaps more of a plant for the bigger rock-garden. A hybrid between these two, 'Bric-a-Brac' (A.M.) lies almost between the two in habit and size of flower truss with a slightly larger reproduction of *leucaspis*'s silvery-white flowers. A little later blooms a treasure for any rock- or peat-garden large enough to give it scale, the attractive (*lutescens* × *moupinense*) 'Bo-peep' (A.M.) with its airy growth and quite large, open flowers of creamy-yellow. All these early flowerers should be planted in shade from the morning sun.

The seed-parent of 'Bo-peep', *lutescens* is, in its F.C.C. form, a wonderful shrub with flights of primrose flowers and bronzy, willow-like leaves. It does, however, make too big a shrub for the rock-garden but is delightful at the edge of a stream or pool.

At the same time (*ciliatum* × *dauricum*) 'Praecox' flowers followed, a fortnight later, by 'Emasculum' of similar parentage but with slightly more substantial and frilly blooms of the same warm lilac-mauve. The 'Praecox' × *moupinense* hybrid 'Tessa' (A.M.) usually coincides its flowering with that of 'Praecox' and is very pretty with rich lilac-pink flowers and dark green leaves that are well set off by the reddish-bronze bark. 'Tessa Roza' is another form of the same cross with bright rose-coloured flowers.

'Fine Feathers' (*lutescens* × 'Cilpinense'), a Bodnant hybrid, is smaller and of more compact growth with pale 'lemon-ice' flowers.

I think it is better than 'Bo-peep' on account of its more shapely habit. It is not too big for the medium-sized rock-garden or peat-terrace.

With the blooming of the Kurume azaleas in April, the gardens take on a gay note. These little azaleas will be fully dealt with in Part II but I am mentioning them here as offering useful colour contrasts to the small-flowered little rhododendrons of the Lapponicum series. Pink cultivars such as the hose-in-hose-flowered 'Kirin', and 'Hinomayo' (which though not one of the original 'Wilson Fifty' is usually considered with this group) look well associated with the starry 'blue' *intricatum* or the lavender form of *hippophaeoides*, while a bolder effect is offered by grouping the lavender-purple *impeditum* with the flame-coloured 'Malvaticum' × *kaempferi* hybrid 'Orange Beauty'. This last effect needs shade as the orange of the azalea fades badly in full sun. Some forms of *impeditum* have grey leaves and these will always be found to be the most dwarf in growth. 'Steel Blue' is a particularly good dwarf clone.

Some people say that the 'Blue Tit', 'Blue Diamond' group of hybrids need sun if they are to flower freely but in my experience 'Blue Diamond', 'Augfast', 'Sapphire' and the others flower well in sun or shade while 'Blue Tit' is a less satisfactory flowerer in any position. Moreover the flowers of 'Blue Tit' fade so quickly to a washed-out grey in sunshine that they are no longer worth having. 'Blue Diamond', 'Augfast', 'Sapphire', 'Bluebird' and the more recently raised 'Bluestone' are lovely anywhere, but in shade their colour is deeper and thus grown 'Blue Diamond' becomes perhaps the bluest of all the small rhododendrons that are at present widely available. Some of these hybrids in time reach four feet or more and so outgrow their space on the smaller rock- and peat-garden. They will easily transplant, if moved with their root balls intact, for use in another part of the garden or they may be clipped back. 'Blue Diamond' and 'Augfast' stand clipping so well that they may be used to form hedges if required. However, 'Sapphire' and the little violet-blue 'Intrifast' are much more compact in growth and are therefore the best choice for the really small rock-garden.

All these blue hybrids associate well with the various forms of *racemosum* and with *williamsianum* with its pretty rounded leaves —bronzy when young—and comparatively large, wide pink bells. The species *williamsianum* is a true Category C rhododendron. It does best in the south and west and is only suitable for specially favoured gardens elsewhere as its young growth is easily frosted.

Also good to group with the blues on the larger rock-garden is the wonderful (*sulfureum* × *flavidum*) 'Yellow Hammer' which makes a rather upright shrub reaching five or six feet in height with little spread. 'Yellow Hammer' has neat dark green leaves and small butter-yellow bells which are perkily borne in the leaf-axils. It is a very hardy little rhododendron and has the advantage in milder areas of flowering twice—in November as well as spring—and so prolific is it that the welcome burst of winter bloom seems in no way to detract from its main flush of colour in April and May.

Another good yellow is (*valentinianum* × *lutescens*) 'Remo' with a lower, mounded habit of growth, slightly larger and more pointed leaves with a bronzy cast and small trusses of brighter yellow, more widely-open flowers.

To place with the small 'blue' species, such as *intricatum*, the lavender form of *hippophaeoides*, *impeditum*, *stictophyllum* and the rest, a yellow member of the same series, *chryseum*. is excellent, particularly in the form Rock 59049—the form that I grow in a former garden—with good yellow flowers enhanced by tan-coloured anthers and leaves that become a warm bronze in winter. With the tiny-flowered white *microleucum* and the reddish-mauve *lysolepis* these species make an attractive drift of colour.

At about this time several hybrids of the often shy-flowering *forrestii* var. *repens* offer a wide choice of size and form. The scarlet (*forrestii* var. *repens* × *griersonianum*) 'Elizabeth', perhaps Bodnant's finest hybrid to date, is, in the F.C.C. form, a magnificent plant for the larger rock- or peat-garden. Well-clothed, with its characteristically dark green leaves, and neatly mounded, it is a plant of first class habit and its trusses of solid, scarlet trumpets are well held up. This form will reach three or four feet in height and is quite fast-growing. For the smaller rock-garden or peat-terrace it should be replaced by its dwarf variety 'Creeping Jenny' which is a low, almost prostrate grower—at its best planted at the front of a peat-terrace so that it may cascade over the wall, or tumbling over a boulder on a rocky slope. Both these forms are extremely free-flowering in spring and usually carry a scattering of bloom from September until frost.

From the Bodnant stable also comes ('F.C. Puddle' × *forrestii* var. *repens*) 'Ethel' (F.C.C.) of low, mounded growth and with double-calyxed flowers of a really intense scarlet. Another *forrestii* var. *repens* hybrid, this time from Exbury is (*didymum* × *forrestii* var. *repens*) 'Carmen'—seldom growing more than about eighteen inches in height and with dark-ruby bells that are brilliant in the sunlight. 'Carmen' should be planted on a high peat-bank or rock-garden ledge where its flowers will catch the sun.

A warm pink for contrast is offered by (*forrestii* var. *repens* × *williamsianum*) 'Treasure', another low-mounded grower with the pretty leaves of *williamsianum* to add to its charms.

Rather taller growing and with larger leaves than *williamsianum* (I do not know its other parent but suspect that it may well be *campylocarpum* from the shape and type of its leaves) is the white-flowered 'Pook' which I got from Mr. Cox of Glendoick and which his list says that he likes very much. I like it, too, and its pristine bells look delightful against a dark peat wall. Incidentally, a good way to grow the taller *forrestii* var. *repens* and *williamsianum* hybrids is to plant them at the bottom of the small rock- or peat-garden with drifts of lower-growers, such as *campylogynum* var. *myrtilloides* or the pretty, shiny-leaved *pumilum*, with its bright-pink bells rising in flights above them.

Carrying the season into July is the deep-red (*didymum* × *griersonianum*) 'Arthur Osborn' which, however, is rather sturdy for all but the biggest rock-gardens; the lower-growing and more compact (*didymum* (?) × *griersonianum*) 'Lava Flow', the name of which aptly describes the habit and glowing, crimson-spotted, scarlet flowers which are carried in quite large trusses; and a Sunningdale hybrid between *campylogynum* var. *myrtilloides* and *lepidotum* which makes a very small mound of tiny leaves with rich, claret 'thimbles' carried rather high on long stalks in bunches of three.

Many azaleas other than the evergreen Kurume type are too big for the rock- or peat-garden and, in time, even the Kurumes may reach two or three feet in height. With their tiered growth, small leaves and typically 'Japanese' look, however, they are unlikely ever to seem out of place. An early-flowering deciduous azalea which is delightful near a rock pool or stream or which would thrive in a cool aspect on a peat-terrace is the grey-leaved *canadense* which used to be known as *Rhodora canadensis* and which is an adorable little shrub, seldom reaching more than eighteen inches in height and bearing a great number of small 'butterfly' flowers in cool-lilac.

In June, the almost prostrate *indicum* 'Balsaminiflorum' will bear its perfect rosette-flowers (rather like those of a camellia) in warm salmon-pink. This is a first-rate plant, taking up little space, with narrow rich-green leaves, covered in silky white hairs, and slowly mounding itself up into a neat hummock.

For those who object to formal flowers even when they are as delectable as these, 'Kokinshita' might be a happier choice. It is as dwarf and slow-growing as 'Balsaminiflorum' but its salmon-orange flowers are of single and flawless shape.

Even a purist, I think, could not object to the frilly double flowers of some of the *simsii* var. *eriocarpum* azaleas—the charming, very dwarf Gumpos which flower in late June or July. Of these 'Gumpo' is icy-white with just that tinge of green that always seems to make a white flower more lovely; 'Jitsu-getsu' is a soft pinky-lavender; 'Pink Gumpo', white tinged with blush and 'Rose Glory' blush suffused and marked with rich pink.

Lovely and exciting though the dwarf rhododendrons and azaleas may be, few people would be satisfied with a rock- or peat-garden containing no other genera. Naturally enough the best companion plants are to be found among those which enjoy similar conditions—moist yet well-drained peaty soil and shade.

Some of the small bulbs offer excellent contrasts. The warm

II. *R.* 'Saint Breward', a beautiful hybrid in which the blood of
*R. augustinii* predominates

rose-purple of *R. mucronulatum's* or *dauricum's* winter flowers are enhanced by the sparkle of a cluster of the tiny orange-gold *Crocus ancyrensis* at the foot. *Narcissus cylamineus* with its slender golden trumpets and sharply reflexed perianth makes an excellent companion for R. 'Praecox', while the dancing white or pink turkscaps of the graceful *Erythronium californicum* 'White Beauty' and *E. revolutum johnsonii* will readily seed in the moist peat to make a carpet of beauty beneath *R. williamsianum*, 'Blue Diamond', 'Bluestone', 'Pook' and other spring treasures.

The Asiatic candelabra primulas are perhaps too tall and out of scale on the smaller rock- or peat-garden. Their place is by the water or in drifts among the larger rhododendrons. *Primula rosea*, however, is not too big to make a splash of warm bright pink by a rock-garden pool. More in scale with the really dwarf rhododendrons is the lilac *P. frondosa* with its fairy whorls and frosty leaves. I find this primula remarkably long-lived and willing. It divides satisfactorily, in our garden stood nineteen degrees Fahrenheit of frost in February 1962 and the more severe winter of 1963, and is easily raised from seed sown on grit-surfaced pans and wintered outside.

Where it does well, the tiny *Soldanella montana*, with its little, fringed, lavender bells, is a charming companion. Shortias are not usually looked upon as easy plants but if the clump is a fairsized when purchased, the white *S. galacifolia* and the pink *S. uniflora* 'Grandiflora' will wax fat on a diet of pine needles and peat.

Gentians, too, make delightful associates for dwarf rhododendrons and azaleas, and the bright blue *G. verna* can usually be persuaded to relish a peat-bed, provided some oak leaf-mould and rotted cow-manure are added before planting. *G. acaulis* does better with the addition of loam to stiffen the peat. *G. acaulis alpina* is a small-flowered but free-blooming form from Mr. Jack Drake of Inshriach which likes an acid soil. The summer- and autumn-flowering Asiatic gentians are, of course, very much at home in the peat. In such ideal conditions the tubby Cambridge-blue *farreri*, and 'Macaulayi'—both in 'Well's Variety' and the smaller but brilliant 'Kingfisher'—and the lovely turquoise 'Caroli' will often succeed as will the late autumn-flowering *G.* 'Kidbrooke Seedling' and *G. sino-ornata*, which in our garden follows it. All these gentians look their best planted to form drifts and pools among, or at the front of, the dwarf rhododendrons.

Of small peat-happy shrubs, several daphnes come at once to mind—the superbly-scented white, *D. blagayana* which likes to have its rather straggly shoots layered by stones; the accommodating *D. retusa* with its quiet purple-and-white flowers; the neat, twice-flowering *D. collina*; *D. cneorum* which sometimes proves tricky but should succeed if the peat is mounded up to layer its stems; and, of course, the familiar *D. mezereum* in purple, old rose, or ivory, and which is not too big for any but the very smallest rock- or peat-bed. All have the family attraction of scent.

Lithospermum *diffusum* 'Heavenly Blue' is, as one might say, a 'natural' to spangle a peat wall with its pure bright-blue starry flowers which look remarkably good, too, covering a flat rock in front of the rich salmon, azalea-rosettes of *R. indicum* 'Balsaminiflorum'. Dwarf brooms must not be forgotten and a waterfall of the creamy *Cytisus × kewensis* cascading down in front of a drift of *R. intricatum* is one of the finest sights the rock- or peat-garden has to offer.

Also good are the whipcord branches of some of the cassiopes with their white, frilly-mouthed bells, the Irish heath—*Daboecia cantabrica* with its white or purple large globular urns as well as those of the newer 'Praegeri' which are between ruby and garnet in colour. They glow with inner fire when the sun strikes them and tend to be carried from mid-autumn on. The gaultherias offer several useful true dwarfs for even the smallest peat pocket. *G. tricophylla* is perhaps the most appealing of all with large, egg-shaped berries of hedge-sparrow blue but the red-berried *G. procumbens* and white *miqueliana* are attractive companions.

On the larger rock-garden, contrasts of texture and form are needed to give solidity and shape. Such conifers as *Juniperus × media* 'Blaauw', the spreading *J. sabina* var. *tamariscifolia* and the conical little 'Christmas trees' of *Picea glauca* var. *albertiana* 'Conica' offer comfortable furnishing. Also to give height, one might plant (in the milder parts of the country) the dwarf *Eucryphia milliganii* which forms a narrow leptospermum-like column of dark foliage six or seven feet in height and generously studded with tiny, fluffy-stamened, white flowers.

Heaths are of course natural companions of rhododendrons in the garden and a larger rock-cum-heather garden might consist almost entirely of these genera with conifers, the dwarf eucryphia, shrubby potentillas, brooms and perhaps the yellow shrub roses and the little creeping pink 'dog-rose' *Rosa nitida* to add contrasting interest.

# CHAPTER 9

# Rhododendrons for the Smaller Garden

⫸⫸⫸⫸⫸⫸⫸⫸⫸⫸⫸⫸⫸⫸⫸⫸⫷⫷⫷⫷⫷⫷⫷⫷⫷⫷⫷⫷⫷⫷⫷⫷⫷

In the past rhododendrons have tended to be linked in the public mind with larger gardens and estates. Some people have felt that rhododendrons grow too big for small gardens or, knowing only the older hybrids, have thought their leaves too heavy and 'depressing' for confined spaces. I hope that what I have already written will have dispelled many of these ideas because, of course, many rhododendrons have beautiful leaves and—like dogs—they come in all sizes; there is the little starry blue *R. intricatum* which with the yellow *chryseum* is as well-fitted to a flat-dweller's balcony (given a trough of peat and pine needles) as is a pekingese to the interior of such an apartment. In the semi-detached garden of the suburbs, the neat and pretty *williamsianum* hybrids will be as much at home as the miniature poodles of the district. The country cottage or bungalow with its quarter-of-an-acre or more of pasture, scrub, or birch-wood can accommodate its 'Fabia' and 'May Day'—and its spaniels.

Of course all the rhododendrons and azaleas mentioned in the last chapter will be quite at home in the small garden. None of them really demand rock-garden conditions and, where there is no free lime in the soil, there is no need to grow them in raised peat-beds. All the dwarf rhododendrons and azaleas will grow well in front of larger rhododendrons in the shrub border, in small beds on their own or in association with daphnes, daboecias, gaultherias and lithospermums. Indeed, flat beds of dwarf rhododendrons can be extremely attractive and can give colour over a long period. Given adequate humus in the soil and planted so that they will soon overlap and grow into each other, the little rhododendrons will form a dense community, sheltering each other from cold and damp or the effects of too much sun, and forming a dense blanket to keep down weeds and to prevent the soil from drying out.

In the late Mr. and Mrs. A. T. Johnson's Bulkeley Mill garden —in front of the old barn, now converted and expanded into a single-storey dwelling—there was a large boat-shaped bed bordered by flagged paths. In the bed, smothered by rhododendron growth with only occasional gaps caused by the loss of an odd plant or two over the years, were various large boulders originally added to retain moisture and give shade and shelter when the plants were young. Many of the plants remain to form a charming and unusual small garden.

At the wider end, a dozen or so purple *R. russatum* were planted to contrast with a group of white Japanese azaleas, thought to be 'Hakatashiro', merging into the apple-blossom pink of Forrest's dwarf *racemosum* 19404. In smaller groups were the blue *scintillans*, the creamy-yellow *hanceanum* 'Nanum'; the blue-purple hybrid 'Prostigiatum' and two members of the Saluenense series—the sometimes-wayward *fragariiflorum* and *chamaeunum* with salver-shaped flowers in pinky plum-colour and bright rose-purple respectively. Next to these were the tiny-flowered snowy *microleucum* and the yellow *megeratum*, some free-flowering forms of *forrestii* var. *repens*, the pinky-mauve *pemakoense* with its comparatively large funnel-shaped blooms, the daphne-flowered *anthopogon*, *campylogynum* with its nodding crimson-purple 'thimbles' and a lemon-yellow member of the aromatic-leaved Glaucophyllum series, *brachyanthum* var. *hypolepidotum*. All are free flowering—several bloom for a second time in the autumn and most, in winter, assume leaf-tones of bronze, russet, purple-red, bright frosty green or steely blue.

In the borders against the grey, sheep's-head, stone walls of the little garden grew several azaleas, the warm yet delicate pink *schlippenbachii*, the large-flowered, dwarf white *mucronatum* and the hybrid ('Hinodegiri' × 'Orange Beauty') 'John Cairns' in vivid Indian red. There, too, were more rhododendrons, 'Blue Diamond', the grey-leaved *calostrotum*, 'Bluebird' and the early-flowering, soft pink (*racemosum* × *ciliatum*) 'Racil' and more azaleas, this time of the Vuykiana group of large-flowered Dutch evergreen hybrids in lavender and pale violet. With these were massed some of the old Gallica and China roses, the pretty dwarf, May-flowering *Rosa pimpinellifolia* varieties with R. 'Canary Bird' and some of the more-or-less continually-flowering Rugosa roses. There were daphnes such as *collina* and the white and old-rose forms of *mezereum* (now in some gardens unfortunately subject to virus), with paeony species to keep them company and in a damp section the immense white and purple flowers of *Iris kaempferi* 'Morning Mist' and 'Purple East', the shaggy orange-gold of a hybrid ligularia (*clivorum* × *veitchianus*) and tall candelabra primulas in yellow and magenta. Viburnums and skimmias added winter and spring fragrance and berries and for height there was the upright form of *Magnolia salicifolia*, *Pyrus salicifolia* 'Pendula', the silver-leaved weeping pear, and the striking and most beautiful February-flowering apricot *Prunus mume* 'Benishi-don' with velvety cherry-crimson, white-stamened flowers that have a strong and delicious scent of hyacinths.

A similar scheme would suit the garden of an old cottage or farmhouse but for a modern bungalow or villa a planting such as that made by Mr. Walter Irvine, described earlier, in Chapter 4, would be more suitable.

For the former backyard of a converted town house, a load or two of woodsy soil planted with bulbs, ferns and primroses, a fairy-like species azalea such as the little mauve *canadense* for early spring, with the dainty *albrechtii* with its larger rose-pink flowers to follow, and the frilly dwarf forms of 'Gumpo' for later blossom would take up but little room. There could also be a succession of dwarf rhododendrons, from the early 'Racil', the creamy 'Moonstone' and deep pink 'Treasure' to the late-flowering 'Arthur Osborn' which would give a long season of interest to be followed by one or two of the double-flowered lings (*Calluna vulgaris* 'H. E. Beale' and 'Alba Plena') and the dwarf red-berried *Pernettya tasmanica*, with the white berries of *Gaultheria cuneata* to complement it. A drift of winter-flowering *Erica carnea* cultivars might wind up the year.

## Rhododendrons for the Smaller Garden

For the more informal small garden—like ours in North Wales—grassy lawns may be edged with winding belts of shrubs (rhododendrons, azaleas, hydrangeas, viburnums, shrub roses, cistuses, heaths, hypericums, pernettyas and potentillas with small shade trees) to form small glades. In such a garden there is no room for massed plantings of rhododendrons or even of deciduous azaleas chosen to flower simultaneously. Nor do I think this the most effective way of using them. Rather one chooses one's favourites from among the smaller species and hybrids, and plants them to flower in succession. A pair of orange-flame mollis azaleas in a green bay between *Philadelphus* 'Virginal' and *Chamaecyparis* 'Triomf van Boskoop' have as much impact and more interest than a conventional semicircle of twenty-four in the more lavish 'adjacent to the golf course', semi-suburban subtopia of pre-war days.

Some of the brilliant honeysuckle-flowered Ghent azaleas are much more effective as single plants than in groups. Of these I think at once of the vivid orange 'Coccinea Speciosa', the orange-and-yellow 'Unique', the strawberry-rose 'Fanny' and coral-red 'Joseph Baumann'. More subtle are the double-flowered, pale pink 'Raphael de Smet' and the double soft yellow 'Narcissiflorum' while the salmon-and-yellow 'Bouquet de Flore' is especially useful on account of its later flowering. We grow it facing north so that it blooms in mid-June, thus usefully prolonging the season for azaleas of this type.

Some of the large-flowered Knap Hill and Exbury azaleas, also, are good enough to stand alone. Two that I use in this way are 'Gannet'—pale blush with an orange flare—and the rather similar but even larger-flowered and yellow-marked 'Buzzard'. Both of these are at their best in shade and both are delightfully scented. All June-flowering azaleas need shade to prevent their flowers from wilting. Another one which has sufficient quality to stand alone is *R. occidentale*. The form we grow is a heavy-textured white with a yellow eye opening from pink buds. There is also a pale pink form. Both have a strong sweet scent with a hint of carnation about it.

There is a wide choice of evergreen rhododendrons for the

smaller garden and some of the newer hybrid groups are particularly suitable. One of these groups has *williamsianum* as a parent, giving a compact, closely mounded habit and pretty rounded leaves. In this group, the flower truss is usually loose and graceful varying from the pendant waxen, cherry-coloured bells of (*haematodes* × *williamsianum*) 'Humming Bird' to the more closely held, tubby bells of (*orbiculare* × *williamsianum*) 'Temple Belle' which has inherited more of the sturdier but still compact growth and Persian-rose flower colour of *orbiculare*. Other good hybrids in this group are the pale yellow, tinged pink (*campylocarpum* × *williamsianum*) 'Moonstone'; (*wardii* × *williamsianum*) 'Cowslip' with creamy-yellow flowers; the taller and slightly later-blooming (mid-late May) soft salmon-pink ('Corona' × *williamsianum*) 'Bow Bells' which has the additional charm of *williamsianum's* bronze-copper young growth; and (? × *williamsianum*) 'Brocade' which, like 'Bow Bells', may reach five feet or more but flowers in early May and still retains the neat, rounded shape which makes it so suitable a plant for a small garden. The flower-trusses are rather larger than those of the other *williamsianum* hybrids, vivid carmine in bud opening to wide, frilly, strawberry-pink flowers that fade to blush with age. As with most pinks the flower-colour is better in shade than sun. All these are hardy although 'Humming Bird' and 'Moonstone', which make their young growth early, are better away from frost pockets.

Another useful group are the *forrestii* var. *repens* hybrids discussed in the last chapter. Of these (*griersonianum* × *repens*) 'Elizabeth' is first class. It is extremely hardy with good leaves and habit and scarlet-crimson flowers. It will eventually make a bush of three feet high with a wider spread. Similar in size is (*forestii* var. *repens* × *neriiflorum*) 'Little Ben' with narrower leaves like those of *neriiflorum* and looser trusses of smaller, bright scarlet, bell-shaped flowers.

'Nereid' (*dichroanthum* × *neriiflorum*) is a hybrid which has occurred naturally in several gardens. It, too, has the long, narrow leaves of *neriiflorum* and lax, drooping trusses of a warm salmon-pink, waxy flowers into which seems to have crept a hint of the milky-orange of *dichroanthum*.

The species, however, which is perhaps the most useful parent of all is *griersonianum*, which seems to confer upon many of its offspring the easy and willing habit that it lacks itself, coupled with great hardiness. Able to put up with almost as wide a range of conditions as any of the old 'ironclads' and beating them for compactness of size and beauty of truss and colour, many of the *griersonianum* hybrids are ideal plants for the smaller gardens of today.

Lovely in the purity of its scarlet flowers is (*haematodes* × *griersonianum*) 'May Day' which, nevertheless, should be kept away from all other reds. Making a well-furnished, compact bush of about five feet and flowering later than 'Elizabeth', 'May Day' is a useful successor to that variety. With eight or nine hanging bells, to 'Elizabeth's' smaller, firmer truss, 'May Day' offers an interesting contrast in style.

The Bodnant hybrid 'Fabia' (*dichroanthum* × *griersonianum*) is, of course, one of the stars of the group. This cross has been made several times and varying forms exist. All are good but outstanding are the Bodnant 'Tangerine' with flowers of vivid terra-cotta tipped with crimson and with a slight double calyx; 'Roman Pottery' with a very lax truss of the most beautiful apricot-orange; and 'Tower Court' which is a bright but soft orange-pink with a warm rose flush at the petal tips. All the forms have good sage-green foliage and a compact but slightly spreading habit. 'Tower Court' is the most dwarf and many people think 'Tangerine' the finest, but my favourite is 'Roman Pottery' which has more of the *dichroanthum* orange in its colour than any of the others. The 'Fabia' grex is late flowering, usually opening at the beginning of June.

Much earlier in our garden is the pink form of 'Goblin' with a rather similar habit of growth and flower-truss but slightly wider-open bells. There are two forms of this and one is scarlet but the A.M. variety is a shade of soft, warm, clear pink. A deeper pink, flowering just a little later than 'Goblin', is found in (*griersonianum* × 'Humming Bird') 'Winsome' which has inherited from (*haematodes* × *williamsianum*) 'Humming Bird' the coppery young growth of *williamsianum*. 'Winsome' has bell-shaped flowers of rich rose.

## Rhododendrons for the Smaller Garden

Hardier than their exotic appearance would lead one to believe, the hybrids of *cinnabarinum*, 'Lady Chamberlain' and 'Lady Rosebery' are, with their slender, compact growth, eminently suited to the smaller garden provided they are given adequate wind-shelter. Mr. A. Sigston Thompson, the Honorary Director of the Northern Horticultural Society's gardens at Harlow Car, Harrogate, Yorkshire, writes to me that they have proved completely hardy in that very exposed garden. There are many forms of 'Lady Chamberlain' varying in colour from 'Golden Queen', which is rich yellow marked with red, to 'Exbury' which is predominantly orange, and 'Salmon Trout' which is the colour of that excellent fish when cooked. 'Seville' is bright orange, the name of 'Apricot' describes itself and 'Chelsea' is orange-pink. All are pleasing and as this is one of the rhododendrons that really pays for grouping, both in and out of flower, when its bluey-green leaves make an attractive foliage pattern, a planting of three or four forms would be rewarding. 'Lady Rosebery' is equally good. Of this grex there is the deep rose F.C.C. form, 'Dalmeny' in soft, satiny pink, 'Pink Beauty' and 'Pink Delight'.

Another hybrid of *cinnabarinum*—this time with *yunnanense*— 'Yunncinn' is a compact plant, light in growth and leaf and with small, airy trusses of rather open flowers that vary from rich lilac-pink to a luscious shade of glowing orchid-purple. With its parentage, 'Yunncinn' should be, and is, a really hardy plant— and it is one with a modern look. It should be more widely propagated as it is a useful plant for the larger rock-garden. Another lovely hybrid is 'Alison Johnstone', a cross between *yunnanense* and the copper-apricot *concatenans* of the Cinnabarinum series. 'Alison Johnstone' often blooms twice, in late April or early May and again in September. It is very hardy, tall growing but slender, and has quite large, well-opened flowers of a pretty pale apricot.

Yellow is a particularly attractive colour in rhododendrons and a selection for the small garden should include the very hardy, though undeservedly rare, old 'Cunningham's Sulphur', which is probably a form of *caucasicum*. It flowers in late April or early May with a close, rounded truss of sulphur-yellow flowers and is small-growing with dark green foliage, but often opens an odd truss or two even earlier. Other good small yellows are the distinctly 'different' upright-growing (*sulfureum* × *flavidum*) 'Yellow Hammer' described in the last chapter and (*valentinianum* × *lutescens*) 'Remo' which flowers a little later and makes a mounded shrub of perhaps three feet with neat, slightly bronzy, dark leaves and bright yellow flowers about the size of those of 'Blue Diamond'. It is supposed to be less hardy than the other two, although in our garden it was unhurt in the winter of 1962–3 by frosts that scorched an odd leaf or two even of 'Yellow Hammer'.

As tough as any, is the June-flowering ('Lady Bessborough' × *wardii*) 'Hawk', of which the original clone is a compact plant, well-furnished and with neat trusses of deep yellow flowers tinged with red in the throat. 'Crest' is an improved clone from a second raising and is also compact, while 'Jervis Bay', with the brightest yellow flowers set off by a vivid scarlet eye, is rather taller growing.

A fine late yellow, carrying the season on until July, is ('Bustard' × 'Fabia') 'Iviza', a neat, small plant with glossy, unusual, spoon-shaped leaves and long Fabia-type bells of nankeen-yellow which open from coral-tinged buds.

Another late-flowering, small rhododendron is (*didymum* × 'Moser's Maroon') 'Impi', with neat trusses of satiny dark red. Rather larger growing and brighter in colour with tubular scarlet flowers spotted with black is ('Essex Scarlet' × *eriogynum*) 'Beau Brummell'. Eventually reaching six feet or so in height but slow growing is the fine (*griersonianum* × 'Soulbut') 'Vanessa' with open trusses of warm salmon-pink flowers enhanced by a crimson eye.

From late-blooming rhododendrons to winter flowerers— (*arboreum* × *caucasicum*) 'Nobleanum', in the crimson type, the soft, bright pink 'Nobleanum Venustum' and the white 'Nobleanum Album', are compact enough for the small garden. In very bleak parts of the country I suspect their blossoms may be a constant frost-loss but in the south and west they are delightful, coming at just the time of year when a five-foot rhododendron in full flower is a warmingly exotic sight. With us 'Nobleanum Venustum' begins to open its flowers in November and will usually carry on in a long succession of bloom until February, when the crimson 'Nobleanum' itself takes over. Of course—even in the west—some of the blooms are occasionally frosted but there are always other buds to open and so, in all but the coldest districts, these useful old hybrids cannot fail to give a reasonable return. The more compact (*caucasicum* × *nobleanum*) 'Jacksonii' is more plebeian in aspect, being of a rather 'blue' pink, but very useful, flowering a little later, usually with the first daffodils. It is not as pretty, however, as 'Praecox' and 'Emasculum', which I mentioned in the last chapter, with their lilac-mauve, azalea-like flowers and airy growth.

Another useful member of the early spring groups is (*racemosum* × *ciliatum*) 'Racil', an extremely hardy little plant with small, rounded, dark green leaves and neat, tight trusses of flowers, larger than those of *racemosum* and, in colour, blush flushed with deep pink at the edges. Pretty, too, is (*ciliatum* × *moupinense*) 'Cilpinense' with larger flowers of soft, pale, pink, dappled and spotted with rose.

Some readers might feel that many of the older 'hardy hybrids' have not been given sufficient emphasis in this chapter. The reason for their omission is that I feel they have been surpassed by equally hardy varieties of better colour and foliage. Why, for instance, plant the blue-crimson 'Britannia' with its unattractive yellow-green leaves when one can plant 'May Day' in its place. Why choose the large-growing 'Pink Pearl' with its blousy trusses of candy-floss pink when one can have the compact and elegant 'Goblin', 'Naomi' or 'Nereid'? Even 'Goldsworth Yellow' has with its rather untidy habit been surpassed by 'Hawk', 'Canary' and the rest.

Certain of the so-called 'hardy' hybrids will always have their place. Among these I would list the deep 'Purple Splendour' and 'Moser's Maroon' because of their unique colour, 'Susan', 'Fastuosum Flore Pleno', 'Blue Danube', 'Blue Peter' and 'Countess of Athlone' for the cool 'blue', and lilac, effect of their flowers in shade. Most of these, however, are too big for the small garden. Their place is in, or at the edge of, the woodland.

The old 'hardy hybrids' may be 'out' for the small garden but certain of the species are very much 'in', among them some of the lightly-built Triflorum series of which *yunnanense* is a plant for

## Rhododendrons for the Smaller Garden

'Everyman's Garden' with its semi-deciduous habit and narrow leaves—a built-in resistance to sun and wind—its graceful growth, and light trusses of white or blush 'butterfly' flowers, tinged with lavender and freckled with chestnut-brown. A cultivar known as 'Openwood' is now in commerce and is even more attractive, with lavender flowers that have the typical chestnut speckling. Another species of the same series, *exquisetum*, is one that I find pleasing with silvery blue-grey flowers carried on a more compact, dense shrub than *yunnanense*. For maximum garden effect, *exquisetum* should be planted where the light will strike it against a dark background. *Oreotrephes*, too, is lovely and like *yunnanense* and *exquisitum* very hardy and wind-resistant. In its best forms it is pinky lilac with blue-grey young growth. *Exquisetum* has now been merged with *oreotrephes* but for garden purposes good forms of the two must remain distinct.

The finest species of the series, *augustinii* and *chasmanthum*, again to be merged, are of variable hardiness. They were not a success in Mr. A. T. Johnson's Bulkeley Mill garden which suffers severely from May frosts. At Bodnant, however, on the other side of the Conway valley, a considerable grouping in a sheltered place on a slope with good air-drainage is usually unharmed. In my garden, a mile and a half from the sea on the exposed North Wales coast, *augustinii* was untouched by a frost that severely cut back the extremely hardy *mucronulatum* which was making young growth at the time of the frost but which quickly recovered and sent out new shoots.

It seems to me that the hardiness of the more tender members of the Triflorum series, including the pink *davidsonianum* and yellow *lutescens* as well as *augustinii* and *chasmanthum*, varies considerably over the years. Damage done to these species sometimes seems to have no logical basis; for instance a group of the F.C.C. form of *lutescens* (reckoned to be the most tender form of this species) growing in the dell at Bodnant was severely damaged in the winter of 1961–2. Now it is a fact, I think, that parts of the Bodnant dell act as a frost-bottom and seem to hold the frost—yet a few miles away at Bulkeley Mill, in an equally frost-ridden position in an even colder garden—a clump of this same form was cut only slightly. In my garden, which experienced nineteen degrees Fahrenheit of frost (−7°C), the F.C.C. form of *lutescens* was in full flower yet, although the flowers were reduced to pulp, the growth was cut back only slightly and the remaining buds were unharmed and in fact opened to perfection after the frost was over. My plant was growing in comparatively full exposure. By the same token, at Bodnant, *davidsonianum* in the reputedly more tender F.C.C. form, its warm-pink flowers spotted with chestnut, was almost untouched by frost. Admittedly this plant was growing in a sheltered place yet many other forms of this species at Bodnant were either killed or badly damaged, irrespective of shelter. On the other hand Mr. A. Sigston Thompson, Honorary Director of the Harlow Car Gardens, Harrogate, in his own Yorkshire garden finds *davidsonianum* 'the hardiest of all'. All this amounts perhaps to a warning. *R. augustinii, chasmanthum, davidsonianum* and *lutescens* are not for the coldest gardens. In the south and west, away from frost-traps, these species are a fair risk. It has been said that they are hardiest in full exposure and in this may lie the clue to the unscathed survival of the Yorkshire *davidsonianums*, the sap of which, following a customarily hard early winter, was well down when frost struck. At Bodnant on the other hand, after the usual mild, wet November and December, sap was high and so the plants were badly damaged

I would be inclined to risk *davidsonianum* in all but the bleakest places and to try it in full exposure because there is really no substitute for this delectable species. The wise, however, in a cold garden would not risk *augustinii* and *chasmanthum* but would plant instead 'Blue Diamond', 'Blue Beard' or the newer 'St. Breward'. All of these hybrids are fine plants and very floriferous, giving a good 'blue' effect, particularly in shade. Over the years 'Blue Diamond' will make a tall and striking columnar shrub reaching to six or seven feet in height.

One might think the February–March flowering *lutescens* useless for any but the mildest gardens on account of its early flowering. Yet at Bulkeley Mill, where frosts of below zero Fahrenheit have been experienced, it succeeds where *augustinii* so often failed. Many gardens which catch the May frosts have spells in February or March of comparatively frost-free weather so that anyone who finds, as I do, the early primrose flowers of the F.C.C. form of *lutescens* quite irresistible must take their chance. It may help, as at Bulkeley Mill, to plant *lutescens* on the well-drained bank of a stream of running water which, if unobstructed by overhanging branches, will offer a channel down which the frost may drain away.

In *yakushimanum*, which forms a dense mound never more than three feet high with rosettes of dark green shiny leaves (with a fawn indumentum below) and round trusses of charming apple-blossom tinged flowers, we have a species that is first class in its own right. Its hybrids which are now coming to the fore offer an interesting range of small-garden rhododendrons.

In an exposed place in sun such as most gardens have to offer, *dichroanthum* will succeed where some of its hybrids would fail. Extremely hardy and drought-resistant with good neat growth, dark green leaves, silvered beneath and rich orange flowers on a pinky-yellow ground this is, in a good form, a plant to catch the eye. Under *scyphocalyx* which has now been merged into this species I know one or two exceptional forms.

In *wasonii*, too, the species offer something the hybrids cannot give. *Wasonii* is a sturdy, hardy shrub with foliage of distinction. With their rusty-brown indumentum beneath and a sprinkling of orange-gold on their upper surface, the young leaves prick up and look at you like a pony's ears. And like the other species mentioned in this chapter *wasonii* does not take an unconscionably long time to flower. Its pale yellow, red-spotted flowers are produced when it is about five years old.

I cannot stress too strongly that in the average new small garden of today, fresh from the bulldozer and builder's rubble, every care must be taken over the preparation of the soil (on the lines suggested in Chapter 6) and in the provision of wind-shelter.

# CHAPTER 10

# Woodland and Larger Gardens

⤞⤞⤞⤞⤞⤞⤞⤞⤞⤞⤞⤞⤞⤞⤞⤞⤞⤞⤞⤜⤜⤜⤜⤜⤜⤜⤜⤜⤜⤜⤜⤜⤜⤜

Lucky is the gardener who has a piece of woodland to plant with rhododendrons and azaleas. There he should find the spongy, woodsy, acid soil that they love. Even in woods overlying limestone the soil often has a neutral-to-quite-acid reaction due to the slowly decaying fallen leaves and vegetation. In the limestone area of North Wales, several woods with open limestone outcrops all around and above them have a thriving population of self-sown *R. ponticum* along with *Helleborus foetidus*, hart's tongue ferns, yew and other typically limestone flora. The limestone woodlands rising behind Colwyn Bay will be familiar to anyone who has spent a holiday in the district and there, too, one may see species and hybrid rhododendrons (in this case purposely planted) growing freely and well and without any chlorotic symptoms.

Almost as important as the soil texture and content, a natural woodland offers wind-shelter and a branch canopy to act as a blanket and to protect the plants to some extent from frost. All but the smallest-leaved rhododendrons appreciate such a situation and even the dwarfs will grow well at the edge of woodland, although too protected and airless a position will cause them to ail and die.

Ideal though a woodland site may be, for the best results it needs careful preparation before planting. As a start the trees must be thinned. Often it is possible to be selective about this, leaving some oak, mountain ash, hollies and conifers along with a silver

III. Dwarf azaleas at Wisley

birch or two for beauty of stem. Beech and sycamore are greedy trees with which few plants can associate happily and so they should be removed. Elms sooner or later become dangerous or fall victim to disease and it is better that they should be cut down at once rather than later on when their falling would damage the rhododendrons. *Ponticum* rhododendron may be left on the outskirts of the wood to cut off draughts at ground level. It may be left also within the wood in one or two places to shelter young plants or to form strategic wind-breaks in the lee of which one may place a large-leaved rhododendron or one such as 'Loderi' or *diaprepes* whose large and delicate blooms need wind-shelter. *Ponticum* seedlings, however, can be a nuisance and this must be borne in mind when deciding whether the plants should be left or not. Care must be taken in thinning, so that one does not remove too much lower growth and so let in the wind. The considerable shade and top-hamper of most woodlands must, however, be reduced. Many of us, I am sure, try to grow our rhododendrons in too much shade. The exact amount of shade needed varies over the country. What would be reasonable in Sussex or Kent with their comparatively dry, sunny summers would result in drawn-up spindly growth and a reduction of flowering in North Wales or the west of Scotland where the rainfall is heavier and the hours of sunshine less. The correct amount of shade can be learned only by experience and by looking at other gardens. If one goes round a garden and sees most of the rhododendron stems bare at the base with the leaves and flowers well above one's head then either there is too much shade in that garden or the plants have been set too close and not later moved to proper distances apart. Some rhododendrons are inclined to be more leggy than others, but in the right situation, without being overshaded or overcrowded, most of them will make reasonably well-furnished shrubs. Others such as *falconeri* are tree-like in habit and so naturally will reveal more of their usually handsome stems and bark.

In a garden well known to me, considerable heavy thinning has been carried out over recent years and I have been amazed to see how much better many of the rhododendrons have been for it. Of course, there has been the reverse side of things, too, and wind funnels have been opened up causing the loss of several tender species and hybrids. The rule, then, is to thin carefully, always with an eye to the wind and with due regard to the local sunshine and temperature records.

Care must be taken not to plant too closely. In the past, when new species were coming in from the East and new hybrids were constantly being created, one did not know how big any particular rhododendron would grow and consequently in many of the older gardens plants were set too close together. The owners and their gardeners were too busy raising and planting out new rhododendrons to move and thin the old and the result today is often crowded thickets of straggly, bare-stemmed rhododendrons flowering quite well but only above one's head where the daylight can reach them. To help to prevent this state of affairs occurring again, I have tried to give the height and breadth that the various species and hybrids may be expected to reach.

When cutting down and thinning timber it is important not to leave sawn-off or fallen branches lying about. Wherever possible, too, tree-stumps should be grubbed up and very large ones may, with the proper safeguards, have to be dynamited. Old decaying tree-stumps and fallen branches result in the invasion of honey fungus (shoestring fungus, bootlace fungus)—a killer, and the trouble most dreaded in woodland rhododendron gardens (see Chapter 14).

Brambles and other weeds must, of course, be removed. Ferns, ivy, bluebells, wood anemones, primroses, woodrush, vaccinium, etc., are all an asset to the prospective woodland garden and should be left wherever possible. Ivy is a useful and harmless ground cover, blanketing the soil, trapping leaves to mulch and feed the plants and making an attractive and helpful association for hardy cyclamen, snowdrops and other bulbs. I do not think, however, that it should be allowed to climb up trees. Where ivy was smothering the trees in a woodland, I would saw through its stems to weaken it and pull it away from the trunks wherever possible, but would never disturb ivy covering the ground.

A short cut to ridding the woodland of its scrubby undergrowth might be sought in the newer weedkillers and brushwood sprays.

Such chemicals, however, might kill desirable underlings such as ferns and woodrush along with the undesirables. They might also damage the trees that were to be retained. Many weedkillers have a longer and more far-reaching effect than one expects or wants and I have known plants killed when planted as long as a year after the ground has been chemically treated. Maples in particular seem susceptible to damage and die at the first sniff of hormone weed-killer or sodium chlorate.

In large gardens where no natural woodland exists, rhododendrons and azaleas are most happily accommodated in a 'natural' glade-like planting scheme in association with other shrubs, perhaps bamboos, and small shade-bearing trees with wind-breaks of conifers, holly and other evergreens.

Bonfires should never be lit near to rhododendron beds nor should rhododendrons be planted near or on the site of old bonfires. Bonfire ash contains much calcium and potassium which, rain-washed into the ground, produces a magnesium deficiency in rhododendrons and azaleas.

Dr. Henry Tod relates that some years ago when he was at Easter Park looking at some of Mr. Younger's fine rhododendrons he came upon one which was showing severe chlorosis and Mr. Younger said to him that he was not at all surprised that it was looking sickly because his gardener had built a bonfire far too near it the previous spring. This interested Dr. Tod, who asked why he said that. Mr. Younger replied that when he was a young man a very old gardener said to him: 'Mind this, laddie, *never* plant a rhododendron where there has been a bonfire.'

Dr. Tod was interested in the idea and thought the cause of the trouble was the high level of calcium and probably potassium in the ash tending to produce a magnesium deficiency in the plant. He tested the leaves of the affected rhododendron and found that they were indeed magnesium deficient.

I was recently shown some plants of 'Matador' and 'Cornish Cross' which, formerly healthy, had swiftly deteriorated and were showing extreme chlorotic symptoms. On inquiry I learned that a dressing of bonfire ash had a few months earlier been given to the rhododendrons in the mistaken hope of providing them with a tonic! *Sequestrene Plus* and magnesium sulphate in the form of a dressing of Epsom salts was recommended.*

Two types of rhododendron seem especially suited to woodland planting—the airily built 'earlies' such as ('Cilpinense' × *lutescens*) 'Fine Feathers', and 'Praecox', and the tall-growing, often scented species and hybrids with large leaves or particularly wind-vulnerable flowers. In this last category come the Falconeri and Grande series, the fragrant early-flowering *sutchuenense* and its allies, the various forms of (*fortunei* × *griffithianum*) 'Loderi', with their very large flowers, the July-flowering, tree-like *auriculatum*, its hybrid 'Polar Bear', and *diaprepes*.

In the woodland and in similar shelter offered by established 'natural' plantings, the overhead canopy formed by the bare branches of deciduous trees offers the frail blossoms of the early-flowering rhododendrons considerable protection from frost. In such a situation the various clones of (*arboreum* × *caucasicum*) 'Nobleanum' and the lightly built *mucronulatum* with its rosy-purple flowers will usually fit in at least one burst of bloom between 'cold' spells. Cornish gardens and those on the favoured coast and sea-lochs of western Scotland and Ireland will often be able to boast the ruby-flowered *arboreum* and its hybrids. The tight, dark purple trusses of the hardier, silvery-leaved *niveum*, too, are worth waiting for, although care must be taken to keep this species away from the bright reds which would make a baroque but unpleasing clash with its colouring.

Of the popular deep reds (*thomsonii* × *barbatum*) 'Shilsonii' is one of the hardiest and is likely to succeed in woodland conditions in most areas although, as with all early-flowering rhododendrons, there is a risk that the flowers will sometimes catch the frost. In the south and west *barbatum* with its waxy, blood-red flowers and *strigillosum* with its comparatively large trusses of brilliant scarlet are among the most striking.

There is something special, too, about the flowers of *stewartianum* and *eclecteum*, those medium-sized shrubs of the Thomsonii

* I am glad to say that a year later when I again visited the garden the plants were again a healthy green. The correct chemical treatment had saved two fine rhododendrons.

series with the typical bell-shaped flowers of that series in shades of yellow, cream, rose, champagne ringed at the mouth of the bell with pink and clear, pale gold. These species often flower in February when *lutescens* is vying with the primroses in displaying the sulphur-yellow of early spring. The dark-blotched lilac (*praevernum* × *sutchuenense*) 'Geraldii', the smaller-growing *praevernum*, the pale blush flowers of which are blotched with wine; the lilac-pink *oreodoxa* and the paler pink, beautifully spotted with red, *fargesii* are four fragrant rhododendrons to spread through the woodland or garden to surprise the eye and greet the nose with delight.

The Bodnant early yellow hybrids—('Cilpinense' × *lutescens*) 'Fine Feathers' mentioned earlier; (*chrysodoron* × *leucaspis*) 'Chrysaspis' and (*leucaspis* × *valentinianum*) 'Valaspis' are reasonably hardy in woodland and will add the charm of the unexpected if tucked into bays between larger rhododendrons or planted at the junction of paths or at bends where, turning a corner, one may come upon them suddenly.

A large shrub which is delightful in the early spring garden is (*fargesii* × *irroratum*) 'Carex', a neatly-furnished pyramidal bush with soft grey-green leaves and pale-blush bells spotted with chocolate inside. The lightly-built, pinky-mauve 'Emasculum' will be in flower at the same time and as this goes over the buds on the big-leaved tree rhododendrons will be beginning to open their tight-trussed flowers. A good pink form of *hodgsonii*, the purple-throated, rose-coloured *rex*, and the fine daffodil-yellow *macabeanum* are some of the easiest to satisfy, while the huge shiny leaves of *sinogrande* and the orange-felted foliage of *fictolacteum*, the massive leaves of *falconeri* and the silver undersides of *rex* and *hodgsonii* will give pleasure during the years while one is waiting for them to attain maturity and for their flowering to begin.

The tall, beautifully-barked *thomsonii* is one of the loveliest species that flower at the beginning of the main spring flush. With its blood-red bells, the creamy-buff trusses of the very hardy *campylocarpum* hybrid 'Unique' make a not-too-glaring contrast. There are two forms of 'Unique', but the best and most usually grown is Slocock's form. This makes in time a tall bush of ten feet or more in height, densely furnished to the ground with healthy, shapely, dark green leaves. Associated with these two rhododendrons at Bulkeley Mill are the creamy-belled (*campylocarpum* × *griffithianum*) 'Penjerrick', one of the loveliest of all rhododendrons, and the tall azalea species known as *reticulatum* with rich butterfly-flowers of magenta-purple.

Elsewhere in the woodland, the graceful pink *vaseyi*, the deeper rose-coloured *albrechtii*, and *schlippenbachii* with its larger, pale flowers will, with the pretty white *atlanticum* make delightful, airy groups. Out of sight of the azalea species, drifts of the yellow-and-cream Knap Hill and Exbury azaleas would make a pleasing foreground to the green of later-flowering rhododendrons. Some of the Ghent azaleas, in time, make very large bushes and are strong enough in floral mass and colour to be planted alone, making solitary bright incidents between other shrubs. The later-blooming, pale-flowered *occidentale* hybrids, 'Exquisitum', 'Gloriosum', 'Irene Koster', etc., are worth planting alone or in groups for their scent. Their pale effect and that of the July-flowering *arborescens* and *viscosum* is cool and lovely in a shady green part of the garden.

In early May some of the best of all rhododendrons are in flower. Among them the old pink-fading-to-white 'Loder's White' and the milky-white, chocolate-speckled 'Dr. Stocker' make big bushes that look well in woodland but which are—like the azaleas mentioned above—quite hardy and equally at home in any garden big enough to offer them room. Not so the clones of the famous (*fortunei* × *griffithianum*) 'Loderi' cross. Basically hardy, these must have adequate wind-shelter if their sweetly-scented, outsize trusses are not to suffer. Large though the flowers and trusses of 'Loderi' may be, there is about them a quality that is lacking in the smaller but coarser trusses of that other *griffithianum* hybrid 'Pink Pearl'. By 1956, twenty-four different clones of the 'Loderi' grex had been registered. All are good but I would especially recommend 'King George', the solidly-textured, delicate blush-coloured flowers of which fade to white with a hint of green at the throat. 'Venus' which with its smaller soft-pink flowers may appeal to those who find the enormous trusses and flowers of 'King George' and of the frilly blush 'Fairyland' a little too big for their taste. 'Sir Joseph Hooker' is another good clone in which the background colour of the petals is white with conspicuous pink veining while 'Julie' has creamy-sulphur tones that always appeal to me.

Among the more modestly-sized rhododendrons that flower at this time ('Aurora' × *fortunei*) 'Naomi' is outstanding and here again one has various clones from which to choose, ranging from the satiny 'Pink Beauty' to the buff-and-lilac shaded 'Nautilus' and the 'Exbury' form which also has buff and cream tones in its basic pink and lavender. The clone 'Glow' is useful in sheltered gardens because it flowers three weeks earlier than the type. Other fine modern hybrids which like 'Naomi' enjoy woodland conditions but are hardy enough to do well without them are the champagne-coloured ('Naomi' × *campylocarpum*) 'Carita' with the petal edges tinged with pink; the pale apricot (*yunnanense* × *concatenens*) 'Alison Johnstone'; (*discolor* × *campylocarpum* 'Lady Bessborough', with its extremely shapely firm trusses of frilly, creamy-yellow flowers, and its pink clone 'Roberte'; the fine yellow (*campylocarpum* × 'Dr. Stocker') 'Damaris'; 'Souvenir de W. C. Slocock', another *campylocarpum* hybrid with compact trusses that are rosy-pink in bud opening to cream with a ray of crimson; and the first-rate, very hardy (*wardii* × *decorum*) 'Ightham Yellow' with its good foliage and habit.

Associating well with these yellows, but looking equally good on their own among green foliage, are several first class reds—the waxy-flowered crimson (*griersonianum* × *strigillosum*) 'Matador' with its dark green hairy leaves; the tall-growing scarlet *griffithianum* hybrid 'Gill's Crimson'; ('Cornish Cross' × *haematodes*) 'Sussex Bonfire'; (*thomsonii* × *eriogynum*) 'Chanticleer'; the scarlet form of the loose-trussed ('Break of Day' × *griersonianum*) 'Goblin'; and (*haematodes* × *griersonianum*) 'May Day' —one of the best and hardiest of all red rhododendrons. Not to be forgotten, either, is the unique, tall-growing (*thomsonii* × *griffithianum*) 'Cornish Cross' with its uncommon and very large waxy flowers of carmine-pink.

A rich array of May-blooming species adds to the range. In yellows we have the firm-trussed *wightii* with its handsome leaves, and the lax *campylocarpum* followed by the later *wardii* with more open, cup-shaped flowers that are particularly rich and bright in the more recently introduced Ludlow and Sheriff form which has a vivid purple eye. The clear pink *souliei* has flowers of a similar, lovely shape and there is also *callimorphum* with more bell-shaped flowers of rose-pink and small, pretty leaves. The Triflorum series offer a choice of pinks, blues, lavenders and white for the more open and sunny parts of the woodland but these have been fairly fully discussed in the last chapter. A rhododendron bred from *augustinii* and its variety *chasmanthum*, in this series—'Electra'—is one of the bluest rhododendrons. Unfortunately it seems to be even more tender than its parents, but for gardens that are comparatively free from May frosts it offers a lovely contrast for the early May-flowering white cherry 'Shirotae'.

Farther into the woodland or by the waterside where colours must be subtle if they are to be in tune with their surroundings the various lavender-blues of the so-called 'hardy hybrid' section are useful in shady places to give the 'blue' effect of wood-smoke. Excellent for this purpose is the dark eyed lavender 'Susan', 'Blue Peter', the lilac-pink 'Countess of Athlone' and the pale lavender 'Lady Grey Egerton' to be followed later by the very old but indispensable 'Fastuosum Flore Pleno'. Some of these are a little crude in colour when the buds first unfold but after a day they quickly fade to more becoming shades.

As May gives way to June (*dichroanthum* × *griersonianum*) 'Fabia' comes into flower along with the lovely *cinnabarinum* hybrids 'Lady Rosebery', 'Lady Chamberlain', 'Bodnant Yellow' and 'Lady Berry'. The species of the Cinnabarinum series are no less lovely; and especially to be sought after are *cinnabarinum* var. *roylei* and *concatenans*. Slightly earlier in flower but appropriate in the more open parts of woodland and garden are (*cinnabarinum* × *oreotrephes*) 'Oreocinn', a slender shrub of medium height with wide-open apricot flowers and attractive blue-grey leaves and (*chartophyllum* × *cinnabarinum roylei*) 'Ernestine', a more vigorous-growing shrub of similar character with pretty lilac-pink flowers.

With 'Fabia' in June, bloom two large-growing, pale-flowered hybrids with a delightful scent. They are ('Loderi' × *discolor*) 'Albatross', with huge flat-topped trusses of enormous white flowers, flushed and spotted with green in the throat, and (*discolor* × *fortunei*) 'Avocet' with long, handsome leaves that have the purple petioles of *fortunei* and a looser truss of glorious pale-blush coloured flowers. Other good hybrids flowering at this time are 'Damozel', a spreading, not-too-tall Exbury hybrid of *griersonianum* with narrow dark green leaves and elegant trusses of deep rose-crimson flowers: (*griersonianum* × 'Loder's White') 'Flamingo', a hybrid of Sir James Horlick's raising, with shapely rich rose-coloured trusses; ('Lady Bessborough' × *souliei*) 'Halcyone', with pinky-cream, cup-shaped flowers slightly blotched with pinky-brown and pretty *souliei*-type leaves. The yellow ('Dido' × 'Lady Bessborough') 'Jalisco', with rather broad leaves and good trusses of waxy, buff-yellow bells, and (*dichroanthum* × *elliotti*) 'Golden Horn' var. 'Persimmon'—a fine rich red without the double calyx of 'Golden Horn' itself which is orange in effect but more clumsy in flower than the elegant 'Fabia' grex.

Later still, taking the rhododendron season well into July, and even into August in the north and west, are the splendid late-flowering Exbury reds which combine the brilliance of the late-flowering species of the Irroratum series with the hardiness of their other chosen parents. Outstanding among these are the moderate-sized (*eriogynum* × *haematodes*) 'Grosclaude', (*elliotti* × 'Moser's Maroon) 'Grenadier' and (*eriogynum* × 'Moser's Maroon') 'Romany Chal'. Even better than these is the excellent habited (*eriogynum* × *griersonianum*) 'Tally Ho' with the true geranium-scarlet flowers of *griersonianum* and dark, soft-green leaves. Hardy enough in Wales and the west, this is said not to be hardy in Surrey and Berkshire where it might be replaced by (*griersonianum* × 'Romany Chai') 'Vesuvius', a Sunningdale hybrid of smaller growth and similar colouring.

The well-known Bodnant pink (*griersonianum* × 'Soulbut')

'Vanessa' flowers at the end of July and makes a neat, compact bush, better furnished than *griersonianum* and with an open truss of rich salmon-pink flowers with a darker freckling and a crimson eye. A Sunningdale hybrid (between 'Vanessa' and 'Roberte' of the 'Lady Bessborough' grex) 'Coromandel' is another neat grower with widely bell-shaped, slightly frilly flowers of creamy-yellow, faintly spotted with red.

In a category on their own—cool, scented, and tree-like—are (*griffithianum* × *discolor*) 'Angelo', a very hardy plant with pink buds which open to enormous trumpet-shaped white blooms, and (*auriculatum* × *diaprepes*) 'Polar Bear' which will grow to thirty feet or more under favourable conditions and has large, bold trusses of pure white, long-tubed *auriculatum*-type flowers a yellow eye. Either of these will scent the woodland or garden for a considerable distance.

# CHAPTER 11

# Greenhouse and Mild Climate Cultivation

⋙⋙⋙⋙⋙⋙⋙⋙⋘⋘⋘⋘⋘⋘⋘⋘⋘

Some of the loveliest, often scented, rhododendrons are unfortunately hardy only in the mildest part of the British Isles. The graceful, large-flowered *ciliicalyx*, the lily-like *lindleyi* and the superb *taggianum*, *sinonuttallii* and *rhabdotum*, with its wonderful, striped trumpets, need wall-cultivation even in favoured Cornish gardens. Others such as the bright yellow *burmanicum*, the paler *johnstoneanum* (especially attractive in the double-flowered form of which a few plants may usually be found in any batch of selfed-seed) and the scented *bullatum* with its apple-blossom tinted flowers and deeply impressed leaves are satisfactory in the open in sheltered gardens in the south-west, near the coast in Wales, and along the western coast of Scotland. *Edgworthii*, however, which is very near *bullatum* in type, needs a wall and has been given one even at Brodick Castle in the favoured climate of the Scottish island of Arran. Such hybrids as (*edgworthii* × *formosum*) 'Fragrantissimum', (*ciliatum* × *edgworthii*) 'Princess Alice', 'Lady Alice Fitzwilliam' and the exotic-looking (*formosum* × *nuttallii*) 'Tyermannii' should also be given wall protection.

In the colder areas of the country it is useless to attempt these plants outside. Luckily, however, like most rhododendrons, they are ideal subjects for a cool greenhouse or conservatory, while small specimens may even be accommodated in any room of the house that is free from gas-fumes, coke-stoves or a too fiercely-hot central heating system, just as may be grown the ordinary indoor evergreen azaleas that one gives and receives at Christmas.

In a large greenhouse where adequate shading can be given in summer the tender rhododendrons may be planted in the border in a suitably spongy compost of four parts rhododendron peat, spruce needles, rotted bracken, or leaf-mould from broad-leaved trees growing on acid soil, to one part of loam and one part of coarse sand.

In smaller greenhouses and conservatories it is usually more convenient to grow the plants in pots—or, better still, in teak boxes (in which adequate drainage holes have been made) which have less tendency than pots to dry out. After flowering the plants may stand outside for the summer, their pots or boxes being plunged in ashes.

Some of the members of the Maddenii series are epiphytes, in nature growing in the tropical forests where in order to be near the light they perch in the tree-tops with their roots thrust into moss and rotted leaves that has accumulated in the forks of the branches or in cracks in the bark. In the greenhouse these species can best be pleased if they are given aerial perches or boxes of slatted teak and grown in a very open compost of coarse rhododendron peat and sphagnum moss, much as one might grow an orchid. Their containers should be kept on the small side and they should never be over-watered. Such treatment suits also such non-epiphytic members of the series as *taggianum* and *rhabdotum*.

### Tender Rhododendrons for Greenhouse Cultivation

*bullatum*—white or pink, scented, small
*burmanicum*—yellow, dwarf
*chrysodoron*—bright yellow, dwarf
'Chrysomanicum' (*chrysodoron* × *burmanicum*)—yellow, dwarf
'Countess of Haddington'—blush, scented, small
*crassum*—white, scented, large
*dalhousiae*—pale chartreuse, scented, medium
*edgeworthii*—white, scented, small
'Fragrantissimum'—white, scented, small

*johnstoneanum*—pale yellow, sometimes double, fragrant, taller

'Lady Alice Fitzwilliam'—blush, deeper stripes, delicious scent, very compact

'Princess Alice' (*ciliatum* × *edgworthii*)—white, scented, apt to straggle

*rhabdotum*—white, striped deep pink, scented, taller

*sinonuttallii*—white with yellow eye, wonderful scent, large

*sulfureum*—rich yellow, small

*taggianum*—white with yellow eye, scented, medium

'Tyermannii' (*nuttallii* × *formosum*)—white, scented, taller

In addition to these there are the Javanicum rhododendrons from Malaysia which need warm-house conditions, and a constant temperature and an even day-length obtained by artificial heating.

The tender rhododendrons of the Edgworthii and Maddenii series and also the tender hybrids do not need high temperatures. They will be quite satisfactory in a cold-house in all but the very bleakest areas and even there only enough heat should be given to keep out the frost. Some, such as the attractive little *moupinense* with its wide-open, azalea-like flowers in milky-white or pink, may be brought into bloom early by removing in early January to a temperature of fifty or sixty degrees, or to the warmth of an indoor room.

Some of the older hybrids such as 'Christmas Cheer', 'Chevalier Felix de Sauvage', 'Handsworth Scarlet', 'Jacksonii', 'Nobleanum' and 'Unknown Warrior' may also be forced, but they take up a good deal of room and in a small greenhouse it may be better to concentrate upon the smaller growing evergreen azaleas, and the lightly built 'Praecox' and *moupinense*. After flowering they should be returned to a cooler atmosphere and gradually hardened off before being placed out of doors for the summer.

Those who want to grow the tender evergreen double-flowered azaleas in a warm greenhouse may find the following lists useful.

FOR CHRISTMAS FORCING

'Princess Beatrix'—salmon

'Eric Schaeme'—pink and white
'Theodor Findeisen'—red
'Madame Petrick'—pink and white

CHRISTMAS TO EASTER FORCING

'Vervaeneana Rosea'—pink and white
'Vervaeneana Saumona'—salmon and pink
'Vervaeneana Rubra'—dark red
'Vervaeneana Alba'—particularly lovely white

Many new greenhouse varieties are now being bred in America and it is hoped that these will soon be widely available in this country. Forcing, however, is not really necessary as there are a wide selection of species and hybrids which, provided frost is excluded, will come into bloom from January on.

A fine plant to have in flower under glass in January is the semi-deciduous rosy-purple *dauricum* which is usually less vigorous in growth than the related *mucronulatum* which is, however, the better choice for out of doors. Two species to follow on are *moupinense*, mentioned above, and the smaller, silver-salvered *leucaspis* set off by its dark anthers. The hybrid between the two, 'Bric-a-Brac', is also good, and when it is over 'Praecox' will be ready to give its display of airy, lilac-mauve blooms. None of these really need any heat at all. They will flower well in an unheated alpine house, but a temperature of thirty to forty degrees Fahrenheit will bring them into bloom just a little earlier.

Not everyone has a greenhouse or conservatory with sufficient room to accommodate the taller-growers. For the small, cold greenhouse, or conservatory, or alpine house, where there may be room only to accommodate two or three of the taller rhododendrons I would choose 'Praecox', 'Lady Alice Fitzwilliam' and 'Fragrantissimum' along with as many of the really dwarf, peat-garden rhododendrons as I could afford or easily propagate. In such conditions, evergreen azaleas of the *simsii* type may easily be brought into flower by Christmas provided (after being plunged out of doors in not-too-shady a place for the summer) they are moved under glass at the beginning of September, kept reasonably moist, and syringed. In November they should be given a light and preferably sunny window in a moderately heated room. Care must be taken to see that they do not dry out. I find that they flower better if they are not repotted too often. A top-dressing of rotted bracken given every November will keep them healthy and growing well.

In most parts of the country such early-flowering rhododendrons as *leucaspis* and *moupinense* are always a frost risk and so they are a natural choice for the cold greenhouse or alpine house where one can enjoy their blossoms unspoiled. Cold winds also can spoil the later-flowering of *racemosum*, of which Forrest's dwarf form should be selected. *Virgatum*, too, is vulnerable as is *williamsianum*, while such brilliantly-coloured dwarf azaleas as 'Hinodegiri' and 'Orange Beauty' may have their blooms spoiled by the weather. Moreover, there is something especially satisfying about growing these little rhododendron species and some of the evergreen azaleas under glass, raised to a height at which one can study them closely and enjoy their perfection, while for those who garden on alkaline soil, a small greenhouse offers the chance to grow a collection of rhododendrons and azaleas in suitable compost and, provided hard tap-water is not used, without the need to counteract the ever-present problems of alkalinity. In very cold gardens, too, some of the gay Kurume azaleas may not be reliably hardy, while the wonderful yellow-flowered dwarf rhododendrons of the Boothii series—*chrysodoron* and *sulfureum*—need protection in most areas as does *valentinianum* of the Maddenii series; and most attractive they are, too, with their small neat leaves and brilliant-yellow, small flowers.

Not strictly needing protection, some of the tiny species of the Lapponicum series are nevertheless delightful under glass. Such are the starry lavender *intricatum*, the grey-leaved *impeditum*, the snowy *microleucum* and good forms of the yellow *chryseum*. Other pleasing species for the purpose are the pinky-purple *imperator*, the closely allied *pemakoense*, the deep pink *pumilum*, the lilac-mauve *uniflorum* and the creeping *radicans* with its large flat, purple flowers. Free-flowering forms of *forrestii* var. *repens* are also worth growing as is the dwarf clone of its hybrid with *griersonianum*, 'Creeping Jenny', and that with *neriiflorum*, 'Little

Ben'. The sometimes difficult Anthopogon series does well under glass provided an airy atmosphere is maintained. Particularly attractive are the pale yellow *sargentianum*, the rich pink *anthopogon* itself and the more prostrate *cephalanthum crebreflorum*. Also attractive is the 'thimble'-flowered *campylogynum* in its various forms. Of the evergreen azaleas, all the Kurumes are ideal with their tiny leaves and small, butterfly-shaped, bright flowers. Special favourites of mine are the hose-in-hose 'Kirin', the crimson 'Ima-shojo', 'Kure-no-yuki' with its larger white hose-in-hose flowers, the rosy lavender 'Irohayama', 'Hatsugiri' in magenta-purple and the pale pink 'Hinomayo'. Not all of these are members of the 'Wilson Fifty' but I think they are near the true Kurumes in character and type.

As mentioned earlier, stout wooden boxes are better than pots for the cultivation of dwarf rhododendrons and azaleas under glass. Where the cost of teak seems prohibitive, a compromise can be made by using some of the dwarf tubs offered in the garden press, and where good cultivation is more important than mere appearance, the dwarf species have been successfully grown in kipper boxes, small five-pound tea chests of the sort in which China tea is sometimes sold and various other wooden boxes. Failing any of these, of course, large alpine pans and half-pots and ordinary clay flower pots can be used. Care must be taken, of course, to see that the containers are clean. They should be well crocked and I like to put a layer of sphagnum moss above the crocks before filling in with spruce needles, rhododendron peat or acid leaf-mould, acid loam and sand in the proportions given earlier (4:1:1). Some growers prefer leaf-mould to peat. I myself like to mix spruce needles, rhododendron peat and rotted bracken but some acid loam (fibrous if possible) and coarse sand should be used for all but the epiphytes and forcing azaleas, which seem to do best in ninety per cent coarse rhododendron peat and ten per cent sphagnum moss. (Too frequent repotting disturbs the plants and should be avoided so it is best to select pots a little bigger than the root ball, leaving perhaps half an inch to an inch to spare all round. Wooden containers may be even bigger.

It helps to not fill the containers with compost right to the top

17. 'Pink Coral', one of the Leonardslee clones of the wonderful *griffithianum* hybrid 'Loderi', this form is sweetly scented and of refined form

18. *R. johnstoneanum*, a cream- or yellow-flowered species with a pleasing double form

19. A Knap Hill azalea hybrid with large, fragrant flowers and good autumn colour

20. *R.* 'Alison Johnstone', one of the newer hybrids between the Cinnabarinum and Triflorum series with lovely apricot-coloured flowers and appealing foliage

but to leave two or three inches to accommodate the top-dressing that should be applied in the autumn or winter each year. I think there is nothing finer for top-dressing than rotted bracken. Spruce needles also are good, as is leaf-mould from broad-leaved trees on acid soil. Rhododendrons and azaleas for forcing may also be given a little liquid manure as they are coming into bud Care, however, must be taken with artificial fertilizer compounds because of the risk of their having an alkaline content. Cold tea is a safe tonic for all rhododendrons and azaleas and is particularly beneficial to those grown under glass.

The actual pH of the potting compost for rhododendrons and azaleas should be about 5, although a little either side of this ideal will not cause harm.

Sometimes the plants outgrow their space in the greenhouse particularly if their containers are rather on the large side. When this happens they may be cut back after flowering to leave shapely bushy plants. This cutting-back may be as severe as necessary. If cut back to the bare stems, new buds may be persuaded to form by constant syringing and will eventually give a shapely compact plant.

During the summer the plants should be removed and plunged into a shaded frame, or the pots and boxes may be stood in the lee of a north wall or hedge. If they have to remain under glass, the house must be well shaded and ventilated and the plants syringed morning and evening. In fact, syringing and damping down will be necessary even in March and April on sunny days as the sun's heat is so accentuated by the glass. I found, however, as mentioned before, that in North Wales, at any rate, forcing azaleas bloom earlier if the pots are plunged in a sunny place and this, of course, means that extra care must be paid to watering.

Raising plants from seeds and cuttings will be discussed in the next chapter.

# CHAPTER 12

# Propagation

᠉᠉᠉᠉᠉᠉᠊᠊᠊᠊᠊᠊

For the amateur with only a small garden, layering offers the easiest method of increasing rhododendron and azalea stock. Many of the small-leaved, dwarf rhododendron species and hybrids may be increased by a simple form of mound layering such as one might use for heaths. By this method such rhododendrons as *racemosum*, *calostrotum*, *radicans*, *chryseum impeditum*, 'Blue Tit', 'Sapphire' and 'Yellow Hammer', with the evergreen azaleas, may be relied upon readily to give a supply of sturdy new plants within eighteen months to two years. This method is successful only when the plants are young and when there are plenty of young shoots pushing out at ground level. One prepares a fine compost of rhododendron peat, rotted bracken and acid loam and works it well down among the branches, burying the side shoots for about an inch and a half of their length. When only three or four new plants are wanted it is helpful to bend outwards each of the shoots required, anchoring them down into the rooting compost by large stones. By this method I have had no difficulty in raising as many plants of suitable dwarf azaleas and rhododendrons as needed.

Not all dwarfs respond to this method, however, and for 'Humming Bird', 'Little Ben' and the other *williamsianum* and *forrestii* var. *repens* hybrids more conventional methods must be used. For these and for the larger rhododendrons and azaleas it is necessary to select a branch which may easily be bent to the ground, and scoop out a shallow trench filled with two parts of

130

peat to one of sand. One then slits the bark on the underside of the branch for an inch or two (according to the size of the plant) to make a little 'tongue' where it is expected to root, pegging, or weighting-down the branch with a stone, so that it is embedded in the rooting mixture. The end of the shoot should then be staked as near upright as possible to ensure the sharp bend necessary to impede the sap-flow from the parent plant and so encourage the shoot to make its own feeding arrangements by sending out roots. This sharp bend also helps to hold open the 'tongue' although some people like to wedge a stick into the slit as well. I have never found rooting hormones to make any difference whatever to the number of layers rooted by this method or by the next which is the one employed by nurserymen when numbers of plants are to be raised.

Few of the larger rhododendrons have more than two or three branches conveniently placed near the ground—nor does it improve a plant's appearance to strip it of its lower branches. If one has a large garden in which it is desired to establish ten or more plants of a species or hybrid it pays to follow the nurseryman's method which entails sacrificing one's original plant to some extent to produce a practically limitless supply of sturdy young layers. The parent plant should be placed on its side in a shallow trench with a compost of peat and sand heaped over its branches while the shoots to be layered are turned upright and pegged down into the mixture. By this method a good supply of rooted plants will be available the second autumn after layering and should then be severed and grown on for a further year in a nursery bed before being planted out to take care of themselves.

Deciduous azaleas may be propagated by a slightly different method. The stock plants must be on their own roots and should be grown in sandy soil and peat and well fed to produce strong growth. In the spring, the stock plants should be cut down to within a foot of the ground to encourage the production of new shoots from the base. Nothing further need be done until the autumn of the following year when sandy, peaty soil is mounded over the plant, leaving only the tips showing. During the next

year the shoots root into the mound. By the autumn of the following year they should have made enough root and may be
severed from the parent plant and set out in rows to grow on.
The parent plant is allowed a year of rest and then the process is
repeated. By this means as many as a hundred layers are obtained
from some of the really old stock plants every three or four years.

When a large garden or park has to be stocked such mass-
production methods are well worth considering. Where only two
or three layers are wanted and there are no suitable branches at
ground level, the required plants may be obtained by air-layering
in polythene.

Ground-layering may be carried out from autumn to spring but
air-layers seem to succeed better if started in April. The necessary materials are moist sphagnum moss; the larger size of
polythene bag of the type sold at a stationer's to hold sandwiches,
or—better still—a supply of tube-flat polythene; some waterproof insulating tape; a child's paint brush, and a tin of hormone
rooting powder. (Very large-leaved rhododendrons need a
stronger hormone powder than the others but this is indicated on
the instruction leaflets which should be studied before purchase.)

The selected shoot should be of the previous year's growth and
should be sliced part-way through towards its tip for about two
inches. The cut should go about halfway through the shoot and
should then be held open with a small twig while one brushes the
hormone powder on to the cut surfaces. Care should be used so
as not to get too much powder on to the cut, as an overdose seems
to impede rooting rather than to help. The sphagnum moss
should then be squeezed free of surplus water (too much moisture
prevents rooting, though the moss should be thoroughly damp)
and pressed into the cut, which should still be held open by the
twig as otherwise the cut tends merely to heal instead of sending
out roots. A good layer of sphagnum is wrapped round the stem
and held in place by an assistant while one pulls into place the
polythene tube. If using a polythene bag, of course, the end
should have been removed.

If one has no assistant it is as well to pull the tube over the
shoot before starting to layer. This is very simply done by strok-

ing one's hands up over the leaves of the terminal rosette so that they form a cylinder over which the polythene tube is drawn. The leaves will usually hold the tube in place while one prepares the cut.

Once the polythene is finally in position one should bind the top and bottom with waterproof insulating tape, continuing for about an inch above and below the ends of the polythene to exclude air and rainwater. The sphagnum moss will keep sufficiently damp and by autumn enough roots may have formed for the layer to be severed and start life on its own. Sometimes roots will not form until the following summer or even later and a close watch should then be kept and as soon as the moss is seen to be well threaded with white roots the layer should be severed. This is where the difficulties begin. It is comparatively easy to get air-layers to form roots, but these roots are water-roots and great care is needed to get the young layers established and thriving in normal conditions. I have found them to do best if potted into a compost of ninety per cent rhododendron peat to ten per cent sand; the mixture then being just laced with spruce needles for nutriment.

The young layers must be kept well-watered, shaded and close. If no closed frame or greenhouse is available, a bell-jar placed over the pots will help. Failing a bell jar, a polythene bag may be used, being secured over the pots with strong rubber bands. I like to leave the condensation on the glass or polythene to drip back on to the plants and soil, approximating as near to mist conditions as possible. Gradually—very gradually—air is admitted, but the plants should receive protection for their first winter and it is best to delay transferring them to nursery rows until the following autumn. It is impossible to overstress the importance of the transition period.

Much prominence has lately been given to the mist technique of raising rhododendrons in quantity from cuttings. The best results are obtained from a high, well-drained cutting bench with the cuttings in trays at intervals of two inches apart and the water, heated to the optimum air temperature of about fifty degrees Fahrenheit, set to come on and off at regular intervals.

By this method cuttings are rooted in four to six weeks. However, cuttings raised in mist need care in establishing. As with air-layers rooted in sphagnum-encased polythene, their roots are mainly water-roots and so the cuttings need a further period in weaning houses, with the time-intervals between the mist spray gradually increased until at last the young plants are ready to be potted on and transferred to a cool greenhouse or cold frame.

Naturally such a method is rather costly but small-scale amateur apparatus is now available which need not be too expensive for the serious enthusiast. Mist propagation means that quantities of plants may be raised *on their own roots* for sale to the public and it is to be hoped that nurserymen using mist will be encouraged to raise more of the easy species and hardier new hybrids. The gardening public needs only to see such hardy hybrids as 'Fabia', 'Elizabeth', 'Unique', 'Letty Edwards', 'Blue Diamond' and 'Temple Belle' in nurserymen's exhibits at shows and to see them in the general lists in the catalogues to order them freely. That species such as *yunnanense, mucronulatum, fortunei,* good orange forms of *dichroanthum* and its sub-species *scyphocalyx,* and such azaleas as *vaseyi, albrechtii, canadense, viscosum, occidentale,* and the evergreen *mucronatum* would likewise quickly capture the public's imagination, I feel sure.

Let no one feel, however, that mist equipment is essential for the raising of rhododendrons from cuttings. The water supply in the gardens at Bodnant is unsuitable to use in the mist technique, but nevertheless—under the able direction of Mr. Charles Puddle—rhododendrons of all types are raised in some quantity from cuttings, including even the difficult large-leaved members of the Grande and Falconeri series. Nor are hormone rooting compounds found necessary to their successful rooting. (Air-layering is the only method of propagation in which they seem to play an essential part.)

Some authorities state that certain types of rhododendron strike best at certain times of the year, beginning perhaps in August with the hybrids, taking cuttings of the Triflorum series in September and ending with the members of the Lapponicum series in December. However, Mr. Puddle tells me that he finds that any time from July to December is suitable so long as those species which make their growth late in the season are given time enough to loose their first sappiness. In fact, with bottom heat, the striking of medium and larger-leaved rhododendron cuttings is comparatively easy. The cuttings, however, should be wounded so as to form as large a callous as possible. Mr. Puddle recommends a compost of one part of peat to two parts of sand, but adds: 'The larger the leaf, the more the peat.'

The frames must, of course, be kept close and moist until the cuttings are well rooted, the admission of air and hardening off being gradually accomplished and the young plants remaining in the frame until the next summer.

Rooting of cuttings of small-leaved mountain and moorland rhododendrons and of the Kurume azaleas is somewhat different in method. I have had considerable success with near-sand-frame conditions using a compost of peat and sand in a small, close frame standing in full sun. My cuttings have been taken in July and August but I have always shaded the frame during really hot sunshine, watering three or even four times a day and never wiping the glass as I firmly believe that in such conditions the moisture-drip assists rooting. Hybrids such as 'Bluebird', 'Augfast', 'Sapphire', 'Yellow Hammer' and 'Pink Drift' are easily rooted in these conditions, as are the species of the Lapponicum, Saluenense, Virgatum and Campylogynum and Anthopogon series along with the dwarf evergreen azaleas. I like to take cuttings about two inches long with a heel and I do not remove the bottom leaves as I think they help to anchor the cuttings in the soil. I just push the shoots firmly into position, leaves and all. . . . These dwarfs may also be struck in November, being inserted round the side of pots in a cold-house, or under a bell-glass in a north border.

Rhododendrons, as a rule, come easily from seed but they interbreed so freely that unless one uses only seed from a deliberately self-pollinated plant or seed resulting from a deliberate cross between two good forms of a species (made perhaps to obtain greater hardiness, more depth of colour, to capture a desired blotch, or to get bigger flowers) the results are unlikely to be true. Hybrid seed, except in the hands of those who have made a careful cross and thoroughly understand what they are aiming for, is useless. Many species are so variable, too, and interbreed so freely that seedlings, unless grown from seed from a self-pollinated plant or a special cross between selected forms, are mostly useless. This is one reason why one should never buy seedling forms of any species unless guaranteed from selfed-seed and why one should, whenever possible, insist on good clonal forms grown from layers or cuttings and so on *their own roots*. Buying seed also is not a good proposition unless it is guaranteed *selfed-seed*.

In one's own garden, however, it is possible to obtain true seed by self-pollinating a good form of a species or by crossing two good forms of the same species. Seed from deliberately self-pollinated flowers of good modern hybrids such as 'Fabia', 'Carita', 'Elizabeth' or 'Hawk' is also worth growing on, as the offspring will usually be good and of even quality, although perhaps not quite as outstanding as their parent. Rhododendron seed must be cleaned before sowing and usually germinates easily. It may either be sown in January or February under glass in a small propagating case with a bottom heat of fifty-five to sixty degrees Fahrenheit or—in the case of the dwarfer and smaller-leaved types—in boxes or in a cold frame at the end of March.

It sometimes happens, however, that the seed does not come up and so, after two or three months they should be removed from the propagating case and plunged in the cold frame until the following spring. Seed should never be thrown away. A winter's freezing and thawing will often induce the most stubborn seed to germinate when removed to heat again in the spring.

As the seed germinates so thickly, shallow boxes are better than pans. The boxes should be half-filled with washed crocks and topped with a compost of sieved rhododendron peat passed through a quarter-inch sieve and mixed with a little silver sand. The peat should be packed well down to within half an inch of the top of the boxes and then surfaced with a layer of peat passed through a finer sieve. The boxes should be well watered at night before sowing the following morning and—certainly where the tap-water contains lime—and preferably in all cases, rain-water should be used. Except for rhododendrons with the largest seeds the seed should be sown on the surface and covered only by a scattering of silver sand.

When sowing seed to germinate in a cold frame, a compost of equal parts of granulated peat and lime-free loam should be used with a surface layer of finely sieved peat and silver sand. However, exceptionally good results can be obtained from sowing in deeper boxes of spruce needles, packed well down and topped with a layer of finely sieved peat or mould from rotted spruce needles. After thinning, the seedlings may be left to grow on in the spruce needle compost until the following spring when they will usually be found to have made exceptionally good growth.

Many rhododendron and azalea seeds take about fourteen days to germinate in heat. As soon as the seed leaves appear, silver sand should be scattered over the pans to anchor the seedlings. A little air should then be admitted and water given as necessary by immersing the boxes in rainwater. After a further fourteen days the seedlings will be ready for removal from the propagating case to a warm greenhouse. The dwarfs, however, should leave the propagating case as soon as they begin to germinate, and their boxes may then be placed on the bench and covered with a sheet of glass.

With both cuttings and seedlings it is important to keep them growing well, and to keep the seedlings growing freely it is help-ful to place them as near the glass as possible so long as they are shaded from the midday sun. In early April light shading should be painted on the glass and on mild, sunny days the boxes should be syringed in the morning and afternoon. It helps also to damp down the paths. Greenfly is a constant danger at this stage and at the first signs of infestation, fumigation should be carried out, using a nicotine compound. Routine fumigation to stop the trouble before it starts might well be the rhododendron raiser's aim.

When the true leaves appear in April the seedlings may be pricked out into boxes. After crocking, it is as well to put in a layer of medium coarse peat before filling the boxes with a compost of two parts of lime-free loam, one part of sieved peat, one part oak leaf-mould (not from trees growing on alkaline ground) and one part of coarse sand. If there is any doubt about the calcium content of the leaf-mould it is safer to substitute sieved rotted spruce needles or sieved rotted bracken.

After pricking out, the young seedlings should be kept rather close for a fortnight. When large enough (usually about the middle of July) they should be gradually hardened off for the winter and then planted out in cold frames, using either the same compost as above or a six-inch layer of rotted bracken. It is helpful to remove the lights of the frame when rain is not too heavy, and also at night during autumn to admit the dew. Natural rain and dew seem to do the seedlings more good than any artificial watering although this, of course, is necessary too.

Hitherto grafting has been widely practised in the nursery trade but in the days of easily-rooted cuttings there is no excuse for its use. The only permissible form of grafting is root-grafting which does away with the possibility of the occurrence of troublesome suckers. Where it is desired to grow difficult species such as *lacteum* in unsuitable soil better results may be obtained if they are root-grafted on to *ponticum*. The process may be used also to speed up the flowering of some species which take many years to mature. Some experts think, too, that the species of the Maddenii series are easier to grow under glass when root-grafted on to *ponticum* stock.

In January and February, selected understocks of *ponticum* are brought into the greenhouse. They consist of pencil-sized pieces of root with tufts of fibrous root at the end and may readily be found among naturalized coverts or windbreaks of *ponticum* where many seedlings occur and where there are many natural layers.

The understocks are potted into a compost of rhododendron peat, fibrous lime-free loam and sand in equal parts, kept moist and given a temperature of sixty degrees Fahrenheit. In these conditions they will quickly make more roots. After six weeks they should be shortened to leave only about an inch and a half of pencil-thick rootstock above the fibrous root ball. Scions of the desired species of hybrids should be about five inches long and should be strong, straight shoots. They are slit for about an inch up the middle, slipped over the sharpened points of the root-stocks to form saddle-grafts, and taped into position. They may then be placed in pots with the union beneath the surface of the compost (equal parts sand, loam and peat as given above). They should be kept close and moist for three to four weeks and then gradually hardened off.

# CHAPTER 13

# Hybridizing

❯❯❯❯❯❯❮❮❮❮❮

In the smaller gardens of today few of us have room to grow on the necessary number of seedlings to make a selection of the best from a cross between the larger species and hybrids. But those who have room would find it worthwhile to hybridize, trying to concentrate on lines which have not yet been fully exploited or even making crosses between good forms of the same species in order to raise better and hardier plants. Those with smaller gardens, too, might find it rewarding to raise new hybrids from the smaller species and hybrids. There is a great need for hardy, compact and adaptable rhododendrons of quality in present-day gardens.

Before deciding upon potential crosses, however, these are one or two basic principles which the prospective hybridizer needs to assimilate:

1. Lepidote (scaly) and elepidote (non-scaly) rhododendrons do not readily cross.

2. The number of chromosomes in a rhododendron also governs its ability or failure to cross with other species. Most species have thirteen pairs of chromosomes (26 chromosomes in all) but some have many more. Those with 26 do not cross readily with those with more. When crossing species with a dissimilar chromosome count, the species with the larger number of chromosomes should always be the pollen parent. Species with extra chromosomes are listed below:

| | |
|---|---|
| *ambiguum* 52 | *edgarianum* 52 |
| *augustinii* 52 | *fastigiatum* 26 or 52 |
| *calostrotum* 26 or 52 | *flavidum* 26 or 78 |
| *chameunum* 26 or 52 | *heliolepis* 78 |
| *chartophyllum* 78 | *intricatum* 26 or 52 |
| *augustinii* var. | *lapponicum* 26 or 52 |
| *chasmanthum* 52 | *maddenii* 52 or 78 |
| *cinnabarinum* 78 | *oreotrephes* 78 |
| *concatenans* 78 | *pemakoense* 26 or 52 |
| *concinnum* 52 | *rubiginosum* 52 or 78 |
| *crassium* 52 or 78 | *russatum* 52 or 78 |
| *davidsonianum* 78 | *saluenense* 26 or 52 |
| *desquamatum* 58 | *xanthocodon* 78 |
| *diaprepes* 'Gargantua' 39 | *yunnanense* 78 |

A glance at the above table will show why such successful crosses have been made between *oreotrephes* and *yunnanense* of the Triflorum series with those of the Cinnabarinum series. All have 78 chromosomes. It also explains the success of the *augustinii* crosses made with some members of the Lapponicum series —probably the 'lapps' used had 52 chromosomes.

3. Hybrids are usually hardier than their parents. Possibly, being raised from seed in this country they become acclimatized. This has also been found to be the case with successive generations of seed-raised species.

4. First crosses between species give the highest proportion of good plants.

5. The best results come from mating species and hybrids that are near to each other in character and habit, e.g. the very successful crosses aforementioned between some members of the Triflorum series and those of the Cinnabarinum which are very nearly related, the species *xanthocodon* being thought by some authorities to bridge the two. According to Sir Edmund Loder, creator of the wonderful Loderi grex—success is more or less certain where a dominant species such as *griffithianum, fortunei, thomsonii* or *barbatum* (and I would add *griersonianum* and *williamsianum* to these) is mated to an allied species or to a hybrid

which does not contain a strain of an undesirable species (in this context I think perhaps the old muddy-coloured *catawbiense* hybrids might be construed as containing undesirable blood).

6. To get the deepest and truest colours, red should be mated to red (providing one uses pure reds with orange rather than blue in their make-up), yellow to yellow or cream, pink to pink, and lavender to lavender. Yellow and red will sometimes produce orange. One can also use species with orange in their flower colour such as *dichroanthum, concatenans* and *cinnabarinum* to get this result. Both *concatenans* and *cinnabarinum* are lepidote, however, and therefore only *dichroanthum* is left to cross with the more common elepidote range. It may be noted that red crossed with white is usually a disaster from the point of view of colour.

7. There are certain *classic* parents which pass on very desirable characteristics to their offspring, viz. *forrestii* var. *repens*, which transmits its brilliant flower-colour and a freedom of flowering it may not itself possess. R. *williamsianum* and *orbiculare* usually transmit their pretty shape of leaf as in 'Humming Bird', 'Moonstone', 'Treasure' and 'Temple Belle'; *cinnabarinum* tends to transmit something of its attractive flower shape together with a lovely blue leaf-sheen; *thomsonii* gives a well-shaped flower truss; *fortunei* and *discolor* give scent; the rose colour of *orbiculare* dominates in the first generation of seedlings, subsequent crosses would probably give a wider colour range; *haematodes* and *dichroanthum* produce in their offspring a large, fleshy calyx.

Some species yield offspring that will flower at an earlier age than others. Notable among these are: *griersonianum, decorum, campylocarpum, williamsianum,* the members of the Triflorum and Cinnabarinum series and most of the dwarfs. Among the best parents may be listed *griersonianum, williamsianum, haematodes, neriiflorum, forrestii* var. *repens, augustinii, yunnanense, cinnabarinum, dichroanthum, fortunei, discolor, griffithianum* and the members of the Lapponicum series. In view of the success of the progeny of *augustinii* crossed with the members of the Lapponicum series it seems that further crosses between other Triflorums and the members of this series might be worthwhile. For instance, *lutescens* might be worth crossing with *chryseum*,

*chryseum* × *microleucum* also might be interesting, and *davidsonianum* could be mated to a mauve *hippophaeoides* or one of the pinker forms of *tapetiforme* or *ravum* to give a small-leaved pink hybrid with the neat character of 'Blue Diamond'.

Scent is a very desirable characteristic and it may often be bred into pale-coloured rhododendrons by the use of *fortunei* or *discolor*. It may sometimes, however, be recessive in the first generation of seedlings but can usually be brought out either by selfing the best of the seedlings or by crossing the seedlings one with another. Scent so far is mainly confined to pale pink or white rhododendrons so more fragrant yellow or orange hybrids would be worth striving for. Mating some of the outstanding yellow elepidote hybrids and the oranges of the 'Fabia' group with the various scented members of the Fortunei series or with 'Loderi' should give some interesting results and, of course, if one could combine fragrance with a flower colour of brilliant scarlet such a hybrid would be a fantastic success. A more probable development in the lepidote section might result from crossing (*yunnanense* × *concatenans*) 'Alison Johnstone' with one of the scented members of the Maddenii series.

The crosses should be made a day or two before the flowers of the seed parent open but when the buds are nearly fully developed and have coloured fully and when no rain is expected for at least three hours. Using a pair of nail scissors carefully cut through the base of the corolla, just above the ovary, removing the cut-away portion of the bloom and gently pulling away the remaining tube. Next cut off the stamens to prevent self-pollination taking care not to brush any pollen against the stigma. Now only the stigma, style and ovary remain. In case of accidents it is as well to prepare several flowers in this way, removing from the truss all those flowers which one does not intend to pollinate.

If the stigma is sticky, pollination can be carried out at once, otherwise it is necessary to wait a day or two until the sticky secretion appears. Meanwhile there is no need to bag the blooms as, in the absense of petals, insects are unlikely to be attracted to the flowers.

As soon as the stigma is found to be sticky the stamens should be removed from the opening blooms of the pollen parent and brushed lightly over the sticky surface visibly to coat it with pollen. If the pollen is not readily yielded the anthers may be split or rubbed between the fingers to obtain it.

After the pollen has been applied the plant should be clearly and indelibly labelled, listing both parents of the hoped-for offspring and indicating the seed parent with a circle and a cross.

Often, of course, the flowering of the pollen parent does not coincide with that of the seed parent. Pollen, however, may be stored in a thermos flask at an even temperature as long as eight or nine weeks. In *Rhododendrons of the World* Mr. David G. Leach suggests placing the stamens from the nearly-open flowers into empty medicine capsules with a little calcium chloride bought from a chemist.

The capsules should be not more than half-full. Each set of capsules is then put into a bottle which has been previously one-fifth filled with coarse calcium chloride, loosely held in place with cotton wool. The bottle should be tightly corked and then the calcium chloride will dry the pollen and so preserve it. Dry pollen, taken before the flowers open, will even keep for a fortnight in an envelope in ordinary room conditions and it may be sent through the post. This means that intending hybridizers may often obtain from other gardens pollen of species or hybrids they do not themselves possess.

Should the pollen parent normally bloom later than the seed parent, the flowering can sometimes be persuaded to coincide if one lifts the pollen parent and brings it into a warm greenhouse, at the same time placing the seed parent in a temperature of thirty-four degrees Fahrenheit until just before it is needed to bloom. Generally, however, it is much easier to reverse the roles, using the earlier-flowering plant as pollen parent and storing the pollen in the way described until required.

The seed of most species and hybrids will be ripe and ready for harvesting at about the end of October. The species and crosses of the Lapponicum and Triflorum series are usually the first to ripen their seed but the seeds of late-flowering rhododendrons such as *auriculatum, discolor* and some of their hybrids

21. *R. sinonuttallii*, a scented, tender species for a warm wall or for the greenhouse except in the most favoured districts

22. *R.* 'Susan' is one of the best of the lavender-blue, so-called 'hardy hybrids'

23. The form of *R. tephropeplum* known as *deliense* has almost strawberry-coloured flowers and willow-shaped leaves, waxy-white beneath. It is a most attractive, small species

24. *R.* 'Broughtonii Aureum', a fine and extremely interesting old azaleodendron with a very sweet scent

may not be ready until late December. When the pods are dry and brown and show signs of opening it may be assumed that the seed is ripe. It should be harvested and kept in a dry cupboard until the end of January when the seed should be cleaned and sown in a propagating frame with a bottom heat of fifty-five to sixty degrees Fahrenheit as described in the last chapter.

So far, in Britain, the full theory of scientific plant-breeding has not been applied to rhododendrons. What is not generally realized is that in the first generation of hybrids from any given cross some of the desired characteristics, e.g. scent, hardiness, red or yellow flower colour, large flowers, compact habit, blue foliage, etc., may be recessive and will not appear until a second generation has been bred by selfing or, preferably, by crossing the two best seedlings of the first generation. It is sad to think that through failure to appreciate this truth many seedlings, in which the desired trait may have been inherent, have been consigned to the bonfire by disappointed breeders. The raising of a second generation has not so far, to my knowledge, been done with many of our most outstanding hybrids such as 'Hawk', 'Carita', 'Fabia', 'Naomi', 'Lady Bessborough' and the rest. If it were done some truly outstanding rhododendrons might be expected to result.

Unfortunately, however, some first-generation hybrids will neither self nor interbreed. When this is the case one should choose another parent known to contain the desired—but, so far missing—characteristics. Suppose, for instance, that one had mated 'Carita' with *discolor* in the hope of introducing scent and obtaining an even larger flower but that the resultant seedlings were self-sterile and would not interbreed one with the other. One might then try mating the 'Carita' × *discolor* seedling back to *discolor* in the hope of strengthening the scented strain and bringing out the scent. One might at the same time get larger flowers but the yellow flower colour might be weakened so that one might then be faced with the possibility of having to back-cross yet again, this time to 'Carita's' *campylocarpum* parent or out to the nearly related *wardii* in its deepest form to deepen the yellow colour.

More simply, however, one might decide to cross the 'Carita' × *discolor* seedling with another hybrid that carried in its genes both the yellow strain and also the large-flowered, scented trait of *discolor*. The hybrid (*campylocarpum* × *discolor*) 'Lady Bessborough' might well be the one that mated with 'Carita' × *discolor* might bring out the recessive scent—in double strength—because is not 'Carita' herself the offspring of the slightly fragrant 'Naomi' and *campylocarpum*?

One of the best of all hybrids, the outstanding 'Hawk' grex was produced by crossing 'Lady Bessborough' (*campylocarpum* × *discolor*) with the good yellow *wardii* to deepen the yellow colour. If, however, 'Lady Bessborough' had been crossed with one of its sister seedlings such as 'Roberte' or one of the other clonal forms, scent might have resulted from the double dose of *discolor* blood. Another good hybrid (*wardii* × *decorum*) 'Ightham Yellow' might also be expected to give a proportion of scented offspring with exceptionally good flower colour if crossed with (*campylocarpum* × *discolor*) 'Lady Bessborough'. This is a cross I should particularly like to make as 'Ightham Yellow' with its vigorous habit and fine foliage is a great favourite of mine.

It is a good practice to back-cross either to the parent with the most desired trait or to a similar species with that trait.

Of course, it takes several years at least to raise a rhododendron of flowering size and this may be one reason why rhododendron breeding programmes have not always been carried through to their logical genetic conclusions.

Present-day breeders, however, are lucky in that they do not necessarily have to start from scratch. Often the first crosses have already been made and one can go on from there, carefully choosing their mates so as to enhance their best and most desirable characteristics. The waiting time may also be shortened by green-grafting in August, using scions with floral buds in order to get a bloom—and therefore the required seed—the following spring.

A young plant of *ponticum* is selected, potted and placed in a shady place. In late June all but one of the terminal branches of its current growth should be removed. The remaining branch is shortened and split and the wedge-shaped base of the scion is held in place with grafting tape. The graft should then be wrapped round with moist sphagnum moss from which all surplus water has been squeezed, covered with a polythene bag which, in turn, is bound into place with waterproof insulating tape. In the spring the buds begin to open. Then all but two of the flower-buds should be removed. As soon as the remaining buds are fully covered and about to open, the corolla should be stripped, the stamens removed. Pollination should be carried out as soon as the stigma is sticky. Unless the cross is incompatible seed will then ripen in the normal way.

Certain lines in rhododendron breeding seem to have been carried as far as possible and the intending hybridizer needs to proceed in new directions. For instance, with the introduction of 'Bluebird', 'Blue Diamond' and now 'St. Tudy' and 'St. Breward', I do not think these 'blue' lepidote crosses can be carried much further. I think, too, that it would be difficult to improve on some of the Bodnant reds or on the later-blooming geranium-scarlet 'Tally Ho' and the hardier 'Vesuvius' of the same colour. Deep yellows, however, are wanted. There are some excellent but sometimes 'difficult' yellows with good flower colour and handsome foliage like 'Mariloo' and 'Joanita' with the blood of the Lacteum series in their make-up. I think, though, that *caucasicum* has both toughness and inherent depth of colour (often recessive but coming to the front in 'Cunningham's Sulphur') to give a good depth of colour to its offspring. The bright 'Canary', after all, is a *caucasicum* cross. True, *caucasicum* passes on the defect of its somewhat papery flowers but if it were mated to a good, waxy *wardii*—perhaps the deep-coloured Ludlow and Sherriff introduction with its splendid purple blotch —I am sure we would see something good, and I am sure too that Wisley will produce some fine dwarf yellows from their *chrysanthum* hybrids.

A study of the rhododendron stud book—*Rhododendron Handbook*, Part II, of the R.H.S.—will often suggest some useful lines on which to work. One which seems to me to have stopped short of its goal was that started at Exbury by the mating of the orange *dichroanthum* to the scented pink (*discolor* × *fortunei*) 'Avocet'. I think perhaps that Mr. de Rothschild hoped to get a scented, large-flowered orange from this cross, but the resultant 'Melrose' is pale pink. Two seedlings of this grex might be crossed together to yield the desired, scented, orange hybrid. I would like, however, to make the cross again, using the fine orange form of *dichroanthum*, sub-species *scyphocalyx*, at Bulkeley Mill and my own exceptionally deep-blush, very strongly scented 'Avocet'. If the desired characteristics did not then show in any of the seedlings, crossing the two best of these should do the trick. And, of course, with *dichroanthum* as parent, plus the extra-hardy 'Avocet', ironclad toughness would be assured.

Not all hybrids, however, are an improvement on their parents and I for one do not accept the criterion that a rounded flower-truss is necessarily an improvement on the lax and graceful trusses of some of the species. God made rhododendrons in varying shapes—most of them lovely—and although the argument may be true that loose trusses do not show to advantage on the bench they are undeniably beautiful in the garden and look exotic and 'out of this world' in appropriate containers indoors. The tight, round trusses of the large-leaved species are undeniably right but I should hate to see an 'improved' 'Fabia' with its fluidity lost—its grace encased in a rigid 'bun'.

Hardiness and a good habit, however, are general requisites. Although slightly tender rhododendrons may be grown and enjoyed in favourable garden climates I do not think any rhododendron with leggy, ungainly growth should be given an award however good its flowers. The committee might even say that they would like to see a further cross of the hybrid concerned suggesting a back-cross to the parent with the better habit of growth.

Foliage, too, is important and, in this, the new *yakushimanum* hybrids should excel. I should like, too, to see 'Joanita' and 'Mariloo' crossed with an easier-to-please yellow—'Ightham Yellow' comes at once to mind—with the hope that some, at least, of the offspring would retain the Lacteum series quality of leaf and flower. 'China', too, is a yellow with good leaves but it has very pale flowers and might be crossed with 'Canary' or even 'Cunnungham's Sulphur' itself to gain more depth of colour.

# CHAPTER 14

# Diseases and Pests

꘡꘡꘡꘡꘡꘡꘡꘡꘡꘡꘡꘡꘡

Rhododendrons and azaleas are not normally miffy or mimpish plants, and in Britain, so long as they are growing in a well-drained acid soil with sufficient moisture, and given shade and wind shelter according to their individual requirements, they are not subject to many ailments. The few diseases that do affect them are either fungoid in origin or else due to some fault in their growing conditions such as bad drainage or a magnesium and iron deficiency. Like most other plants that we grow in our gardens these days, however, both rhododendrons and azaleas are troubled by a number of pests which though annoying are seldom serious; the damage that they do causing unsightliness rather than real harm. These pests range from the few rabbits that are still with us, the bullfinches and slugs, to the rhododendron fly and leaf-hopper and will be dealt with later on in this chapter.

To simplify the diagnosis of rhododendron ills the symptoms will be clearly given.

## FUNCTIONAL DISORDERS

CHLOROSIS

*Symptom.* Yellowing of the leaves beginning with interveinal chlorosis and increasing until whole leaf surfaces have a sickly yellow look.

*Diagnosis.* Either too much lime is present causing the plant to absorb it to the exclusion of iron, magnesium and manganese, or the soil is acid but deficient in magnesium.

*Treatment.* Test the soil. If pH 6·5 or above apply *Sequestrene Plus* as directed on the container, following up the treatment by watering in several fortnightly applications of Epsom salts (magnesium sulphate) at the strength of an ounce (approximately two tablespoonsful) to two gallons of water. Also, in the evening of a dull day, spray the foliage with a solution of sulphate of manganese (one ounce to two and a half gallons of water). If the soil is acid, water in several fortnightly applications of Epsom salts at the above strength.

### Bad Soil Drainage

*Symptom.* Premature yellowing and dropping of leaves, often of the current year, in early autumn.

*Treatment.* Dig up the rhododendron with leaf-ball intact and replant on a layer of gravel or granite chippings in a compost containing a high proportion of moist peat, spruce needles, or bracken, and sand mixed with the natural soil. It is important to prepare a site much larger than is actually needed and also to mix the prepared compost well with the surrounding soil. In very heavy, wet soil, land drainage should be carried out before rhododendrons or azaleas are planted.

*Note.* Sometimes clogging of the mulch can cause suffocation with symptoms similar to the above. If this is suspected the mulch should be pulled back from the collar of the plant, leaving the ₒop of the root ball clear.

### Drought

*Symptom.* Tight leaf-curling and browning, followed by leaf dropping.

*Treatment.* Water heavily, apply a mulch of moist peat and give some shade from the hottest sun. Mulching with four to six inches of moist peat or rotted bracken while the soil is still wet in spring will help to prevent this trouble.

FOLIAGE SCORCH

*Symptom.* Burnt tips to the leaves.

*Diagnosis.* This may be caused by frost damage in winter. If it occurs in hot weather it may be due to drought. It also results after too-heavy a dosage of sequestered iron compound.

*Treatment.* If an overdose of iron is suspected, heavy watering may help. It goes without saying that no further iron should be given for several years. If, however, the scorching is due to sunshine it may be advisable to replant the rhododendron in the autumn in a shadier place.

BARK SPLIT

Some rhododendrons, particularly those with *arboreum* or *griffithianum* blood may suffer bark splitting as a result of spring frosts when the sap is rising. Only if the whole of the bark is lifted away from the stem by the split, causing virtual ring-barking, is it likely to kill the plant.

*Treatment.* Grafting wax may be applied if the split is bad.

FAILURE TO FLOWER

This may be due to immaturity but it can also be due to planting in too much shade. Sometimes moving the plant will help, or removing overhanging branches to give it more light may be tried. Sulphate of potash may be given as a stimulant. It should be remembered, though, that many of the best rhododendrons do not flower freely when young. Some of the tree rhododendrons may take fifteen years to flower and even hybrids such as 'Hawk', 'Carita' and 'Avocet' are shy and may be biennial or even triennial bloomers in their early years. Provided the plants are healthy and one is sure that they have enough light I think it is best not to interfere. Bracken mulching definitely helps the plants to produce flowers.

# FUNGUS DISEASES

## Azalea Gall

*Symptom.* Disfiguring and unsightly reddish swellings of the leaves of evergreen azaleas which make them look as if they were afflicted by elephantiasis.

*Treatment.* Pick off and burn all the affected leaves and spray the bushes with a copper fungicide at the directed strength in spring or autumn.

## Bud Blast

*Symptom.* The flower buds are at first discoloured in the autumn and later turn black. Tiny hair-like spores may be seen on the surface. In severe cases the growth buds also are affected.

*Treatment.* Rigidly pick off and burn all such buds and cut back all affected growth, taking care to burn the prunings. Fortnightly spraying from June to October with Bordeaux mixture at the recommended strength should be carried out in gardens where an attack has occurred.

It is thought that this disease is spread by the leaf-hopper, so an additional spray of D.D.T. should be given every three weeks from August to the end of October to deal with these pests. Bud Blast can be serious if it is not checked.

## Honey Fungus

This is the most dreaded of all diseases that attack rhododendrons although fortunately it does not occur very frequently. However, attacking and killing, as it sometimes does, really old and valued plants in many woodland gardens, all possible preventive measures should be taken.

*Symptom.* The leaves become yellow and droop. Often lichen attacks and the plants slowly die back. If one digs down to the roots long black 'bootlaces' will be seen adhering to them. White fans of the fungus may also be found below ground level.

*Treatment.* For a long time it has been thought hopeless to attempt to treat this disease and that the best cure was simply to dig up and burn the affected plant, destroying all traces of the fungus, too. In America, however, it has been found that the fungus can be kept in check, if not eradicated, by drenching the root area with phenyl-mercuric monoethanol-ammonium-acetate which is sold under different trade names as a spray against apple scab (see *Rhododendrons of the World* by David G. Leach).

*Prevention.* Old tree stumps and dead branches lying on the ground seem to attract this disease, so all old stumps should be grubbed up with a tree-jack and the ground should be kept clean of fallen branches, prunings, etc. Mr. Leach says that only rhododendrons in failing health are attacked but this does not seem to be entirely the case over here where I have seen several thriving plants suddenly become sickly, fail and die from this cause.

## PESTS

### BIRD DAMAGE TO BUDS

This may often be prevented by spraying the shrubs with a few spots of Renardine and soft water. Azaleas and the deciduous or semi-deciduous rhododendrons of the Dauricum and Triflorum series seem to be the most usual victims.

### CAPSID BUG

These are often prevalent where rhododendrons are grown near fruit trees—even the ornamental crab-apples sometimes harbour the pests.

*Symptom.* The leaves are gradually eaten away in large, curved 'bites'.

*Treatment.* Spray with D.D.T. in April and May.

### RHODODENDRON FLY (LACEWING)

This pest attacks rhododendrons growing in full sun and is particularly fond of the old *catawbiense* 'hardy hybrids'.

*Symptom.* Yellow spots occur on the leaves, followed by minute punctures all over the surface. This trouble is serious, destroying the chlorophyll and affecting the function of the leaves and may lead to an affected plant dying during a spell of drought. Dark brown bugs which later develop into the flies will be seen under the surface of the leaves.

*Treatment. Lindex* (or a solution of fifty per cent malathion, two teaspoonsful to a gallon of water, with a spreader-sticker substance added) should be sprayed on the underside of the leaves as soon as the bugs hatch during the latter half of May.

### Rhododendron Leaf-Hopper

*Symptom.* Small punctures in the leaves. The leaf-hopper (an insect like a small grasshopper) may be seen and heard about the bushes. It is a danger because it is thought to spread the Bud Blast fungus and so should be firmly dealt with.

*Treatment.* Spray with D.D.T. every three weeks from August to the end of October.

### Vine Weevil

*Symptom.* The edges of the leaves appear to be 'cut' in a circular pattern—almost as if a leather-punch had been used. The insect is small and dark, feeds at night and hides in the mulch during the day.

*Treatment.* Mr. David G. Leach recommends a spraying with forty-five per cent chlordane emulsion (one and a half teaspoonsful to one gallon of water) with an additional spreader sticker. The spraying should be carried out at the end of June and the whole ground area around the affected plants should also be sprayed.

Alternatively, one may set traps by placing pieces of corrugated paper on the soil around the shrubs. The weevils will hide in the folds during the day and may be picked up and killed. Lead arsenate sprays have sometimes been recommended but the lead arsenate has been found to have a cumulatively harmful effect on the rhododendrons and so should not be used.

### Rabbits

Fir-cones soaked with Renardine and scattered among the plants will successfully deter rabbits.

## SLUGS AND SNAILS

When young rhododendrons are grown in mixed borders and among herbaceous plants I have known slugs and snails to crawl up the stems and eat the young leaves.

*Remedy.* *Slugit* pellets scattered at weekly intervals around the base of the plants will rid the area of slugs. It is necessary to repeat the baiting, as fresh slug eggs are continually hatching out.

A new insecticide, *Rhodon Insecticide Mixture*, has been developed by the Ling Point Rhododendron Research Laboratories, Cobbett's Hill, Weybridge, Surrey to control all rhododendron insect pests and can be coupled at one spraying with *Rhodon Bud Blast Fungicide* which has proved reliable in controlling this troublesome disorder.

# PART II

>>>>><<<<<

## NOTE

In the descriptions of rhododendrons and azaleas that follow it is important to realize that the stars of merit or R.H.S. awards apply only to certain superior forms of the species or hybrid under consideration. Such forms known as 'clones' are vegetatively propagated. If one wants to grow the form of *R. lutescens*, for instance, to which the First Class Certificate of the R.H.S. was awarded, one must be sure to state when ordering that the F.C.C. clone *only* is required.

Many clones of certain hybrids are in existence and some of them vary a great deal in merit. Most of the hybrid clones have now been given clonal names, e.g.: 'Hawk Crest', 'Hawk Jervis Bay', etc. The original cross holds the grex, or umbrella name, 'Hawk', but seedlings of this cross are very variable and so it is unwise to purchase a hybrid named merely 'Hawk'; 'Hawk Crest' or 'Hawk Jervis Bay' should be insisted on. Where no clonal name exists as with 'Humming Bird' it is important to state that 'Humming Bird' F.C.C., or, to give another example, 'Winsome' A.M., is wanted.

# Key to Symbols Used in the Lists

A   Hardy anywhere in the British Isles.

B   Needing wind shelter wherever grown and some shade in the south.

C   Hardy except in frost bottoms, very exposed areas or places where spring frosts are severe and likely persistently to cut the young growth.

D   Hardy only in the milder of the seaboard districts. Elsewhere may be grown against west walls.

E   Mildest districts only—cold-house elsewhere.

t   Tree-like habit of growth.

s   Indicates shrub.

*   Flower of foliage quality.

\*   Reasonable easiness of cultivation.

# CHAPTER 15

# Rhododendron Species for the Garden

ᗡᗡᗡᗡᗡᗡᗡᗡᗡᗡᗡᗡᗡᗡᗡᗡᗡᗡᗡᗡᗤᗤᗤᗤᗤᗤᗤᗤᗤᗤᗤᗤᗤᗤᗤᗤ

Some gardeners and nurserymen in the past have tended not to keep a sense of proportion about the rhododendron species. Either they have grown every and any one of them as they were sent in by the plant collectors and failed to discard the more unattractive, or they have clung to the 'ironclad' hybrids, regarding the species and newer hybrids alike with suspicion as 'difficult to grow'. In fact there are species as easy and tough as any of the older hybrids and often they possess a great deal of charm and grace. To get the best garden value from rhododendrons, I think it is necessary to grow both species and hybrids, carefully discriminating to select only the best.

Because the species have been grouped together by the botanists into affinities with similar characteristics, habitats and needs, it is more satisfactory to consider them in their botanical series. Many of the series differ widely from each other in size and in climatic needs and cultivation requirements so it is necessary to classify them into groups according to their garden needs and to rate them as to hardiness as indicated in the key on page 158.

I shall not attempt to include every species or even every series but only those of outstanding beauty, or easy cultivation and garden worth.

*Note.* The given times of flowering and stated sizes are apt to vary according to district, climatic conditions, and site.

**Exceptionally large-leaved rhododendrons needing maximum shade shelter and good moisture. (Coastal California only in U.S.A.);**

FALCONERI SERIES

******\**R. falconeri* C. s or t (25 ft. × 20 ft.) (April and May flowering).
*****\**R. fictolacteum* B. t (20 ft. × 20 ft.) April–May.
******\**R. hodgsonii* B. t or lge s (15 ft. × 15 ft.) April.
******\**R. rex* B. t (30 ft. × 20 ft.) April.

GRANDE SERIES

*******\**R. macabeanum* B. t (20 ft. × 25 ft.) March–April.
******\**R. sinograne* B but D for optimum growth (30 ft. × 18 ft.) April–May.

**Large-leaved rhododendrons for woodland conditions or equivalent positions in sheltered gardens, i.e. sheltered garden glades or the north or west side of a high hedge or shrub belt. (Hardy to Boston in the United States.);**

ARBOREUM SERIES

*******\**R. insigne* B. s (8 ft. × 10 ft.) June–July.

CAMPANULATUM SERIES

–*******\**R. campanulatum* A. s (12–25 ft. × 12–18 ft.) May.

FORTUNEI SERIES

*******\**R. calophytum* B. s (16 ft. × 16 ft.) April.
*******\**R. decorum* B. t (15 ft. × 10 ft.) late May.
******\**R. discolor* B. t (15 ft. × 10 ft.) late June.
*******\**R. fortunei* A. t (20 ft. × 15 ft.) May–June.
******\**R. fargesii* B. s (12 ft. × 10 ft.) March–early April.
*******\**R. oreodoxa* B. s (12 ft. × 10 ft.) late March.
*******\**R. orbiculare* B. s (3 ft. × 5 ft.) May.

LACTEUM SERIES

    \*\*\*\*Difficult. *R. lacteum* B. s (20 ft. × 18 ft.) early.
    \*\*\*\*\*\*\**R. wightii* B. (15 ft. × 15 ft.)


**Medium-sized species needing shelter in Great Britain. (Coastal California only in U.S.A.);**

AURICULATUM SERIES

    \*\*\*\*\*\*\**R. auriculatum* B. t (20 ft. × 25 ft.) August.
    \*\*\*\*\*\*\**R. griersonianum* C. s (5 ft. × 5 ft.) July.

BARBATUM SERIES

    \*\*\*\*\*\*\**R. barbatum* C. t (12 ft. × 6 ft.) March–April.
    \*\*\*\*\*\*\**R. smithii* B. t (10 ft. × 6 ft.) April.
    \*\*\*\*\*\*\*\**R. strigillosum* B. s (8 ft. × 8 ft.) March.
    \*\*\*\*\*\*\**R. pseudochrysanthum* B. s (2 ft. × 3 ft.) April–May.

BOOTHII SERIES

    \*\*\*\*\*\**R. tephropeplum* B. s (3 ft. × 4 ft.) May.

CINNABARINUM SERIES

    \*\*\*\*\*\*\**R. cinnabarinum* B. s (10 ft. × 5 ft.) May.
    \*\*\*\*\*\*\**R. concatenans* C. s (6 ft. × 4 ft.) May.

IRRORATUM SERIES

    \*\*\*\*\*\*\**R. aberconwayi* A. s (5 ft. × 4 ft.) May.
    \*\*\*\*\*\*\*\**R. venator* B. s (6 ft. × 6 ft.) June.

NERIIFLORUM SERIES

    *R. operantum* B. s (1½ ft. × 4 ft.) April–May.
    \*\*\*\*\**R. didymum* C. s (2–3 ft. × 3 ft.) June–July.
    \*\*\*\*\*\**R. dichroanthum* B. s (4 ft. × 5 ft.) July.
    \*\*\*\*\*\*\**R. haematodes* B. s (3 ft. × 4 ft.—slow) April–May.
    \*\*\*\*\*\*\**R. forrestii* var. *repens* B. s (prostrate) May.
    \*\*\*\*\*\*\**R. neriiflorum* C. s (5 ft. × 5 ft.) April–May.

THOMSONII SERIES

*******R. *callimorphum* B. s (7 ft. × 5 ft.) April–May.
********R. *caloxanthum* B. s (4–5 ft. × 4 ft.) May.
******R. *campylocarpum* B. s (6–10 ft. × 5 ft.) May.
*******R. *souliei* B. s (8 ft. × 7 ft.) May.
********R. *wardii* A–B. s (4–12 ft. × 4–8 ft.) May–June.
*******R. *stewartianum* B. s (8 ft. × 4 ft.) February–March.
*********R. *thomsonii* A–B. t (14 ft. × 6 ft.) April–May.
*******R. *williamsianum* C. s (2½ ft. × 4 ft.) April–May.

TALIENSE SERIES (for foliage beauty)

********R. *bureavii* B. s (6 ft. × 6 ft.) April.
********R. *wasonii* B. s (5 ft. × 5 ft.) April–May.

**For more open positions. Rhododendrons which will stand sun but need some care. (Hardy in Delaware and West Virginia in U.S.A.);**

TRIFLORUM SERIES

*******R. *augustinii* B. s (10 ft. × 6 ft.) May.
********R. *oreotrephes* A. s (6 ft. × 4 ft.) May.
*******R. *lutescens* B–C. s (6 ft. × 5 ft.) February–March.
*******R. *davidsonianum* B–C. s (6 ft. × 4 ft.) April.
********R. *yunnanense* A. s (8 ft. × 5 ft.) May.

DAURICUM SERIES (winter flowering)

********R. *mucronulatum* A. s (5 ft. × 4 ft.) January.

**Tough species to form hedges or wind-breaks. (Hardy to Boston in U.S.A.);**

HELIOLEPIS SERIES

******R. *rubiginosum* A. s (8 ft. × 8 ft.) March–April.

PONTICUM SERIES

*****R. *smirnowii* A. s (8 ft. × 10 ft.) May–June.
*******R. *yakushimanum* B. s (3 ft. × 5 ft.) May.

**Dwarf species for small gardens, rock-gardens and the front of shrub beds and borders. (California coast only in U.S.A.);**

ANTHOPOGON SERIES

*****R. anthopogon* A. (1–1½ ft. × 3 ft.) April.
*****R. sargentianum* A. (2 ft. × 4 ft.) May.

BOOTHII SERIES

*******R. leucaspis* B. (1 ft. × 3 ft.) February.

CAMPYLOGYNUM SERIES

*****R. campylogynum* A. (1 ft. × 1½ ft.) May.

GLAUCOPHYLUM SERIES

********R. charitopes* B. (3–5 ft. × 3 ft.) April.

LAPPONICUM SERIES

*******R. chryseum* A. (2 ft. × 2 ft.) April.
*******R. hippophaeoides* A. (2 ft. × 2 ft.) April.
**–*******R. impeditum* A. (1 ft. × 1½ ft.) April–May.
*******R. intricatum* A. (1 ft. × 1 ft.) March–April.
*******R. lysolepis* A. (2 ft. × 3 ft.) April.
*******R. microleucum* A. (1½ ft. × 2 ft.) April.
*******R. ravum* A. (4 ft. × 4 ft.) May.
********R. scintillans* A. (2 ft. × 2 ft.) April.

MOUPINENSE SERIES

*******R. moupinense* B. (2 ft. × 2 ft.) February–March.

SALUENENSE SERIES

*******R. calostrotum* A. (2½ ft. × 2½ ft.) May.
*******R. keleticum* B. (½ ft. × 1 ft.) June.
*–*******R. nitens* B. (2 ft. × 2 ft.) July.
*****R. radicans* B. (creeping) May–June.

UNIFLORUM SERIES

******R. imperator* B. (prostrate) April–May.

*******R. pumilum* A. (½ ft. × 1 ft.) May.
*******R. uniflorum* A. (1 ft. × 1½ ft.) May.

VIRGATUM SERIES

**–*********R. racemosum* A. (2–6 ft. × 3 ft.) April–May.
*******R. virgatum* C. (4 ft. × 3 ft.) April.

MISCELLANEOUS DWARFS

*******R. spiciferum* C. (3 ft. × 3 ft.) April.
********R. lepidostylum* B. (1½ ft. × 4 ft.) May–June.
*******R. hanceanum* 'Nanum' B. April.


**Tender species some of which survive against north or west walls in North Wales and on south coast. They will grow in open woodland in Cornwall and Western Isles and California and need cold green-houses elsewhere;**

BOOTHII SERIES

****Tender. *R. sulfureum* D. (3 ft. × 3 ft.) March.

EDGWORTHII SERIES

****Tender. *R. bullatum* D. (4 ft. × 4 ft.) April–May.

IRRORATUM SERIES

****Tender. *R. eriogynum* E. (8 ft. × 8 ft.) July.
****Tender. *R. kyawi* E. (8 ft. × 8 ft.) August.

MADDENII SERIES

***Tender. *R. burmanicum* E. (2 ft. × 2 ft.) April.
***Tender. *R. johnstoneanum* D. (3 ft. × 4 ft.) May.
****Less tender. *R. valentinianum* C. (1½ ft. × 2 ft.) April.
***Less tender. *R. ciliatum* C. (4 ft. × 5 ft.) April.
***Tender. *R. crassum* D. (10 ft. × 8 ft.) June–July.
***Tender. *R. maddenii* E. (6 ft. × 6 ft.) June.
***Tender. *R. polyandrum* E. (3 ft. × 3 ft.) June.
****Tender. *R. dalhousiae* E. (5 ft. × 3 ft.) June.
also *R. megacalyx, nuttallii, rhabdotum, taggianum* and *lindleyi.*

Falconeri Series (slow to flower but leaf effect fine)

*******R. falconeri* C. s or t (25 ft. × 20–25 ft.) April–May.
(After Hugh Falconer, Superintendent of a famous
Indian botanic garden.)

A native of the Himalayas where it is found at 10,000 feet,
*R. falconeri* is one of the hardiest of the big-leaved tree rhododendrons. It can be grown in most areas under woodland conditions but care should be taken to see that it is not placed in a
frost pocket. *R. falconeri* sometimes makes a large spreading
shrub but it more commonly assumes a handsome tree-like form
with a rounded umbrella-like top, a flaking trunk and warm
cinnamon-coloured branches. Its leaves are massively textured,
leathery and up to a foot long, with a rich-green, rather-rough
upper surface, deeply inlaid with yellowish veins and a wonderful
foxy-red fur beneath. The flower truss, too, is heavy and full of
substance—in shape a flat-topped bun made up of twenty or
more frilly-edged, creamy-yellow bells, magnificently blotched
with purple at the base. Then, when the flowers are over, the
young growth is lovely—as indeed it is in all the members of this
series—with upright cockades of almost-white kid, while the
young wood is swathed in velvet like a stag's antlers.

In planting this magnificent species it is worth every care to
choose a site where it will be happy. Above all, *R. falconeri* needs
adequate moisture to support its bold leaves and vigorous growth
Magnificent in Cornwall and the Western Isles of Scotland where
it reaches its full height and spread, in drier areas it may remain
only a sparsely branched yet shapely shrub or small tree of
fifteen to twenty feet and its leaves will be correspondingly
smaller. Like many other of the greatest garden treasures,
*R. falconeri* calls for patience on the part of the gardener. It may
not flower until it is fifteen or more years old from seed. Indeed,
an eighteen-inch specimen planted out on one of the woodland
slopes in the late Mr. A. T. Johnson's garden at Bulkeley Mill in
the Conway Valley did not flower for more than twenty years.
Even before it blooms, *R. falconeri* and the other large-leaved
members of the genus are worth their garden space for their

handsome foliage effect. They look best when grouped with lysichitums, bamboos, rheums and other waterside plants with exotic leaves. Among them drifts of moisture-loving candelabra primulas, *Iris sibirica*, *I. ochroleuca* and rodgersias will add colour to heighten the effect.

Rhododendron 'Fortune', an Exbury hybrid between this species and the even more tender *sinogrande*, is tougher than either and a magnificent rhododendron with deep-yellow, dark-blotched flowers borne in the *falconeri* type of truss.

**–*******R. hodgsonii* B. t or lge s (15 ft. × 15 ft.) April.

> (After B. Hodgson—one-time East India Company's resident in Nepal.)

This species is easier than *falconeri* to grow well, and like *falconeri*, it more often assumes the form of a tree than a shrub. Hardy as to cold, it needs only a moist-but-not-waterlogged acid soil and some shelter to protect its foliage from the wind.

Certainly the leaves of *hodgsonii* are worth protecting. They are sometimes as much as eighteen inches long—smooth dark-green and silvery on top, the underside too is pale with fawn-grey indumentum, that shows to fine effect when the leaves catch the breeze. The heavy, well-filled flower trusses are rose-lilac, or even purple-rose in colour with a deeper blotch at their base. The trunks of this species are beautiful, too, with a fawny-bronze papery, peeling bark.

******R. rex* B. t (30 ft. × 20 ft.) April–May.

> (Kingly.)

Some confusion has existed between this species and the nearly related *ficto-lacteum* and some forms previously known as *ficto-lacteum* are now recognized as *rex*. Both have a tighter, more rounded, flower truss than that of *falconeri*.

Good though some forms of *ficto-lacteum* may be—with pale-pink, darkly blotched flowers borne in tight, round trusses and handsome leaves richly felted beneath with rust, *R. rex* is altogether a finer thing. Two forms of *rex*, both grown from seeds of K.W.4509 (formerly known as *fictolacteum*) have been honoured by the R.H.S., the white-flowered form receiving the F.C.C. and the pink one the A.M. Another A.M. clone was grown from Rock 03800 and in varying gardens around Britain many other fine forms exist. *R. rex* has more oval leaves than *fictolacteum*—dark, shiny green and up to a foot in length with a pale buff indumentum that is no less beautiful than the russet felt of the best forms of *fictolacteum*. Its young growth is golden-bronze and its tight, pom-pom flower trusses are firm and lovely, varying from white through blush to a beautiful, warm rose-pink with a rich dark-purple throat. There is a move afoot to merge the two species.

Both species are much hardier, more wind-resistant and easier to grow than *falconeri* and even than *hodgsonii*. For colder, more difficult gardens they are the large-leaved species to choose.

GRANDE SERIES (some members are slow to flower but meanwhile their leaf-effect is fine)

\*\*\*\*\*\**R. macabeanum* B. t (20 ft. × 25 ft.) March–April.

(After Mr. M'Cabe, Deputy Commissioner, Nagu Hills.)

This is the finest yellow among the large-leaved rhododendrons with pale to deep-coloured flowers in globular ten-inch trusses. Its leaves, too, are fine and, though not quite as large as those of the elephant-eared *sinogrande*, they are of a similar dark, shiny green and very thick and leathery in texture with a woolly, silvery indumentum beneath.

As with all the large-leaves species, it is important to leave plenty of space around *macabeanum* at planting time. Perhaps more than any, this species is a spreader, and fully developed specimens have not yet been seen in the British Isles.

Naturally, growing more rapidly in the moister west, *macabeanum*, none the less, does well also in the drier parts of the country. It begins to flower when about seven or eight years old and is very free with its blooms. So freely does it flower that rigorous dead-heading and regular feeding is necessary to conserve and build up its strength. A mature plant with its hundreds of yellow globes glowing through the shelter of light woodland is a wonderful sight. Particularly fine forms exist in Sir Edward Bolitho's garden at Trengwainton in Cornwall (this is the F.C.C. form) and also at Trewithen. Its silvery cockades of young growth are particularly attractive and look for all the world, as Mrs. R. M. Harrison so perceptively said, in her lecture to the R.H.S. in March 1962, 'like little candles on a Christmas tree'. The effect of this silver young growth and scarlet bud-scales on the stems is truly lovely.

*******R. sinogrande* B. (but D for optimum growth) t (30 ft. × 18 ft.) April–May.

(Chinese *grande*.)

*R. sinogrande* is probably the best known of the large-leaved rhododendrons on account of its magnificent foliage. The strikingly shiny, dark green, heavy leaves with their shimmering silvery indumentum may measure as much as three feet long on a young plant in moist gardens in the west; larger and more tropical in effect than those of any other evergreen one sees in British gardens. When the plants reach flowering age, however, the leaves become smaller. It is as if the strength that went into the leaves is now taken up by the effort of flowering. *R. sinogrande* does not flower until it reaches six feet or more in height. This does not take long in the west, as its growth may average a foot a year after it has once got away. In drier and colder parts of Britain it makes very little growth and so may take twenty years or more to flower. The truss is massive, flat-topped and inclined to be looser than in the other large-leaved species but wonderfully effective, composed of many large, heavy textured creamy-white to deep yellow bells with a crimson basalplotch.

Unlike most rhododendrons it does not move easily. Rooting deep into the soil it keenly resents disturbance. With its massive and demanding leaves it is not an easy plant and needs plenty of moisture and nourishment to do well. Some forms make their young growth as late as July and August and so in cold districts are apt to catch the early frosts. The forms from the last collection of Kingdon Ward make their young growth in April and so are much hardier.

*R. giganteum* of the Grande series grown well only in such places as Brodick Castle on the Isle of Arran, and certain other parts of the west coast of Scotland and Northern Ireland. It is a plant for the very mildest gardens and its deep rose-pink flowers are lovely.

**Moderately large-leaved species needing shelter**

ARBOREUM SERIES (Tree-like. The members take a long time to flower)

A hundred-year-old, blood-red *arboreum* is a splendid thing to inherit with a garden. The rich warmth of its reddish trunk and fine green, woolly-felted leaves in winter give pleasure in a way that is only surpassed by the beauty of its upstanding ruby flower-trusses in spring. All the same this species takes so long to flower —up to twenty years—and is so tender that except for climatically favoured gardens its place may be taken by some of its hybrids as will be suggested in the next chapter. Even the hardier, white-flowered, fine-foliaged sub-species *cinnamomeum* may be replaced by the hybrid 'Sir Charles Lemon' with its orange-felted, dark-green leaves, and large creamy flowers which will give one a speedier reward.

*******R. insigne* B. s (8 ft. × 10 ft.) June–July.
(Remarkable.)

Like most of the other members of this series, *R. insigne* takes many years to flower but is very hardy and so perhaps the most worth while of the series for those owners of large gardens who are prepared to wait for it to bloom. Slow-growing but spreading in habit, eventually it takes a great deal of space. With long, narrow, shiny leaves, four inches long by about an inch and a half wide, and silvery beneath with a coppery sheen, in foliage it is interesting to say the least. The flowers too are good, and are carried in loose trusses of clear-pink, spotted with crimson inside, while one particularly good form has flowers of blush-pink, striped and flushed with rose.

CAMPANULATUM SERIES (May take a number of years to flower)

**-*******R. campanulatum* A. s (12–25 ft. × 12–25 ft.) May.
(Bell-shaped.)

This is a very variable species with regard to flower colour, and the 'Knap Hill' form is the one to choose with dark, handsome foliage felted with fawn indumentum beneath and with large, rich lilac-blue flowers that give a very good blue effect in shade or fading light. The form *aeruginosum* with thick blue-green leaves is worth growing as a foliage plant in large gardens and makes an effective contrast with the *arboreum* hybrid 'Sir Charles Lemon'.

For favoured gardens *R. fulgens* makes a compact mounded bush of shining dark green. Its flowers, too, seem to shine and are in a tight truss of deep rich crimson. Hardy enough in itself, it flowers early in February and March and so is a bad risk for gardens where early frosts are prevalent. *R. lanatum*, too, is beautiful but succeeds only in moist west-coast districts. With woolly white leaves and cream or yellow flowers, heavily spotted inside with red, it is a lovely plant.

### Tougher, moderately large-leaved species

FORTUNEI SERIES (Flowering in six years or so from seed)

*******R. calophytum* B. s (16 ft. × 16 ft.) April.
  (Beautiful plant.)

Well deserving its specific name, *R. calophytum* is indeed a most beautiful plant and although its foliage may lack the grandeur of the more massive leaves of the members of the Falconeri and Grande series it is extremely graceful and pleasing with fine rosettes of very long, narrow pendant leaves. These leaves are a smooth, dark green, and their rosettes make elegant collars for the beautifully set, large, loose trusses of widely bell-shaped flowers that vary in colour from white through blush to a warm pale rose, always with a magnificent dark crimson blotch.

Like most other members of the Fortunei series, *R. calophytum* has the incomparable asset of scent. It is completely hardy but flowers in April and so, in some gardens, its blossom may catch the frost. For this reason and also for the protection of its beautiful leaf-rosettes, it should be given a sheltered position in light woodland conditions with, if possible, an overhead branch canopy of a deciduous tree and with a hedge, wall, clump of holly or other dense cover to protect it from the worst winds. Where these requirements are met it is long-lived and an easy and satisfying plant to grow well.

*******R. decorum* B. t (15 ft. × 10 ft.) late May. (Ornamental.)

This is another large-growing, delightfully fragrant species with a strong, sweet scent and grass-green, lance-shaped leaves. Its wide-open flowers are large and very beautiful. They are carried in loose trusses of eight to ten. In the forms most commonly seen, the flowers are icy-white with a greeny-yellow throat but in some the petals may have a pink flush and one or two clear pink forms also exist. Quite unique is the form in the Glendoick Gardens of Messrs. Cox, in Perthshire, with flowers that approach lemon-yellow in colour. This form is known as 'Cox's Uranium Green'.

Often the flowers are borne amid the unfolding young leaves and the effect is delightful, particularly when the blooms are expanded to their full, wide-open extent sometimes with a characteristic and quite charming crinkle of the petals.

Ranging in the wild from Szechuan to Upper Burma, its hardiness varies according to the district from which the parent plant was collected. The forms introduced by Kingdon Ward are generally recognized to be the hardiest and can even be used to form a wind-break or hedge. To use them so, of course, involves the spoiling of many of the flowers so this practice is limited to older gardens where quantities of the species have been originally raised from seed.

*R. diaprepes* (D when young but C when mature) late July. (Distinguished.)

Equally good is the white-flowered *diaprepes* but unfortunately it is not so hardy. Making its young growth too late to ripen in cold gardens and subject to bark-splitting, it is none the less beautiful when mature. Good in leaf and flower, and fragrant, it is worth growing in gardens mild enough for it really to succeed. The Tower Court form 'Gargantua' has more chromosomes than usual and consequently is an extra vigorous form with very large flowers and leaves.

\*\*\*\*\*\**R. discolor* B. t late June.

(Different colours.)

The flowers of this species, though beautiful, are more papery in texture than those of the other members of the series and unfortunately they soon brown. It, too, is subject to bark-splitting. In sheltered gardens it is a beautiful plant but in colder, more exposed sites I would grow its scented blush-pink hybrid with *fortunei*, 'Avocet', which in our garden began to flower when it was barely three feet in height and, although it curls its leaves and looks rather miserable in very cold weather, is none the less extremely hardy in every way.

\*\*\*\*\*\*\**R. fortunei* A. t (20 ft. × 15 ft.) May–June.

(After the plant collector Robert Fortune.)

The name species of the series, *R. fortunei*, is a most useful plant. Very hardy and accommodating, it forms a small tree or a stout shrub with smooth green leaves often set off by distinctive purple petioles. The leaves are smooth and glabrous beneath.

An old but beautiful form, 'Mrs. Charles Butler' (sometimes listed as 'Sir Charles Butler') is still obtainable and, with its loose clusters of soft, rose-pink, delightfully scented flowers, is one of the best forms to choose, although there are also some delightful lilac-pinks to be found. The form 'Mrs. Charles Butler' is the parent of some of the finest hybrids and through 'Soulbut' (*souliei* × 'Mrs. Charles Butler') is responsible for some of the beauty of the classic late-flowering (*griersoniananum* × 'Soulbut') 'Vanessa'.

\*\*\*\*\*\**R. fargesii* B. s (12 ft. × 10 ft.) early April.

(After Père Paul Farges, the French missionary.)

One of the most beautiful of early rhododendrons, this is a great favourite of mine for its scented soft pink, frilly, rather open bells. In the late Mr. A. T. Johnson's garden, *R. fargesii* with its neighbour *R. oreodoxa* (see below) gives a full month of delightful flowers. Both species need wind-shelter to protect the flowers and should be dead-headed to conserve their strength. The blooms and buds are resistant to a few degrees of frost and both species flower extremely freely. For this reason they should be given an occasional feed of dried blood or a bi-yearly mulch of cow-manure. They begin to flower at the comparatively early age of about seven years from seed.

*******R. *oreodoxa* B. s (12 ft. × 10 ft.) March.
     (Glory of the mountains.)

Usually breaking into its scented lilac-pink bloom before *fargesii*, this species should be planted as its companion in every garden where there is room and which escapes severe early frosts. It is an odd fact that those gardens which are hit by May frosts usually escape in March. In our garden near the North Wales coast we missed both but in the Conway Valley, although the various forms of 'Loderi' are usually hit in May, these earlier-flowering species are a success in five years out of six. Where they succeed R. 'Geraldii' which flowers even earlier should be planted as well. It makes a large tree-like shrub of up to sixteen feet with a width of eight or ten feet and has lovely deep-lilac flowers with a handsome brown blotch. Its only drawback is that it takes up to ten years to flower.

*******R. *orbiculare* B. s (3 ft. × 5 ft.) May.
     (Circular leaves.)

This species is much smaller growing and although not noticeably scented is one of the most attractive rhododendrons in cultivation. Its leaves are round, fresh green and need wind-shelter. The whole bush is circular and becomes covered at flowering time with tubby, rose-pink, frilled bells. Spreading widely, as it gets older the bush sprays outward with the result that the sap-flow is restricted to the ends of these branches and die-back results. This may be prevented if the more sprawling outer branches are layered so that they form their own roots and so get a sap supply of their own. If this is done at the age of ten or twelve the bushes should live healthily for a great many more years. There is no need to sever the layers from the parent plant.

Some growers have accused R. *orbiculare* of being a blue-pink and a difficult colour to place in the garden. In the best Bodnant form, however, it is a deep rose. It associates well with the violet-blue hybrid 'Blue Diamond' or with R. *augustinii* itself.

This species usually takes about six years to flower from seed.

The wonderful, large-flowered, scented *R. griffithianum* is too tender to grow without protection in any but the very mildest gardens in Cornwall, Ireland and the Western Isles.

LACTEUM SERIES (Coast of California only in U.S.A.)

****Difficult. *R. lacteum* B. April.

*Rhododendron lacteum* with its dark-green, six-inch leaves and daffodil-yellow flowers is one of the most beautiful rhododendrons. It is also one of the most difficult to grow satisfactorily. Demanding a very acid soil—pH 4·5—a moist climate and a spongy, well-drained-yet-damp, peaty rooting medium it may be expected to succeed only in the west and even there is not as long-lived as other large-leaved members of the genus. Unfortunately, too, it takes a very long time to flower. These factors make perhaps the only excuse for grafting it on to the less demanding *ponticum* stock. Root-grafts only should be made as described in the chapter on propagation.

*******R. wightii* of the same series is an almost equally beautiful and much easier plant which may be grown in its place. It takes ten years to flower but is a reasonably good doer in most gardens although it seems to have the same tendency as *R. lacteum* to be somewhat short-lived. It is a fine plant with felted leathery leaves and flower trusses of a really good yellow.

## Rhododendron species needing some shelter

AURICULATUM SERIES

*******R. auriculatum* B. t (20 ft. × 25 ft.) August.

(Ear-shaped, referring to the lobes on the leaves.)

Easy, but needing wind shelter, moisture, and shade because it flowers so late, *R. auriculatum* is a beautiful and rewarding plant with elegant, lance-shaped, lobed leaves of soft green, a strong, outward-branching habit and large funnel-shaped white flowers with a green eye and very sweet scent. Its young growth does not appear until after the flowers and in the north this is a serious handicap as it never ripens its wood enough to set flower buds. It is therefore a plant for the southern half of England and for the west. Its name refers to the lobes at the base of the leaves.

*******R. griersonianum C. s (5 ft. × 5 ft.) July.

> (After R. C. Grierson of the Chinese Customs—a friend
> of the plant collector Forrest.)

R. griersonianum has the loveliest flower colour of any rhododendron—a soft, true, geranium red. Important as the parent of such fine hybrids as 'Fabia', 'Elizabeth', 'Azor', 'Romany Chai', 'Matador' and 'Tally Ho', it is none the less a wonderful plant in its own right with its loose truss of gloriously coloured flowers and long, narrow leaves of dark, matt-green with a buff indumentum below. Unfortunately it seems tender in the home counties although it is reported as successful in the east of Scotland. Perhaps, like some of the primulas and gentians, it prefers the Scottish air. In the west it is hardy enough but it is definitely shy-flowering in Wales. For my own part I prefer its hybrid 'Tally Ho' with the same lovely flower colour, more vigorous, yet low and mounded, growth and a great deal more hardiness than its rating in the current R.H.S. *Rhododendron Handbook* would lead one to suppose.

BARBATUM SERIES (Seven or eight years to flower)

*******R. barbatum C. t (12 ft. × 6 ft.) March–April.

> (Bearded.)

This species takes seven years or more to flower from an eighteen-inch plant but it is so beautiful that the wait seems worth while when one at last sees its waxy-textured, pure blood-red flower trusses that are similar in shape to those of *arboreum*, although somewhat smaller. Its stems are clothed by the reddish-brown bristly hairs from which it derives its specific name. The leaves are narrow, pointed at the ends, and handsome with deeply impressed veins, and when fully grown the tree-like shape of the plant shows off the smooth, pinky-bronze bark to advantage. Unfortunately it flowers so early and its young growth is so often cut that it is useless for frosty gardens.

*******R. smithii B. t (10 ft. × 6 ft.) April.

> (After Sir James Smith, an English botanist.)

Very like R. barbatum but a little later to flower and so often missing the early frosts, *R. smithii* is a better choice for gardens that catch the March frost.

*********R. strigillosum* B. s (8 ft. × 8 ft.) March.
(Beset with bristles.)

This is the best of the three for many gardens. Although March-flowering, the blooms will stand slight frost and the un-opened buds are completely resistant to damage. It is later to start into growth and if the young growth is cut it is replaced by fresh. Though smaller in truss than *R. barbatum* its flowers are nevertheless of the same fine scarlet.

********R. pseudochrysanthum* B. s (2 ft. × 3 ft.) April–May.
(Like *R. chrysanthum*.)

This is a charming dwarf species, with its apple-blossom coloured buds and bells followed by the ash-grey of the unfolding young leaves. Some forms, however, are not free-flowering. The Formosan form offered by Sunningdale seems to be one of the most reliable in this respect.

BOOTHII SERIES (Flowering young)

*******R. tephropeplum* B. s (3 ft. × 4 ft.) May.

A small, rather twiggily branched shrub with dark willow-like leaves, silvery beneath and a loose truss of tubular-campanu-late flowers varying in colour from white through pink to luminous rose and even magenta, the magenta-rose coloured form that used to be known as *deleiense*, K.W.6794, is prettier than the smaller forms of Forrest's collection. This species flowers in three to four years from seed.

CINNABARINUM SERIES (Flowering young)

********R. cinnabarinum* B. s (10 ft. × 5 ft.) April–May.
(Cinnabar red.)

Although some of the plants originally introduced by Sir Joseph Hooker became very large and spreading, the plants of this species usually seen are slender and almost willowy in growth. Lovely in flower, many forms are almost equally lovely in the intense blue sheen of their leaves. The colour of the pendent, lapageria-like flowers varies from purple, pink, champagne,

25. *R.* 'Yellow Hammer' is an interesting dwarf hybrid of fairly narrow upright habit and small tubular yellow flowers. It is useful for a restricted space

26. *R.* 'Moonshine Supreme' is one of the best of the new yellow hybrids bred at Wisley

27. *R.* 'Carita' in its various varieties is beautiful in shades varying
from biscuit to primrose

28. *R. arizelum* is an aristocrat with handsome foliage and
wonderful tight rounded trusses of flowers

orange, yellow, red and bi-colour combinations of orange and scarlet, *R. c. blandfordiflorum* has buff flowers tinged with red and is a lovely variety, but the most sought-after of all is *R. c. roylei* of dark, cinnabar red. Better still is the glorious *R. c. roylei* 'Magnificum' of Sir James Horlick's garden on the isle of Gigha, and Sir George Campbell's at Crarae, Argyll. This form has flowers of a red-plum purple with a hint of magenta—a colour more likely to be found in certain pelargoniums than in rhododendron species but a lovely glowing colour none the less. The Ludlow and Sheriff forms, also, are good and very varied in colour though less blue in leaf. Asking only wind-shelter, some shade and a site that is not too dry, *R. cinnabarinum* is much easier in cultivation than its exotic appearance might suggest.

*******R. concatenans* C. s (6 ft. × 4 ft.) May. (Flowering in six years from seed.)

(Linking together.)

This species is near to *R. cinnabarinum* but the flowers are more bell-shaped, and may be apricot, veined with purple or sometimes a glowing copper. The striking blue-green of its leaves makes it one of the finest foliage plants in the genus and may be seen to perfection at the lower end of the dell at Bodnant where with other cinnabarinums it makes a vivid leaf-pattern effect. *R. keysii* is more tender with narrow tubular flowers, orange-red, tipped with yellow. It is less attractive than its more accommodating hybrid 'Cinnkeys' with a similar colour scheme. *R. xanthocodon* (C.) is a pale-foliaged edition of *R. cinnabarinum* itself with more bell-like, waxy, pale yellow flowers. It is attractive but definitely needs shelter.

All the members of the series flower when quite young.

## IRRORATUM SERIES

*******R. aberconwayi* A. s (5 ft. × 4 ft.) May.

A comparatively recently introduced species with very pleasant wide-open, saucer-shaped flowers carried in a firm rounded truss. The flowers are white, often flushed with rose, and spotted red on the upper lobe and the leaves are a leathery dark green, stiff and surprisingly brittle. It is a useful garden species—very hardy and adaptable.

*********R. venator* B. s (6 ft. × 6 ft.) May–June.

(A huntsman.)

This species is another reasonably hardy member of a tender series. With its brilliant scarlet, tubular flowers it is worth trying in all but the bleakest gardens provided some protection can be given from cutting winds. It, too, is a good parent. It is a species for which I have a great affection with its neat growth, dark green leaves and soft, yet bright, red blooms. It flowers at about eight years from seed which means that one may have to wait three or four years for a bought-in plant to flower but the waiting is well worth while.

NERIIFLORUM SERIES (Very slow to flower)

This is a series of very fine rhododendrons, of which one or two are reluctant to flower. Where this risk is present it is mentioned in the text. In the main, however, the series is composed of rhododendrons that are beautiful in their own right and valuable to the hybridizer as first-class parents producing offspring that are much more free to bloom.

*R. aperantum* B. s (1½ ft. × 4 ft.) June.

(Limitless—it forms enormous mats of growth.)

Apricot to orange-red, this species seems to flower well only at Bodnant where it has been successfully used as a parent. Being so shy-flowering it is hardly worth including in the average garden.

*****R. didymum* C. s (2–3 ft. × 3 ft.) July.

(Twofold.)

A good parent of late-flowering red hybrids this species is very subject to spring frosts. Usually dark blood-red in colour, K.W.13225 is a form with bright scarlet flowers that offer good possibilities to the hybridizer.

******R. dichroanthum* B. s (4 ft. × 5 ft.) July.

(Two-coloured flowers.)

Valuable as the imparter of orange colouring to its offspring, *R. dichroanthum* exists in so many poor forms that it should itself be planted only if a particular colour form happens to catch the eye. This is, however, a species which will stand more sun and drought than most and for that reason its better forms may be felt to be worth planting in drier, southern gardens. The sub-species *apodectum* is perhaps a consistently more attractive plant, while under the form *scyphacalyx* one sometimes finds a fine orange that is worthy of three stars.

*******R. haematodes* B. s (3 ft. × 4 ft.—slow) May.
(Blood-like.)

A good parent and a good rhododendron in its own right which often begins to flower at only three years old. Its fleshy, crimson-scarlet, long-necked bells are strikingly lovely and its foliage is handsome, dark green and felted fawn-brown below.

*******R. forrestii* var. *repens* (prostrate and spreading) April.
(Creeping.)

On the whole more useful as a parent than in its own right on account of its shyness of flowering. The 'Tower Court' F.C.C. form, however, may be relied upon to flower really freely. With its large, rounded, dark green leaves and big, tubular, bright scarlet bells it is a form worth planting. At its best pouring down a sunny slope.

*******R. neriiflorum* C. s (5 ft. × 5 ft.) May.
(With flowers like an oleander.)

Should one choose to grow only one plant in the series, this species is the one to pick for its distinctive long-tubed, open-mouthed bells of bright scarlet-crimson and elegant, thin, dark green leaves. This species does not take so long to flower as some of the others. It usually begins to bloom at five years old from seed and one plant at Bulkeley Mill started to flower when only a foot high. The form listed as *euchaites* is taller and more tree-like (up to fifteen feet in height) and takes longer to flower. Both need wind-shelter and half-shade.

THOMSONII SERIES (Flowering comparatively young at five to six years from seed)

This series contains some of the loveliest medium-sized rhododendron species. Its members are remarkable for their beauty of leaf and bark no less than for the charm and colour of their flowers.

\*\*\*\*\*\*\*\*R. *callimorphum* B. s (7 ft. × 5 ft.) April–May.

(Beautifully shaped.)

This species is fairly typical of the series with oval, or rounded, bluish-green leaves that have a decorative blue sheen when young. The flowers are held in loose trusses. They are crimson in bud and open to clear pink bells. Like most of the species in this series, R. *callimorphum* is a graceful and extremely pretty plant. Unfortunately although reasonably hardy, however, R. *callimorphum* is more temperamental than some in its dislike of dry conditions or sun-scorching. Even in Scotland it should have some shade.

\*\*\*\*\*\*\*\*R. *caloxanthum* B. s (4–5 ft. × 4 ft.) May.

(Beautiful yellow flower.)

Like the *cinnabarinums* this species is valuable for its blue-green leaf colour. The blueness fades as the leaves age but the summer effect is quite remarkable. It is intensified if the plants are grown on a sunny slope. Plenty of moist peat should be incorporated when planting and care must be taken to see that the plants do not suffer from drought. To my mind this is an even lovelier species than *campylocarpum*, its orange flower-buds usually opening to perfect bells of soft clear yellow, although there are one or two forms with pale orange-coloured flowers.

\*\*\*\*\*\*R. *campylocarpum* B. s (6–10 ft. × 5 ft.) May.

(With bent fruits.)

R. *campylocarpum elatum* is the form usually grown and is a pretty plant and an easy grower with small, rounded, soft green leaves and loose trusses of clear-yellow flowers lightly dusted inside with red spots. The original introduction (Hooker's form) is more bushy in growth and does not exceed six feet in height with large, shiny, dark-green leaves and deeper-coloured flowers of a rich greeny-yellow. A variety of forms intermediate between the two exist and also some which are clearly merging into *caloxanthum*. All are hardy in the west but in colder districts they may be more safely replaced by R. *wardii* which is in my opinion a finer species, although a little later to flower.

*******\*R. souliei* B. s (8 ft. × 7 ft.) May.

(After Père J. A. Soulie, a French missionary in Tibet.)

This is one of the most beautiful rhododendrons with silky-textured, wide-open flowers of delectable shape in loose, flat-topped trusses. The colour varies from pink to white and the leaves are heart-shaped, bright green when young and becoming a wonderful blue as they age.

********\*R. wardii* A–B. s (4–12 ft. × 4–8 ft.) May–June.

(After Frank Kingdon Ward—the plant-hunter.)

This is a very variable species containing many geographic forms and possible hybrids, some of which used to have specific rank. Of these, the form that used to be called *croceum* is good, with leaves that are thicker and more oval than in the rest of the group. Its colour is a deep, bright yellow without a blotch. Another excellent form that can be bought is the more recently collected Ludlow and Sherriff 5679 form with daffodil-yellow flowers with a purple blotch. These two forms are later than most to flower and are certainly the ones to choose for gardens that are subject to May frosts. For hardiness and fine flower colour the 'L' and 'S' form should be used for hybridizing and might be used to impart depth of yellow to the paler *campylocarpum* hybrids. I am sure that such crosses would be hardy in most places where rhododendrons can reasonably be expected to grow in the British Isles.

*******\*R. stewartianum* B. s (8 ft. × 4 ft.) February–March.

(After a curator of the Edinburgh Botanic Garden.)

*Rhododendron stewartianum* and *eclecteum* are for garden purposes very near, with many intermediate forms. For western and southern gardens they are valuable for their early blooming and in many quite frosty gardens, such as Bulkeley Mill in the Conway Valley, these species seem to flower in between the cold spells and so escape unharmed. For northern and midland gardens, unless specially favoured, they are not really worth growing.

The main difference between the two species is to be noticed in the leaves, those of *stewartianum* having a slight layer of hairs on the underside and longer petioles. In flower colour both species have a delightful range from white, yellow and pink to rose and even crimson sometimes with another colour ringing the mouth of the bells. There is an Award of Merit form of *eclecteum* with clear yellow flowers but I do not think it is any more beautiful than the champagne-ringed-pink and pink-shot-with-yellow forms of *stewartianum* that predominated at Bulkeley Mill.

Both species begin to bloom when about five years old.

Like all winter-flowering species they benefit from the shelter of an evergreen bush to the south and an overhead canopy of leaf-losing trees.

\*\*\*\*\*\*\*\**R. thomsonii* A–B. t (14 ft. × 6 ft.) April–May.

(After a superintendent of the Calcutta Botanic Garden.)

Most forms of this species are truly hardy but the more recently introduced Ludlow and Sherriff forms are definitely tender in cold districts and should be rated C. The young leaves are fresh lettuce-green when they first appear and then change to a remarkable blue-green—an effect, however, which is more fleeting than that of *caloxanthum* and *wardii*. The trunk, too, is beautiful, the bark peeling in old plants to reveal a polished fawn and brown surface with pale purple shading. The flowers are in loose trusses—hanging bells of rich blood-red that need the rays of the late afternoon sun to reveal them at their best. For this reason *R. thomsonii* needs careful placing. It needs feeding, too, and dead-heading, for flowering heavily as it does and from a comparatively early age (five to six years from seed) its strength might otherwise become exhausted. A yearly mulch of cow-manure or dried blood as recommended for *fargesii* and *oreodoxa* is the answer to this problem.

\*\*\*\*\*\*\**R. williamsianum* C. s (2½ ft. × 4 ft.) April–May.

(After J. C. Williams of Caerhays.)

Equally at home in the rock-garden or at the front of a belt of shrubs, *R. williamsianum* needs sunlight if it is to flower freely. Its small, round leaves which are bronze when young are among the prettiest of the rhododendron genus and this merit, together with its neat growth and bell-shaped flowers, it passes on in some measure to its deservedly numerous progeny. Its soft pink bells, loosely held in twos or threes, are set off delightfully by the bronzy young growth and contrast well if grouped with the deep-blue of *R.* 'Blue Diamond' nearby. Flowering early and very subject in cold gardens to frost, the answer may be to plant *R. williamsianum* in full exposure so that it flowers later and makes hardier growth.

## TALIENSE SERIES

*********R. bureavii* B. s (6 ft. × 5 ft.) March–April.

(After Edouard Bureau—a collector in China.)

This species is usually grown for its fine foliage. It is sometimes extremely slow to flower and grows to a comparatively large size. It is not, therefore, a plant for small gardens where the greatest effect must be gained from each foot of space. For the larger garden it is valuable for its wonderful leaves—dark matt-green above, with a yellow mid-rib and a thick orange-brown indumentum beneath. It should always be planted on a bank above a path where its wonderful rusty felt may be frequently admired. Its flowers when they are to be seen are perfectly shaped, lilac in bud, opening to blush-pink.

*********R. wasonii* B. s (5 ft. × 5 ft.) May.

(After a friend of the collector E. H. Wilson.)

Almost equally good in foliage, smaller in growth and flowering at a reasonably young age, this is a first-class rhododendron. Silvery cockades of young growth unfold to leaves that are rich green above sprinkled with orange-brown that later fades and disappears. The silver indumentum beneath is replaced by hazel-brown and the mature leaves are pointed and sturdy. The flowers too are worth while and borne in loose trusses of creamy-yellow bells that sport crimson spots or are sometimes flushed with pink. Bodnant has a good deep-yellow form and there is also a rarer pink called *rhododactylum* with clear pink flowers spotted with red. All are full of quality and make really fine plants for the smaller garden. They are very hardy, too, and I know of a well-furnished specimen growing in the open in a North Cheshire garden which survives wind and cold quite unperturbed.

# Rhododendron Species for the Garden

## Species for more open positions

TRIFLORUM SERIES (Flowering at four to six years from seed)

\*\*\*\*\*\*\**R. augustinii* B. s (10 ft. × 6 ft.) May.
(After Augustine Henry.)

In its best forms the willow-leaved *R. augustinii* is one of the bluest of all rhododendrons, yet grey-pink and muddy mauve forms also exist so it is unreliable when grown from seed. Named clones should be bought from a reputable source after which they may be increased by cuttings or layers to give a uniform stock. Unfortunately the deepest blues are reputed to be the most tender. Tower Court and Magor's forms are among the bluest and of these perhaps the Tower Court form is the hardiest. Happy in full sun and standing some wind, *R. augustinii* needs to be sheltered from the east and north. Hardy enough in the south and west, it is nevertheless not a plant for frost hollows or very cold districts. As with many slightly tender rhododendrons it definitely seems hardier if grown in moderate exposure and in nature comes from exposed hillsides in Szechuan and western Hupeh.

R. *augustinii* var. *chasmanthum* C. s (10 ft. × 6 ft.) May.
(With gaping flowers.)

Flowering later than *R. augustinii*, this form, which used to have specific rank, has more rounded and glossy leaves and a bigger truss of equally blue flowers. Unfortunately it is often found to be even more tender. The F.C.C. form with its chestnut-spotted, soft lilac-coloured flowers is so beautiful that it ought to be grown wherever possible. Careful siting on the north of a hedge, wall or large evergreen should secure its survival in all but the bleakest areas. Sun and good drainage work wonders in the west where one's care is sometimes rewarded by an autumnal burst of bloom.

\*\*\*\*\*\*\*\**R. oreotrephes* A. s (8 ft. × 6 ft.) May.
(Mountain bred.)

This is a lovely rhododendron that will succeed in most gardens. Found at 10,000 to 12,000 feet in south-east Tibet it is naturally much hardier than *R. augustinii* which is not usually found much above 9,000 feet and *R. augustinii chasmanthum* which although found at up to 10,000 feet comes from the warmer valleys of south-east Tibet and north-west Yunnan. The leaves of *R. oreotrephes* are lovely—oval shaped, smooth dark green with a bluish bloom above and showing glaucous under-surfaces below when the wind catches them. They set off the lilac or mauve-pink flowers to perfection.

Although undoubtedly hardy, *R. oreotrephes* has been found choosy in some gardens. The complaints as to its behaviour seem to come from the drier areas and from districts exposed to easterly winds. It grows well in Wales and may be one of those plants that do best in the west and south-west. It is said on good authority to resent disturbance when once established—a trait not often found in the genus which as a whole seems to benefit from what the late Mr. E. A. Bowles used to refer to as 'carriage exercise'.

The variety *exquisetum* formerly had specific rank and for garden purposes is distinct with flowers that are more of a silvery lavender that can look grey if wrongly placed. Situated on a bank or in thin woodland where the light will strike it, the unusual flower colour will give a delicate and lovely effect.

*******R. lutescens* B–C. s (6 ft. × 5 ft.) February–March.

*Rhododendron lutescens* in its best forms is one of the most beautiful of early spring shrubs. With its primrose-yellow flowers and willowy leaves it seems to hold all the joyous essence of the season as it catches the thin sunshine. Fortunately, too, it is one of those early species whose blossoms often seem to miss the frost, yet it is not a plant for a frost hollow. In the winter of 1961–2 specimens in the dell at Bodnant were cut to the ground and a thicket of several old plants by the stream at Bulkeley Mill were also damaged though not so severely. In our own garden a three-foot plant of the F.C.C. form was struck by nineteen degrees of frost when just coming into flower. The open blossoms were destroyed and some of the top growth cut back but the buds were unharmed and went on to open well in the next mild spell. It is a plant which will stand twenty degrees of frost but not thirty. This species, like all those of the Triflorum series, is variable from seed which can produce washy greeny-yellows.

So it is as well to choose your plant in flower or else to buy only the F.C.C. vegetatively-propagated form which has wonderfully burnished bronzy-red young leaves to add to its merits. It is, however, supposed to be slightly more tender in growth, although I have found it hardy enough in full sun, standing twenty-one degrees of frost in 1963 without losing a leaf.

*********R. davidsonianum* B–C. s (6 ft. × 4 ft.) April.

(After Dr. W. H. Davidson, a missionary in China.)

About as hardy as the last species, *R. davidsonianum* should give no trouble, except in the bleakest gardens, so long as it is sited where the frost can drain away. An overhead canopy of deciduous trees also helps to protect against frost damage. With flowers of warm pink, spotted with red or chestnut in its best forms, it is a beautiful species and one which associates well with the smaller-flowered blue hybrids such as 'Blue Diamond' and 'Augfast'. The Exbury, Headfort and Caerhays clones are all first class but seedlings should never be bought as they may have disappointingly pale or even white flowers which though pleasing are not what one expects from selected forms of this species.

*********R. yunnanense* A. s (8 ft. × 5 ft.) May.

(From Yunnan.)

This species is one of the easiest and best—a real 'Everyman's' rhododendron, free-flowering, hardy and easy, even in dry and windswept areas. It has the characteristic graceful growth of the series with lance-shaped, olive-green leaves and the usual wide-open, funnel-shaped flowers, lightly and gracefully borne in compact trusses, of either white or blush, tinged with lavender and heavily spotted with rich chestnut colour. *R. yunnanense* 'Openwood' is a particularly good lavender form richly speckled with red that can be obtained from Knap Hill.

DAURICUM SERIES (Winter flowering)

*********R. mucronulatum* A. s (5 ft. × 4 ft.) January.

(With a sharp point.)

Bone hardy anywhere, this is one of the best winter-flowering rhododendrons. Completely deciduous and more than halfway in evolution to becoming an azalea, it is attractive in summer and autumn leaf and delightful in January and February when its wide-open rose-purple flowers hover like decorative butterflies on its bare branches. *R. mucronulatum* usually chooses a mild and sunny spell in which to bloom and its flowers belie the ethereal delicacy of their appearances by being surprisingly resistant to a few degrees of frost. This natural resistance is helped by the presence of an overhead branch canopy of deciduous trees and by being sited to the north of a wall, hedge or large evergreen so that the sun is prevented from striking the blossoms before they have had a chance to thaw and dry after a night of frost. Even if the first lot of flowers are frosted there is a succession of buds to open in the next mild spell. In this, and in the superior showmanship of its flowers being borne while the branches are leafless, it is better than the related evergreen *R. dauricum* from which the series takes its name.

## Tougher Species

### HELIOLEPIS SERIES

\*\*\*\*\*\**R. rubiginosum* A. s (8 ft. × 8 ft.) March–April.
(Reddish brown.)

Allied to the Triflorum series but without their quality, this species and the others in the series are probably natural hybrids between members of the Triflorum series and some other species. The leaves are aromatic and most members of the series are tough. *R. rubiginosum* is one of the hardiest of all and is useful for a shelter or hedge plant where one does not want the heavy leaf effect of the older hybrids. It is not affected by a slightly alkaline soil and is safer than the cheaper grafted hybrids of which too often the invasive *ponticum* stock takes over.

### PONTICUM SERIES

\*\*\*\*\**R. smirnowii* A. s (8 ft. × 10 ft.) May–June.
(After Smirnow.)

A very useful shelter plant, this species is actually tougher than *ponticum* and certainly less invasive. *R. smirnowii* makes a sturdy, wind-resistant bush of dense growth and is useful to form an inner barrier at ground level to stop the gusts that creep beneath the lower branches of outer conifer screens.

\*\*\*\*\*\*\**R. yakushimanum* B. s (3 ft. × 5 ft.) May.
(From Yakushima.)

This species, although most attractive on its own account with round trusses of apple-blossom bells and handsome, shining green leaves thickly felted with fawn on the under-surface, is particularly important as the parent of a new race of low-growing hardy hybrids suitable for present-day small gardens. The equally dwarf *R. chrysanthum* with good yellow flowers is also now being used for hybridization.

## Dwarf Species

### ANTHOPOGON SERIES

\*\*\*\*\**R. anthopogon* A. (1–1½ ft. × 3 ft.) April.
(Bearded flowers.)

This is not one of the easiest dwarfs. Coming from high altitudes in the Himalayas, in southern gardens it must have an open position. It dies back if planted in close conditions among other shrubs or in woodland. In the east of Scotland Messrs. E. H. M. and P. A. Cox of Glendoick, Perthshire, find the whole series rather tender and needing shelter from cutting winds (see *Modern Rhododendrons* by E. H. M. and P. A. Cox). At Bulkeley Mill when grown cheek-by-jowl with other dwarf rhododendrons in a small bed, though given full exposure, *R. anthopogon* became straggly and suffered from the dying-back of leggy branches. An open site on a sunny rock-garden would probably suit it best in all but the coldest districts. It is nevertheless a most attractive little rhododendron, twiggily branched with aromatic small leaves and pretty daphne-like flowers in white or pink. The form K.W.10541 from Sunningdale is compact and sturdy in growth with exceptionally rich pink flowers. Messrs. Cox offer a slightly taller form with cream-pink flowers that makes a useful contrast. *R. cephalanthum* var. *crebreflorum* is a smaller, prostrate grower making a close mat of glossy green leaves which become freely studded with bright pink little flowers in the form K.W. 9591, while there is at Bulkeley Mill a charming creamy-pink known as K.W.6967.

*****R. sargentianum* A. (2 ft. × 4 ft.) May.

(After the director of the Arnold Arboretum.)

This species is reputed to be very difficult in the south but it is easy in the north and in Wales. It again needs an open position. It has the typical daphne-flowers of the series but in yellow. Some forms are pale and creamy but there are some good lemon coloured clones in existence. Messrs. Cox of Glendoick have one that is a more compact grower than the type.

BOOTHII SERIES

*******R. leucaspis* B. (1 ft. × 3 ft.) February.

(White shield.)

A hardy member of what is on the whole a tender series, the only drawback of this species is that it flowers at a time when its blooms are likely to be cut by frost. Growing it in an alpine house or protecting its buds and flowers with a polythene bag or cloche when frost threatens is the solution and its beauty is such as to more than justify this small trouble. With dark-green, hairy leaves and flat, two-inch, silver-white flowers, dusted with brown anthers, it is a most attractive rhododendron. Most forms of the species are good but to be sure of the best one can order the F.C.C. form.

CAMPYLOGYNUM SERIES

*****R. campylogynum* A. (1 ft. × 1½ ft.) May.

(Bent ovary.)

This species, too, is best in full sun. In shade it is apt to grow leggy. With unusual thimble-shaped flowers of which a second crop is sometimes carried in the autumn, *R. campylogynum* is a characterful little plant for a rock-garden or bank nearer eye-level where its flowers can be properly appreciated. Its leaves are dark green on top and waxy-white beneath, and its long-stalked little thimbles vary in colour from clear pink through crushed strawberry to plum-purple. Its variety ****myrtilloides* is completely prostrate in growth, making a plant about ten inches in

189

diameter with plum or rose-pink thimbles that are often less freely borne than those of the type. Its leaves turn to reddish-purple in late autumn, helping to build up a colourful winter pattern of dwarf rhododendron foliage with members of the Lapponicum series and others.

## GLAUCOPHYLUM SERIES

********R. *charitopes* B. (3–5 ft. × 3 ft.) April.
(Graceful of aspect.)

This species is another which in Wales, at any rate, can usually be relied upon to offer a good show of bloom in the autumn. In colder gardens the autumn blooms may be nipped by an early frost but it does not seem to matter as there are always plenty of buds left to open in spring. Pleasant in foliage R. *charitopes* has shiny obovate leaves, dark green on top and with a slightly recurved edge. The under-sides are glaucous and densely scaly. Best of all they give off a delightful aromatic scent with a savour rather like that of bog myrtle but with a sweetness replacing the bog myrtle's sharp tang. In the best forms the flowers are really beautiful—recurving waxy saucers of delicious pale rose with a freckling of red. This species stands so far above the other members of the series as almost to disqualify them from being mentioned. R. *glaucophyllum*, however, is quite pretty with grey leaves and smaller flowers of apple-blossom pink. It, too, carries a quota of autumn bloom.

Both species are good and easy doers for sunny open places in the garden. R. *charitopes*, however, seems to need rather more moisture in the soil than *glaucophyllum*. It will not show to its best on a droughty rock-garden.

## LAPPONICUM SERIES

This is among the most useful and hardiest group of dwarf rhododendrons composed of fascinating, twiggy shrublets whose aromatic small leaves often turn to bronze, blue-purple and frosty green in the winter. Some species have the agreeable habit of flowering regularly in autumn and all are free flowering and healthy with wide-open, starry little flowers in shades of lavender, dark blue, purple, claret, yellow, white and even rose. Completely hardy they will stand full exposure to wind and sun. Coming, however, from the moorlands of Asia where they replace the heather they are used to moist peat at their roots just as is the native ling of our own moorlands. For this reason they must not be allowed to dry out. In hot southern gardens they have sometimes proved difficult and are all the better for being planted on the north slope of a rock-garden or in the shade of boulders.

*******R. chryseum* A. (2 ft. × 2 ft.) April.

(Golden yellow.)

This species varies a great deal in quality, so plants propagated from good clones should always be bought. The one I grow is Rock 59049—a very dwarf and compact plant with strongly aromatic little leaves of dark sage-green that colour to deep bronze in winter. Its flowers are a good daffodil yellow enlivened by tan anthers.

Rock 59189 is also good with pale-anthered, greenish-yellow flowers and a red stigma.

Kingdon Ward 9636 is taller with bold bronzy-green leaves and larger flowers of dull yellow flushed with bright rose. It is worth growing for contrast but should be grouped separately from the true yellows.

*******R. hippophaeoides* A. (2 ft. × 2 ft.) April.

(Resembling sea-buckthorn.)

The best form of this species is 'Haba Shan' with neat grey-green leaves, and comparatively large trusses of lavender-blue flowers. It is a reliable autumn flowerer.

**–*******R. impeditum* A. (1 ft. × 1½ ft.) April–May.

(Tangled.)

Varies in shades of blue and violet purple, sometimes with red anthers and sometimes with a tiny, white, furry zone at the base of the corolla. The foliage is deep bluey-green and very attractive, changing to bronze in the winter. Rock 59263 A.M. is a fine deep violet-purple but I prefer the lighter periwinkle blue forms which can sometimes be obtained. 'Steel Blue' is a particularly dwarf and pleasing clone with grey leaves.

\*\*\*\*\*\*\**R. intricatum* A. (1 ft. × 1 ft.) March–April.
 (Web-like.)

This is an adorable little shrub with small, fluffy-stamened, starry flowers that are almost always a good lavender. Its leaves are grey-green, neat and small and borne on a network of intricate twiggy little branches. Sometimes it is apt to become too twiggy and should then be pruned back before this trait becomes too bad. Most of this series, like *R. racemosum* of the Virgatum series, will stand an occasional necessary trimming.

\*\*\*\*\*\*\**R. lysolepsis* A. (2 ft. × 3 ft.) April.
 (With loose scales.)

Reddish violet in colour and so offering a useful contrast, this species associates well with *chryseum*, *hippophaeoides* and the white *microleucum* described below to make a colourful interwoven tapestry.

\*\*\*\*\*\*\**R. microleucum* A. (1½ ft. × 2 ft.) April.
 (Small, white.)

This is the only white member of the series and very pretty with snowy little flowers and light green leaves.

\*\*\*\*\*\*\**R. ravum* A. (4 ft. × 4 ft.) May.
 (Grey.)

This species is unusual in the series on account of its larger size, larger flowers and pink colouring that in its best forms is a deep rose.

*R. cuneatum* (wedge-shaped) is very like it, though perhaps even taller growing. They do not flower when as young as the other members of the series but once they start they are very free flowering.

\*\*\*\*\*\*\*\**R. scintillans* A. (2 ft. × 2 ft.) April.
 (Sparkling.)

This is the truest blue of the series bearing masses of small, lavender-blue to deep purple-blue flowers. The F.C.C. form is particularly deep and near to a royal blue—a colour that to my mind is more pleasing than the white-centred violet-purple of the much-praised *R. russatum* (*cantabile*).

So blue is a good *scintillans* that it should be separated from

29. Established bushes of the dwarf *R.* 'Humming Bird' with blood crimson bells. This hybrid keeps its dwarf mounded shape into age and will stand clipping

30. Dwarf evergreen azaleas give character and colour to the rock-garden at Leonardslee

31. An eighty to a hundred year old bush of *R. obtusum* shows how this species keeps its distinctive tiered habit into age

32. Japanese azalea cuttings showing good root formation after five months (see Chapter 12 on propagation)

the lavender colours of *hippaphaeoides, intricatum,* etc., by the yellow *chryseum* or white *microleucum.*

Other *lapponicums* worth growing are the neat, lilac-lavender *stictophyllum* and the tiny-leaved *drumonium* with its white-eyed flowers of a richer lilac.

## MOUPINENSE SERIES

*******R. moupinense* B. (2 ft. × 2 ft.) February–March.
(From Moupin.)

The only difficulty with this lovely species is its early-flowering habit which means that its flowers are sometimes spoiled by frost. Bone hardy in growth, it may be given full exposure to retard its flowering until the worst of the frost is past. Also it is small enough to protect with a polythene cloche or bag, removing the protection when the danger is over. With neat, pointed, leathery leaves and wide, azalea-like, heavy-textured flowers of white freckled with red or, even lovelier, soft-pink flowers, it is well worth its place in any garden where there is a chance of its flowers escaping the frost.

## SALUENENSE SERIES

This is a useful series on account of its flowering time—May to July—which is late for dwarf rhododendrons and serves to fill in the gap until the precocious autumn blooms of some members of the Lapponicum and Glaucophyllum series appear at the end of August. Unfortunately the colours of many of the species are not as attractive as in some of the other dwarfs, tending as they do to dark red-purples and magentas.

******R. calostrotum* A. (2½ ft. × 2½ ft.) May.
(With a beautiful covering.)

Neat and serviceable with glaucous leaves and the usual wide-open, rosy-purple, salver-shaped flowers. Its variety *calciphilum* (lime-loving) is found on limestone in the wild and is rather smaller and more compact with paler flowers.

******R. keleticum* B. (½ ft. × 1 ft.) June.
(Charming.)

A tight little mound of a plant with shining green leaves and brighter red-purple flowers, it is useful to carry on the flowering sequence.

\*–\*\*\*\*\*\**R. nitens* B. (2 ft. × 2 ft.) July.

(Shining.)

Later still and in some forms—notably that offered by Messrs. Cox of Glendoick—a much better colour, almost a pinky-rose.

\*\*\*\*\**R. radicans* B. May–June.

(Creeping.)

This is an interesting little species which forms a low mound with its outer branchlets close to the ground and spreading quickly. The form collected by Rock is the best and easiest to grow with dark-green, shiny leaves and purple flowers. It is not quite as good-tempered as some of the dwarfs, needing some shade and plenty of moisture in the growing season. A north-facing boulder near the streamside, or a shady and rather damp slope suits it perfectly. Artificially these conditions may be met by planting the species at the bottom of a north-facing rock-garden slope.

UNIFLORUM SERIES

\*\*\*\*\*\**R. imperator* B. (prostrate) April–May.

(Emperor.)

Hardy and easy if in full sun, this is an attractive dwarf species with quite large pinky-purple flowers similar to those of 'Praecox' but borne on prostrate branches.

\*\*\*\*\*\*\**R. pumilum* A. ($\frac{1}{2}$ ft. × 1 ft.) May.

(Small.)

*Rhododendron pumilum* is an uncommon but pretty dwarf—prostrate branched and with half-inch, hairy, little rose-pink bells.

\*\*\*\*\*\*\**R. uniflorum* A. (1 ft. × 1$\frac{1}{2}$ ft.) May.

(One flowered.)

This species and *R. pemakoense* are almost identical but the latter is a fortnight earlier to flower and thus more likely to have its blooms spoiled by frost. For most gardens, therefore, *R. uniflorum* is the better plant. It has wide, funnel-like flowers and very small neat leaves. The contrast of the large pinky-purple blooms and the little dark leaves makes it a most attractive plant.

VIRGATUM SERIES

**–**********R. racemosum* A. (2–6 ft. × 3 ft.) April–May.
     (Flowers in racemes.)

Usually flowering just before the blue Lapponicum × *augustinii* dwarf hybrids, this is one of the most useful of all species and in most forms is pleasing with trusses of apple-blossom to deep pink flowers and sturdy, red-stalked leaves. Flowers appear also in the axils of the leaves. The dwarf form Forrest 19404 is one of the most popular with pale-centred, deep-pink-edged little blooms with attractively prominent stamens. Glendoick offer a tall, bright-pink form and most specialist nurseries have additional good forms to offer. It is useful to associate with the blue-flowered dwarfs and will make a delightful informal hedge. Such a hedge, raised from seed, at Bulkeley Mill was the joy of the late Mrs. A. T. Johnson's heart. Grown straggly over the years it was severely cut back by the new owners of the mill but is coming again strongly from the base and will eventually, I am sure, make an even finer hedge than before.

*******R. virgatum* C. (4 ft. × 3 ft.) April.
     (Willowy twigs.)

This species is like *racemosum* but with larger, pale-pink flowers and leaves. There are some very pretty forms in existence but unfortunately none are as hardy as the former species. It is a worthwhile plant for gardens in the south and west.

MISCELLANEOUS SPECIES

*******R. spiciferum* C. (3 ft. × 3 ft.) April.
     (Bearing spikes.)

Somewhat similar to *racemosum* but with more downy leaves and rich pink flowers this species is a fine plant for west and south-west gardens. It makes its young growth soon after flowering and this is too often cut by frost in cold gardens for it to be a good risk there. To my mind it is much more attractive a species than the allied *R. spinuliferum* which is more of a curiosity than a garden joy with narrow, upright, tightly tubular flowers of brick-red from which the stamens protrude.

\*\*\*\*\*\*\*\**R. lepidostylum* B. (1½ ft. × 4 ft.) May–June.
(Having a scaly style.)

This is a foliage plant, pure and simple, and the four stars are awarded for the beauty of its blue-green, softly-furry leaves. Its flowers are pale yellow and quite overshadowed by the loveliness of the young leaves. Although listed as B this is rather a warning to avoid cold, cutting winds than a limitation. If grown in full sun it is quite hardy in the north. In the south it may need some shade. A plant in really heavy shade at Bulkeley Mill is lovely pouring down a woodland bank, but there it has a tree canopy and exceptionally good air drainage to protect the soft growth incurred by the shade from frost damage.

\*\*\*\*\*\*\**R. hanceanum* 'Nanum' B. (1 ft. × 1½ ft.) April.
(After H. F. Hance, Consul at Canton.)

The dwarf type of this member of the Triflorum series, known as 'Nanum', is the only form worth growing and is indeed an attractive plant. Easy in half-shade it has dark, shiny leaves and neat trusses of creamy-yellow, orange-anthered flowers freely borne.

**Tender species some of which survive against north and west walls in North Wales and on the south coast, and are hardy in open woodland in Cornwall and the Western Isles and California, but need cold-house treatment elsewhere.**

BOOTHII SERIES

\*\*\*\*Tender. *R. sulfureum* D. (3 ft. × 3 ft.) March.
(Sulphur coloured.)

This is a lovely small species with attractive shiny, dark-green leaves and trusses of four to six bright sulphur-yellow flowers, about an inch across. Even brighter and yet more tender is *R. chrysodoron*.

EDGWORTHII SERIES

\*\*\*\*Tender. *R. bullatum* D. (4 ft. × 4 ft.) April–May.
(Puckered leaves.)

This Chinese species is much hardier than its Himalayan equivalent *R. edgworthii*. It is hardy in North Wales on a sheltered wall and is a lovely plant with dark-green ridged leaves and loose trusses of four or five wide-open, white, wonderfully scented flowers that are sometimes tinted pink. Sunningdale have a pretty pink form of this species. F21564 and Rock 59202 are said to be the hardiest forms and at Exbury these were crossed to produce a form which can be rated at least Category C.

The more tender *edgworthii* is most beautiful in the Ludlow and Sheriff form which is white with a deep-green eye.

IRRORATUM SERIES

    ****Tender. *R. eriogynum* E. (8 ft. × 8 ft.) July.

    (With a woolly ovary.)

Although easy enough in woodland conditions in Cornwall, Ireland and the west of Scotland, for most of us this species and the similarly brilliant scarlet *elliottii* are of interest mainly as the parents of some of the late-flowering scarlet hybrids such as 'Tally Ho', 'Fusilier', 'Romany Chal', 'Grenadier' and 'Grosclaude'. Flowering late they are not really suitable for cold-houses.

    ****Very Tender. *R. kyawi* E. (8 ft. × 8 ft.) August.

    (After a Burmese collector.)

Even later to flower and yet more beautiful with larger scarlet flowers this is a species for very favoured gardens.

MADDENII SERIES

The members of this series are superb greenhouse or conservatory shrubs mostly with large, lily-like flowers in white, blush or yellow. Often they are scented. The later-flowering members are useful to grow in tubs to be taken outside from the end of May until autumn, which treatment, of course, suits all cold-green-house rhododendrons and azaleas.

    ***Tender. *R. burmanicum* E. (2 ft. × 2 ft.) April.

    (From Burma.)

This species has less scent than most but is attractive with pale-yellow flowers and neat, dark leaves.

***Tender. *R. johnstoneanum* D. (3 ft. × 4 ft.) May.

(After Mrs. Johnstone—wife of an official in Manipur.)

Hardier in growth but not always satisfactorily free to flower except in the mildest gardens. White, yellow and double-flowered forms of this species exist and most are pleasant with a delicate, sweet scent.

****Less tender. *R. valentinianum* C. (1½ ft. × 2 ft.) April.

(After a missionary in China, Père Valentin.)

Hardy in some parts of Surrey this is a dwarf species with small dark leaves and the richest yellow flowers of the series. Several equally good hybrids have been raised from it (see following chapter). The Rock form is, to my mind, the less pleasing of the two types in cultivation.

***Less tender. *R. ciliatum* C. (4 ft. × 5 ft.) April.

(Fringed.)

Hardy in many gardens but apt to be caught by frost this species is best grown in full sun in the north and in the south given the protection of a north-facing wall or evergreen. Its slightly scented, wide-open flowers are pink in the bud, opening to blush. It is really happiest in the west and is quite satisfactory in Wales.

***Tender. *R. crassum* D. (10 ft. × 8 ft.) June–July.

(Fleshy.)

This species is fairly hardy even in Perthshire but the flower buds are often cut by frost. It is too big for most greenhouses so is a satisfactory proposition only for the fortunately mild gardens of Cornwall, western Scotland and Ireland. This is a pity because the leaves are as handsome as those of most of the series and the flowers are lovely—long, funnel-shaped, scented and in the best forms are white with a distinctive yellow eye.

***Tender. *R. maddenii* E. (6 ft. × 6 ft.) June.

(After Lt.-Col. E. Madden.)

Much more tender than *crassum* and again rather large for most greenhouses for which a better plant is:

***Tender. *R. polyandrum* E. (3 ft. × 3 ft.) June.

(Many stamens.)

An equally pleasing species with long, narrow, dark leaves and five-flowered heads of large, waxy, white, lily-like blooms.

****Tender. *R. dalhousiae* E. (5 ft. × 3 ft.) June.

(After Lady Dalhousie.)

One of the most exciting species with pale-green leaves and lime-green buds opening to huge greeny-yellow trumpets. This species has a particularly fine scent and is an excellent greenhouse plant.

Among other lily-flowered species for greenhouses are the nutmeg-scented *R. megacalyx*; *nuttallii* with the largest flowers in the series, creamy, pale yellow or white, often striped green on the outside; the pink-striped *rhabdotum* and *taggianum* which is similar to *dalhousiae* but hardy enough to grow out of doors in favoured places on the Solent, and in Devon and Cornwall, as well as the west of Scotland and the milder Irish gardens.

# CHAPTER 16

# Hybrid Rhododendrons

⟫⟫⟫⟫⟫⟫⟫⟫⟫⟫⟫⟫⟫⟪⟪⟪⟪⟪⟪⟪⟪⟪⟪⟪⟪⟪⟪

## Winter-Blooming Hybrids—Medium to Large

\*\*\*\*\*\*\*'Nobleanum', Award of Garden Merit (*arboreum* ×
    *caucasicum*) (8 ft. × 8 ft.) crimson.

\*\*\*\*\*\*\*'Nobleanum Album' (white).

\*\*\*\*\*\*\*'Nobleanum Venustum' (pink).

This is a group of extremely useful, very hardy old hybrids
which should be given some protection to save their winter
blooms. The north or west sides of a hedge, building, or large
evergreen will suit them well and they may also have a large sheet
of heavy polythene to cover them, should frost threaten to spoil
the flowers.

The clear, bright pink 'Nobleanum Venustum' is the first to
begin to flower. Indeed as I write this at the end of November,
a five-year-old plant of this clone, outside in the garden, has one
truss expanded and is opening a second with six or seven more
to follow.

'Nobleanum' itself follows, with its bright crimson-red trusses,
just after Christmas in North Wales, with 'Nobleanum Album'
flowering later, towards the end of February.

All the clones are rather slow-growing with narrow leaves that
have a tendency to roll. They are particularly sensitive to lime.
The stars are awarded for general usefulness and for creating a
bright and lovely picture in the winter garden rather than for any
intrinsic quality of bloom which has a certain flimsiness of texture that is no doubt derived from their *caucasicum* parent.

# Hybrid Rhododendrons

## Very Early Spring

LARGE

*******'Cornubia' A.M. (*arboreum* × 'Shilsonii') C.—large, red.
A magnificent red with compact blood-red trusses but hardy
enough only for milder districts.

MEDIUM

******'Jacksonii' (*caucasicum* × 'Nobleanum') A. (5 ft. × 5 ft.)
pink.
Coarser in flower than 'Nobleanum' but a useful plant all the
same, 'Jacksonii' blooms in March with the early daffodils and
carries a great many soft-pink, heavily spotted flowers, striped
with red on the outside of the petals. Unlike 'Nobleanum' and
'Nobleanum Venustum' which open their buds over a long
period, 'Jacksonii' opens almost all its flowers at once.

## Winter-Flowering Medium-Sized, Lightly Built Hybrids

*******'Praecox' A.G.M. (*ciliatum* × *dauricum*) A. (6 ft. × 4 ft.)
lilac-pink.
Semi-deciduous in some forms, 'Praecox' is an extremely
tough, undemanding and rewarding little rhododendron. Lightly
built and with small, neat leaves, it is airy enough in appearance
for a large rock-garden and yet may eventually reach six feet in
height. Its lilac-pink, frilly, 'butterfly' flowers are rather thin in
texture but they have great charm and give a most welcome hint
of spring. In our garden we enhance the blue tinge of the flowers
by underplanting with *Pulmonaria* 'Mrs. Moon' and Mr. Bowle's
plue periwinkle—*Vinca minor* 'Le Grave'. At Edinburgh Botanic
Garden there is a famous hedge of 'Praecox' that might well be
copied in others. Dwarf rhododendrons of this type are not used
nearly as much for hedges as they might be. Sturdy and floriferous, they stand clipping well. The species *racemosum* in some of
its taller forms makes a very pretty hedge and some of the small-
leaved 'blue' hybrids, 'Blue Diamond' and 'Augfast' in particular, are attractive and easy hedging plants.

# Hybrid Rhododendrons

*******'Tessa' A.M. ('Praecox × moupinense) A. (3 ft. × 3 ft.)
lilac-pink to pink.

This hybrid is even hardier than 'Praecox' and its flowers are
more resistant to frost than those of *moupinense*. With well-
shaped, dark leaves, a reddish-bronze bark and hosts of deep
lilac-pink flowers with a ray of crimson spots, 'Tessa' is an
excellent plant for any garden. Sunningdale offer a clone known
as 'Tessa B' with clear pink flowers.

## Winter and Very Early Spring-Flowering Small Hybrids

*******'Bric-a-Brac' A.M. (*leucaspis × moupinense*) B. (2 ft. ×
2 ft.) white.

This is a fine early-flowering Exbury hybrid with milky-
white, salver-shaped flowers set off by chocolate anthers. Hardy
enough in itself, like all early-blooming rhododendrons, 'Bric-
a-Brac' should be planted where the early-morning sun will not
strike its flowers after a night of frost. It is, however, a handy size
to cover with a large polythene bag.

*******'Cilpinense' A.M. (*ciliatum × moupinense*) B. (2–3 ft. ×
3 ft.) pink and white.

Flowering a week or more later than 'Bric-a-Brac', the Bod-
nant-raised 'Cilpinense' is a little larger in growth and makes a
very neat, bushy plant with shining leaves and pinky-white
flowers opening from deeper buds. It is one of the best of the
early dwarf rhododendrons and hardy and easy enough for any
garden where its flowers may be protected from frost.

******'Racil' (*racemosum × ciliatum*) A. (3 ft. × 3 ft.) blush.

As hardy as *racemosum* but with neat, tight trusses of larger
blush-pink flowers edged with rose, this is a pleasing little plant.
Very hardy.

## March and Early April Flowering, Large Growers

*******'Carex' (*fargesii × irroratum*) B. (12–15 ft.) white or blush.

A large-growing hybrid, 'Carex' is a good, early flowering
plant for the larger garden. With soft grey-green foliage it makes

a well-furnished pyramidal bush. It has neat trusses of pink flowers that open white and are enhanced by dark anthers. The inside of the bells are spotted with red. In 'Carex Blush' the flowers are blush-pink.

However, if I could spare room for only one large pale-coloured early-flowering rhododendron, I would choose the equally hardy and free-flowering *oreodoxa* which adds fragrance to the charm of its lilac-pink flower trusses and good foliage. Where there is room for more than one, 'Carex' is a charming rhododendron that is well worth a place.

*******'Choremia' F.C.C. (*haematodes* × *arboreum*) C. (6 ft. × 6 ft.) scarlet.

'Choremia' is really only a medium-sized shrub but I have placed it here where it may be considered along with the other early but taller-growing reds of its type.

This hybrid is sometimes placed in category D but it is hardier than that. It is not, however, suitable for exposed gardens or for bleak, frosty districts. Sheltered woodland conditions enable it to stand below zero Fahrenheit frosts in North Wales.

******'Cornubia' A. M. (*arboreum* × *Shilsonii*) C. (20 ft. +) scarlet.

Perhaps a little hardier than 'Choremia', this hybrid is much larger growing and makes a cheerful and impressive sight in woodland gardens. Its flower trusses are smaller than those of 'Choremia' and tightly globular, but of a warm, bright scarlet.

******'Gill's Crimson' (*griffithianum* × *arboreum* ?) C. (15 ft. × 15 ft.) red.

This is, I think, a little hardier than the other early red hybrids so far mentioned and is a handsome shrub; compact in growth and with fine dark-green foliage and loose trusses of large scarlet flowers.

********'Shilsonii' A.M. (*barbatum* × *thomsonii*) B. (14 ft. +) scarlet.

Probably the hardiest in the group, 'Shilsonii' is a splendid plant for the large garden with *barbatum*'s barbaric-scarlet waxen flowers, the handsome leaves of *thomsonii* and a fine cinnamon-coloured trunk.

\*\*\*\*\*\*'Endsleigh Pink' B. (18 ft. +) pale rose.

An old *arboreum* hybrid, this makes a useful large-growing rhododendron for colder districts where the early reds may not prove hardy. The pale-rose flowers are carried in neat, tight trusses and it has dark-green *arboreum*-type leaves, slightly silvered below.

There are also the old clones known as 'Caucasicum Album' and 'Caucasicum Pictum' which flower early but these are so poor in individual flower as to be not worth garden space in any but the bleakest, most exposed and shadeless places.

## March and Early April-Flowering Medium-Sized Hybrids

\*\*\*\*\*\*\*'Bo-peep' A.M. (*lutescens* × *moupinense*) B.(6 ft. × 4 ft.) pale yellow.

Hardy and with the narrow bronze leaves of *lutescens*, 'Bo-peep' has not the depth of colour of the best forms of that species. It has, however, the flower size of *moupinense* and the effect of a bush covered with these open, azalea-like, creamy-yellow flowers is very effective.

\*\*\*\*\*\*'Crossbill' (*spinuliferum* × *lutescens*) B. (5 ft. × 3 ft) yellow. 'Crossbill' is bright in the colour of its yellow, apricot-tinged flowers but these have the closed, globular shape of *spinuliferum* with protruding anthers. It makes an uncommon and curiously attractive, slightly built shrub.

\*\*\*\*\*\*\*'Emasculum' (*ciliatum* × *dauricum*) A. (6 ft. × 4 ft.) lilac-pink.

Flowering a fortnight later than the very similar 'Praecox' and having the same parentage, 'Emasculum'—in my opinion—is the better shrub. Its slightly frilly flowers have more substance than those of 'Praecox' and are borne in a bigger truss. Yet 'Emasculum' has never been given its richly deserved Award of Garden Merit and it is not grown nearly as widely as it should be. In every garden where I planted 'Praecox', I would plant 'Emasculum' to succeed it and to complement the yellow of the long-blooming *lutescens*.

\*\*\*\*\*\*\*'Fine Feathers' ('Cilpinense' × *lutescens*) B. (5 ft. × 3 ft.)
   pale yellow.

This early yellow Bodnant hybrid is a delightful shrub. Hardy
enough to grow almost anywhere, only its flowers need the shelter
that should be given to all early-blooming plants. 'Fine Feathers'
has larger leaves than 'Bo-peep'. It has a pretty habit and large,
open, shapely flowers of pale lemon-ice.

\*\*\*\*\*\*'Seta' (*spinuliferum* × *moupinense*) B. (5 ft. × 3 ft.) pink
   and white.

An attractive and erect-growing plant, perhaps leaning more
towards *moupinense* in flower than does 'Crossbill', its bells are
nevertheless narrow in shape and are white tipped with vivid pink
at the lobes.

\*\*\*\*\*\*'Spinulosum' A.M. (*spinuliferum* × *racemosum*) B. (5 ft.
   × 3 ft.) deep pink.

Another of the *spinuliferum* group, more like *spinuliferum* in
shape with deep-pink tubes and protruding anthers. It is quite a
colourful garden plant.


## April and Early May—Flowering Tree-like Rhododendrons for Woodland and Large Gardens

\*\*\*\*\*\*'Barclayi' (*thomsonii* × 'Glory of Penjerrick') D.
   (12 ft. +) scarlet.
   (The clone 'Robert Fox' was given the Award of Merit in
   1921.)

This magnificent scarlet rhododendron really is too tender for
most districts. Sheltered Cornish gardens and those in Ireland
and the west of Scotland are the only places where it may be
planted without risk as it is too large to be given the protection
of a wall. The Bodnant 'Redwing' F.C.C. ('Barclayi' × 'Shilsonii')
offers a better chance of success in sheltered gardens elsewhere
and, being a perfectly hardy plant in North Wales, might be
expected to prove satisfactory in many of the southern counties.
Unfortunately this fine hybrid is rare in commerce.

\*\*\*\*\*\*'Boddaertianum' (*arboreum album* + *ponticum album*) B.
   (14 ft. +) blush-white.

When fully grown this is a handsome rhododendron with long, dull-green, lance-shaped leaves with a faint golden indumentum beneath and round trusses of blush-white flowers freckled with crimson. The chocolate-tipped anthers of the stamens enhance the effect.

*******'Cornish Cross' (*griffithianum* × *thomsonii*) C. (10 ft. × 10 ft.) carmine-pink.

Bred by that wonderful old gardener, Smith, at Penjerrick, this is one of his famous six hybrids described by the late Lord Aberconway as among 'the finest ever raised'. 'Cornish Cross' has the beautiful pinky trunk of *thomsonii* and huge waxy flowers of rich carmine-pink. Although I have listed it here among rhododendrons of tree-like proportions, 'Cornish Cross' is not too big to grow against a sheltered wall and it was in such a position that the plant at Bulkeley Mill thrived.

*******'Dr. Stocker' A.M. (*caucasicum* × *griffithianum*) B+. (12 ft. +).

This is a very hardy hybrid that will succeed in any garden not ridden by early May frost. Its fairly large, mossy-green leaves deserve some wind shelter. 'Dr. Stocker' is an old hybrid that should be more widely grown, particularly in large gardens where room can be found. Its flowers are milky-white and borne in the large, loose trusses of its *griffithianum* parent. Unfortunately they lack the substantial texture of *griffithianum* but 'Dr. Stocker' is none the less a delightful shrub.

******'J. G. Millais' ('Ascot Brilliant' × 'Pink Pearl') B+. (12 ft. × 10 ft.) crimson-red.

Not as exciting as some of the more tender reds this is nevertheless a useful hybrid of real hardiness with the decorative leaves of *thomsonii*, inherited through 'Ascot Brilliant' and good trusses of deep crimson-red flowers with a freckling of a darker colour.

********'Penjerrick' A.M. (*campylocarpum* × *griffithianum*) B. (10 ft. × 8 ft.) cream or pink or white.

Another of the 'Smith Six'. I—and many others whose judgment is better than mine—consider this to be the most beautiful hybrid of all. Good foliage, beautiful coppery bark and perfect bell-shaped, dark-anthered flowers on long, richly coloured pedicels—'Penjerrick' has everything.

There are varying shades of flower colour from pale yellow, through cream and white to a delicate salmon-pink just tinged with yellow. All are good and choice is a matter of preference. If I had room, I would grow every 'Penjerrick' I could find.

       \*\*\*\*\*\*\*'Sir Charles Lemon' (*arboreum* × ?) B–C. (10 ft. × 12 ft. +) cream-white, handsome foliage.

This is a handsome hybrid, worth growing for the beauty of its leaves alone. These are richly textured, dark green with showy orange indumentum beneath. The flower-trusses, too, are good—rounded and composed of large creamy-white flowers that contrast well with the magnificent foliage. Hardy in many places it is one of those that catch the spring frosts in parts of Surrey and Berkshire. In North Wales it is completely satisfactory and I have never seen its young growth damaged.

## Hybrids of Medium Growth (April and Early May Flowering)

      \*\*\*\*\*\*'Cunningham's Sulphur' (*caucasicum* clone ?) A. (5 ft. × 5 ft.) sulphur yellow.

Able to stand full exposure to sun and wind and making a sturdy mound of dark green, slightly curled foliage with shapely trusses of pale yellow rather papery flowers this is an old plant that has unfortunately become rare. It should be more widely planted and is worth using more often as a parent of yellow hybrids. It is a good carrier of the yellow colour that always lurks in the genes of *caucasicum* and will also impart the priceless virtue of hardiness to its progeny. Unfortunately it is rather light in petal texture but that could be counteracted by crossing again to a more waxy yellow such as the Ludlow and Sheriff form of *wardii*.

'Canary' an offspring of *caucasicum luteum* (which is not very different from the above clone) and *campylocarpum* has these very characteristics and is a pretty shrub with neat leaves and bright, deep-yellow flowers. It is one of the hardiest yellows but needs to be crossed again, either with *wardii* or with a yellow of substantial texture such as 'Carita', to improve the flower.

*****'Dairymaid' A.M. (*campylocarpum* × ?) B+. (6 ft ×
    6 ft.) creamy-yellow, flushed pink.

One of the Slocock hybrids, 'Dairymaid' is a very pale yellow
with a pinky flush and red spots in the throat. Like many of these
hybrids, 'Dairymaid' is compact, with quite good foliage and a
rounded flower truss.

******'Diane' A.M. (*campylocarpum* × 'Mrs. Lindsay Smith')
    A. (8 ft. × 8 ft.) primrose.

Perhaps 'Diane' has a little less quality than 'Dairymaid' and
the flower trusses tend to be overcrowded but it is a plant of
undoubted hardiness and seems slightly deeper in colour—due no
doubt to the olive-yellow markings at the throat of the flowers.

*******'Damaris' A.M. (*campylocarpum* × 'Dr. Stocker') B.
    (10 ft. × 10 ft.) yellow.

There are several clones of this very fine hybrid. All are good
but vary in size and flower colour. Most are vigorous with
pointed, dark green leaves and seem very hardy. The 'Logan'
form is particularly pleasing, with large trusses of bell-shaped
Dresden yellow flowers.

****'Earl of Athlone' F.C.C. C. (5 ft. × 5 ft.) bright red.

One of the better Dutch hybrids but it is somewhat tender
and a weak grower. Its colour is good—brilliant red, but on a
blue rather than an orange base. It is worth planting in a sheltered, green part of the garden or woodland where its flowers
can be lit up by the sunlight but where they are out of eye-shot
of other red rhododendrons. Its only possible companion is a
buff-yellow such as 'Unique' which follows alphabetically later
in this section.

********'Ibex' A.M. (*griersonianum* × *pocophorum*) B. (5 ft. ×
    5 ft.) scarlet.

This Rothschild hybrid is a much better garden plant than
'Earl of Athlone' and it is finer in foliage and growth with the
narrow, sage-green leaves of *griersonianum* enhanced by a rusty-
orange felting below. Its flower-trusses are shapely and made up
of brilliant scarlet-crimson flowers.

********'Joanita' (*caloxanthum* × *lacteum*) B. (7 ft. × 8 ft.) yellow.

This is a very fine hybrid which has inherited a little of the difficult temperament of *lacteum* which means that it demands a moist, woodsy, acid soil of pH 4·5 to pH 5. It makes a low, rounded bush with handsome dark green leaves and has fine trusses of daffodil-yellow, crimson-eyed flowers that open from orange-yellow buds. I think it should be crossed to the Ludlow and Sheriff form of *wardii* with the object of deepening its remarkable flower colour while at the same time improving on its constitution and achieving a good-tempered garden plant.

*********'Marcia' F.C.C. (*campylocarpum* × 'Gladys') B+. (8 ft. × 8 ft.) deep yellow.

Another fine yellow and said to make eight feet, although the plant I know best has been rather slow-growing. 'Marcia' has round trusses of rich-yellow flowers with a small red eye. It seems very hardy.

*********'Mariloo' A.M. ('Dr. Stocker' × *lacteum*) C. (8 ft. × 8 ft.) soft yellow.

This *lacteum* hybrid seems to have inherited many of *lacteum's* good qualities without its difficult temperament. A plant of 'Mariloo' at Bulkeley Mill grew fast and easily into a sizeable shrub. Flowering at quite an early age 'Mariloo' carries rounded trusses of very large, soft-yellow flowers. Another glory is its handsome, felted leaves and it is to protect these that it is classified 'C', meaning that it should be planted away from frost-pockets and given wind-shelter.

********'Matador' (*griersonianum* × *strigillosum*) B. (6 ft. × 8 ft.) red.

This hybrid has been raised at both Bodnant and Exbury and though it was introduced by Bodnant, some may prefer the colour of the Exbury form in which the waxy, long-tubed flowers are a lighter, brighter red. The flowers last for a long time and the leaves, like those of *strigillosum* are long, narrow, pointed and hairy. It is a bold, outstanding plant and reasonably hardy.

*********'Naomi Glow' ('Aurora' × *fortunei*) A–B. (5 ft. × 7 ft.) pink.

A hardy pink of quality, flowering three weeks ahead of other members of the grex.

*******\*thomsonii* × *orbiculare* B+. (8 ft. × 6 ft.) rose-pink to rose-red.

This is an unnamed hybrid which can sometimes be bought. Several good forms of this cross grew at Bulkeley Mill and Messrs. Hilliers of Winchester stock it. It has always fascinated me although I know that it has occasionally been decried by the purists. Its rose-pink to cherry-pink bells have a pleasing stridence and its kidney-shaped leaves are very fine.

## Small-Growing Hybrids—'Blue' (April and Early May)

********\*'Augfast' (*augustinii* × *fastigiatum*) A. (5 ft. × 3 ft.) 'blue'.

This and 'Blue Diamond' are, in my opinion, two of the best of the taller-growing, small-leaved 'blue' hybrids. Bred from the scaly species they are entirely different in character from the larger-leaved, large-flowered 'blue' hybrids of the elepidote (non-scaly) section—'Susan', 'Blue Danube' and their fellows.

Like the other small-leaved hybrids that have their origin in the tiny-flowered, extra-hardy, very small-leaved species of the Lapponicum series and the larger-flowered, taller, willow-leaved, more tender *augustinii*, the best 'blue' of the Triflorum series, 'Augfast' fulfils the objects that must have been in the minds of the hybridizers who worked on these lines. Its flowers are a good, dark lavender-blue—among the 'bluest' to be found in any rhododendron—and though they are not as large or individually as beautiful as those of *augustinii*, the effect of a bush in full flower is very fine. Much more compact in growth than *augustinii*, the neat, dark little leaves make it an attractive plant even when out of flower. It is undeniably hardy and I have found it to be very free in flower and to flower regularly every year.

*******\*'Bluebird' A.M. (*intricatum* × *augustinii*) A. (4–5 ft. × 4 ft.) 'blue'.

Paler in flower colour than 'Augfast', in leaf this hybrid has a yellow tinge and despite its Award of Merit it is not to my mind as satisfactory a plant. Nor does it seem to flower so reliably. Awards of Merit, however, are given on the appearance of a good spray in full flower, and in flower, 'Bluebird' is undeniably good. I do not care for the leaf colour but the small compact trusses of soft lavender-blue 'butterfly'-shaped flowers deepen to a very 'near-blue' indeed. I think it should be crossed to 'Augfast' or 'Blue Diamond' in the hope of retaining the excellent flower quality and gaining healthier leaf-colour and freedom of bloom. 'Blue Beard' (*augustinii* × 'Blue Tit') suffers from neither of the above drawbacks but is nearer mauve in flower-colour and so, I think, slightly less attractive.

\*\*\*\*\*\*\*\*'Blue Diamond' F.C.C. ('Intrifast' × *augustinii*) A. (8 ft. × 3 ft.) 'blue'.

This, in my opinion, is the real pick of the basket. Eventually making dark columns of attractive foliage, in flower 'Blue Diamond' is the 'bluest' of the lot and, in some ways, quite as attractive as even a good *augustinii*. Moreover, it is as hardy as any.

\*\*\*\*\*\*\*'Bluestone' (*augustinii* × 'Bluebird') also is good but less hardy.

\*\*\*\*\*'Blue Tit' (*augustinii* × *impeditum*) A. (3 ft. × 3 ft.) 'blue'.

'Blue Tit' loses quality stars for lack of depth of flower-colour which suffers from comparison when planted near the others of the group and which in sunlight quickly fades to an ashy grey. It loses an outline star, used to denote garden-worth, because I find it to be rather shy in flower. With us it flowers tolerably well one year and the next has only a sparse scatter of bloom. This is forgivable enough in a 'Penjerrick' or an 'Avocet' but from these small hybrids one expects more reliable behaviour.

\*\*\*\*\*\*\*'Intrifast' (*intricatum* × *fastigiatum*) A. (1½ ft. × 1½ ft.) 'blue'.

More of a plant for the small rock-garden than the others, lacking the influence of the taller *augustinii*. 'Intrifast' is an attractive dwarf plant with starry lavender flowers and brilliantly-blue young leaves.

\*\*\*\*\*\*\*\*'Sapphire' ('Blue Tit' × *impeditum*) A. (2–3 ft. × 3 ft.) 'blue'.

I have seen 'Sapphire' described as a vigorous grower but my plant is slow growing with darker, larger leaves than those of 'Blue Tit' and deeper flowers which are yet paler than those of 'Augfast'. It is a most pleasing dwarf blue.

\*\*\*\*\*\*\*\*'Songbird' ('Blue Tit' × *russatum*) A. (4 ft. × 4 ft.) 'blue'.
This hybrid comes from Sir James Horlick on the Isle of Gigha on the west coast of Scotland. It is very hardy. Strong-growing yet neat, it has deep violet-blue flowers in small, compact trusses.

A recent introduction, 'St Breward' promises to be the finest of the group—better even than 'Blue Diamond'—but is not yet in commerce. 'St. Tudy', from the same raiser, is also a good blue.

It seems likely, however, that these two, resembling as they do *augustinii* in habit and growth, will eventually make sizeable plants.

These 'blue' dwarf hybrids form a closely knit and distinct family. That is why I have decided to keep them together and to deal with the other early-flowering small hybrids in another alphabetical list as below.

### Small and Dwarf Hybrids in Colours other than Blue

\*\*\*\*\*\*'Brocade' ( ? × *williamsianum*) B. (5 ft. × 5 ft.) pink.
Handsome of leaf, in flower 'Brocade' is rather frilly and over-large for a plant of its character. It is useful, though, in a small garden where a free-flowering and pretty plant is wanted. Its carmine buds open to strawberry-pink flowers which fade to blush and are borne in trusses of nine or ten. With the vivid buds, strawberry-coloured newly-opened flowers and paler older ones, it has a pleasantly chintzy effect.

\*\*\*\*\**calostrotum* hybrid 'Rose' A. (5 ft. × 5 ft.) lavender-rose.
This hybrid does not seem ever to have been given a name. It occurs in various gardens and catalogues and, being raised from collected seed sent home by Farrer, is apparently a natural hybrid. It makes a quite large, mounded bush with close, twiggy growth and small leaves. Its flowers are salver-shaped like those of *calostrotum* but are slightly smaller than those of that species and are of a pale and quite pretty lavender-rose. It is not, however, as useful as 'Impeanum' listed below. The very dwarf *scintillans* × *calostrotum* hybrid 'Pink Drift' in its best pink-lavender form is also a more valuable plant.

## Hybrid Rhododendrons

\*\*\*\*\*\*\*'Cowslip' (*wardii* × *williamsianum*) B+. (4 ft. × 5 ft.) creamy-yellow.

This is a typical *williamsianum* hybrid with pretty, rounded leaves, a little larger than those of its parent. It makes a rounded, compact little plant with pink buds opening to loose clusters of the palest creamy-yellow bells. In cold gardens frost may sometimes cut the young growth but the plant seems to stand this and recover.

\*\*\*\*\*\*'Impeanum' F.C.C. (*impeditum* × *hanceanum*) A. (1 ft. × 2 ft. +) pale lilac.

A real rock-garden rhododendron of almost prostrate growth, 'Impeanum' has neat leaves and comparatively large trusses of pale lilac.

\*\*\*\*\*\*\*'Dormouse' ('Dawn's Delight' × *williamsianum*) B+. (4 ft. × 5 ft.) pink.

Larger than *williamsianum* with handsome, rounded leaves and with loose clusters of pretty, delicate pink bells, this is an attractive and characterful hybrid.

\*\*\*\*\*\*\*\*'Elizabeth' F.C.C. (*griersonianum* × *forrestii* var. *repens*) A. (4 ft. × 6 ft.) scarlet.

One of the best and hardiest of all small hybrids, 'Elizabeth' is the rhododendron *par excellence* for the modern small gardens of today. Shade from the hottest sun in the south and a soil without free lime are its only requirements. With good, dark-green leaves and a neat, compact habit, 'Elizabeth' makes a prosperous-looking, well-furnished shrub. Its comparatively large flowers are gloxinia-shaped and bright scarlet-red. It is not too large a plant for a big rock-garden but on a smaller—or to cascade down a peat or sandstone wall—its nearly prostrate clone 'Creeping Jenny' would be more suitable. Both are extremely free-flowering and often bear a few flowers in the autumn. The flowers of 'Creeping Jenny' are perhaps a little smaller than those of the type. It has proved itself hardy in many bleak and exposed situations all over the country.

\*\*\*\*\*\*\*\*'Ethel' F.C.C. ('F.C. Puddle' × *forrestii* var. *repens*) A. (1½ ft. × 2 ft.) scarlet.

Another of the splendid Bodnant dwarf reds, 'Ethel' is no less brilliant than 'Elizabeth'. Its flowers are of a similar intense

213

scarlet but in shape are more like those of *forrestii* var. *repens* although they have a double calyx. It is a very compact, neat plant and excellent for a peat-terrace or sandstone rock-garden.

\*\*\*\*\*\*'Fittra' A.M. (*dauricum* × *racemosum*) A. (3 ft. × 2 ft.) rose-pink.

A Hillier hybrid that is splendid for the larger rock-garden or planting of dwarf rhododendrons. Useful as any early dwarf it nevertheless lacks that touch of quality which would make one award it four stars.

\*\*\*\*\*\*\*\*'Little Ben' F.C.C. (*neriiflorum* × *forrestii* var. *repens*) A. (2 ft. × 4 ft.) scarlet.

Possibly a little less free in flower than 'Elizabeth' and 'Ethel', this is none the less an excellent dwarf and one that appeals very much to me, having something of its *neriiflorum* parent in the shape and poise of its brilliant scarlet flowers. Low and spreading it is a splendid plant for a bay among larger rhododendrons, or to place on a large rock-garden or at the foot of a peat-wall. It also looks well grouped in a community bed with other dwarfs. It is a very hardy, good-tempered plant.

\*\*\*\*\*'Little Bert' A.M.—the reverse cross with the taller form of *neriiflorum*, *euchaites* used instead of *neriiflorum* itself—is, as might be expected, less dwarf and its flowers are nearer crimson than scarlet. It, too, is a good plant although it has sometimes been accused of not being too free-flowering. Mr. Sigston Thompson writes that both are popular and succeed well at the Northern Horticultural Society's Gardens at Harlow Car.

\*\*\*\*\*\*\*'Moonstone' (*campylocarpom* × *Williamsianum*) B. (4ft. × 4 ft.) yellow.

Another of these fine *williamsianum* hybrids, 'Moonstone' makes a rounded, neat bush with the small, pretty leaves of *williamsianum* and bell-shaped flowers of soft yellow tinged with pink opening from orange-pink buds. Like most *williamsianum* hybrids it seems reliably hardy in most districts, the only danger to its well-being is the risk of frost or searing winds persistently cutting its young growth.

\*\*\*\*\*\*\*\*'Remo' (*valentinianum* × *lutescens*) B. (3 ft. × 4 ft.) yellow.

One would expect from its parentage that 'Remo' would be a

mild-area plant. Yet, with us in North Wales, 'Remo' was not touched by a frost that slightly cut back *lutescens* and even browned an odd leaf-tip or two of 'Yellow Hammer'. It withstood the severe and prolonged frosts of 1962 and 1963 without harm so I have no hesitation in rating it 'B'. It is a lovely little rhododendron with pointed, slightly hairy leaves of dark bronzy-green and clusters of bright-yellow flowers, deeper in colour than the best forms of *lutescens* and borne, of course, a month or more later.

*******'Rosy Bell' A.M. (*ciliatum* × *glaucophyllum*) B. (4 ft. × 4 ft.) blush.

Not an outstanding rhododendron but a pleasing and worthwhile plant of quiet charm. 'Rosy Bell' is a very old hybrid with glossy green small leaves and neat trusses of pretty blush-pink flowers with darker speckling.

********'Temple Belle' (*orbiculare* × *williamsianum*) A–B. (3 ft. × 5 ft.) rose-pink.

Mr. Sigston Thompson of Harlow Car writes to me that he has found this to be a very hardy rhododendron and his seems to be the general experience. Handsome in foliage with the larger rounded, matt-green leaves of *orbiculare* and with trusses of bell-shaped flowers in rich Persian-rose, it is a fine hybrid and one that fits admirably into the present-day, small garden picture. It should, however, be kept away, at all costs, from other pinks and preferably from reds. I think its best companion for pictorial effect are the deep 'blue' small-flowered rhododendrons of the 'Blue Diamond' type, the foliage and habit of which would offer a useful contrast.

*********'Yellow Hammer' (*sulfureum* × *flavidum*) A. (5 ft. × 3 ft.) yellow.

Four stars are given by me to this hybrid not only for the distinction of its little butter-yellow, brown-anthered bells but for its pretty, narrowly-oval, small leaves with their hint of bronze and for its pleasing habit—upright with an occasional arching spray of leaves and flowers. In our North Wales garden it was exposed to the strong and often bitterly cold winds that blow in winter from all quarters and the only damage it showed was an occasional brown leaf-tip. It is especially loved for its habit of flowering quite freely in November and again bearing a seemingly undiminished crop in spring.

## Mid to Late May-Flowering Hybrids (Large-Growing)

\*\*\*\*\*\*'Ascot Brilliant' (*thomsonii* × ?) A. (15 ft. +) red.

A good old 'hardy hybrid' of rounded growth and well-furnished with leaves that show some trace of its *thomsonii* descent. Its flower trusses are rich glowing crimson and it is exceptionally free-flowering. It is still well worth growing, especially where a substantial bush is needed to shelter smaller and more tender rhododendrons from the wind or in natural woodland where the soil is poor and where its vivid colouring will show to advantage amid the general greenery.

\*\*\*\*\*\*\*'Carita' A.M. ('Naomi' × *campylocarpum*) B+. (10 ft. × 8 ft.) cream, yellow and pink forms.

'Carita' is a hybrid that with me has proved capable of standing considerable exposure to wind. It is a pretty plant with rich-green, oval, shiny leaves but it is columnar and perhaps a little straggly in growth. In leaf it is excellent and in flower it is impossible to find any fault. Mushroom-pink buds open to a loose truss of purple-stalked bells of champagne-yellow tinged with pink at the petal edges.

There are also cream and pink forms of this hybrid. 'Carita Pink' seems to be smaller in growth and more compact with similar, beautifully-shaped flowers of soft lilac-pink.

\*\*\*\*\*\*\*\*'China'A.M.(*wightii*×*fortunei*)A.(8 ft. × 10 ft.)buff-ivory.

The result of a cross between two outstanding parents. 'China' is a good hybrid from the firm of Messrs. W. C. Slocock. To handsome leaves and a good, yet spreading, habit—which means that it must be given plenty of room—'China' adds the beauty of its large trusses of red-throated, buff-ivory flowers. There is an 'A' clone which is taller-growing. Both are quite easy plants to please.

\*\*\*\*\*'Cynthia' A. (15 ft. +).

Listed as rosy-crimson by the nurserymen, but I think

'magenta-puce' would be nearer a true description. 'Cynthia' is a hybrid of such glaring colouring that I would never plant it. Of undeniably vigorous and healthy growth, however, had I a large plant of it in the garden it would take a harder heart than mine to cut it down. In older gardens where it exists, it should be left as a shelter-plant. Only rhododendrons flowering at a different time, or those of creamy-yellow or ivory-buff (definitely *not* white) should be allowed within eye-shot.

*******'Goldfort' ('Goldsworth Yellow' × *fortunei*) A. (8 ft. × 8 ft.) pale yellow.

Unmarred by the leggy growth of 'Goldsworth Yellow' and having inherited the good leaves of *fortunei*, 'Goldfort' is a fine hybrid with creamy-yellow, apricot-tinted flowers opening from pink buds. It is hardy and vigorous.

********'Loderi' grex (*fortunei* × *griffithianum*) B. (10 ft. × 12 ft.) white or pale pink.

There are many varieties of this famous cross and all are good. A typical 'Loderi' has dull-surfaced, well-shaped, mid-green leaves furnishing a spreading yet shapely bush to the ground. The flower-trusses and individual flowers are enormous, yet full of quality and of good texture. All have a cool and delicious scent.

Among the most popular varieties are 'King George' (blush fading to white with a green eye), 'Sir Edmund' (blush-white), 'Fairyland' (frilly blush), 'Venus' (not-too-large soft pink), 'Sir Joseph Hooker' (pink), 'Helen' (soft pink), 'Pink Diamond' (not too large delicate pink), 'Julie' (white flushed sulphur-yellow).

'Loderi' is much hardier than one would expect and good reports have reached me of its behaviour in the exposed Harlow Car Gardens at Harrogate.

*****'Loder's White' (*arboreum album* × *griffithianum*) B+. (15 ft. +) pink, fading white.

This old hybrid is much hardier than its parentage might lead one to expect. It makes a well-furnished mound with good leaves and handsome trusses of beautifully-shaped pink flowers which take some time to fade to white.

*******'Mrs. A. T. de la Mare' A.M. ('Halopeanum' × 'Mrs. Charles Butler') A. (10 ft. × 10ft.) white.

Another attractive white of considerable hardiness and with a scent almost equal to that of 'Loderi', 'Mrs. A. T. de la Mare' has handsome rosettes of *fortunei*-type leaves and rose-pink buds opening widely to pure white flowers with a slight greeny blotch.

*********'Susan' F.C.C. (*campanulatum* × *fortunei*) A. (8 ft. × 10 ft.) lavender-blue.

The best, to date, of the large-flowered 'blues' of the elepidote section, 'Susan' has handsome foliage and a good habit as well as considerable flower charm. Rather bright mauve when opening, the flowers mercifully pass quickly from this shade to a cool lavender, spotted with browny-maroon. At this stage they are delightful. 'Susan' is a useful plant in woodland where one does not want 'to disturb the nightingales'—as the late Mr. A. T. Johnson used to say—by using rhododendrons of too bold a colour.

### Medium-Sized Mid to Late May-Flowering Hybrids

*********'Alison Johnstone' (*yunnanense* × *concatenans*) A–B. (7 ft. +) pale apricot.

With soft pinky-apricot, rather open, flowers in neat trusses, and glossy *concatenans*-type leaves, this is a really lovely hybrid with a 'modern' look. Particularly attractive are the prominent azalea-like stamens and stigma which lick out of the flower with a graceful curve. It is extremely compact, neat in habit and very hardy, doing well in a fairly open and not too-shaded position. One of the best hybrids to fill an important place in a small garden or to contrast with rhododendrons of a heavier type in a large one.

********'Blue Peter' F.C.C. A. (7 ft. × 8 ft.) 'blue'.

Good leaves and a hardy hybrid-shaped flower truss of fifteen widely funnel-shaped flowers that are slightly frilly at the petal edges make this a worthwhile plant. Officially described as 'cobalt violet' with an almost white throat and maroon spotting on the upper petal this is the nearest in colour-effect to 'Blue Diamond' to be found in the larger-flowered, non-scaly group of hybrids.

'Blue Peter' flowers towards the end of May.

Flowering earlier—at about the middle of the month—'Blue Ensign' A.M. is another good 'blue' hybrid that can be relied on to give a similar effect.

\*\*\*\*\*'Blue Danube' flowers concurrently with 'Blue Peter' and is good enough to plant in woodland. Lacking the lighter colouring at the throat, however, it is not so good in garden effect.

\*\*\*\*\*\*'Lady Grey Egerton' A. is another in this colour group and is a pretty rhododendron with rather frilly flowers of soft, pale lavender which need shade.

\*\*\*\*\*'Countess of Athlone' A. (8 ft. × 12 ft.) mauve pink.

Included here only for the cool lilac-pink to which its flowers, I thought crude on opening, quickly fade, this old hybrid is another healthy, hardy, well-furnished shrub for woodland planting where cool, smoky colours are needed.

\*\*\*\*\*\*\*'Day Dream' A.M. (*griersonianum* × 'Lady Bessborough') B+. (8 ft. × 12 ft.) rose-and-yellow.

A very fine plant with soft green, slightly hairy leaves and elegantly held, rather wide flowers which open rose and change to creamy-yellow with a rose eye, giving a delightful effect.

\*\*\*\*\*\*'Electra' A.M. (*augustinii* var. *chasmanthum* × *augustinii*) C—. (10 ft. × 6 ft.) 'blue'.

'Electra' is a truly lovely plant that is hopeless in the average garden. Smitten almost yearly by May frost in the Conway Valley, only the perfection of its very 'blue' butterfly-shaped flower ensured its place in the garden. In really mild gardens it is a delightful shrub with slender leaves, vigorous growth and great freedom of flower. To see it at its best it should be used to underplant the *Prunus* 'Shimidsu'—the last to bloom of the ornamental white-flowered cherries.

\*\*\*\*\*\*\*'Flashlight' (*callimorphum* × *campylocarpum*) B. (5 ft. × 9 ft.) apricot, changing to yellow.

This is a hybrid with a 'species' look and, as might be expected from its parentage, it is a lovely rhododendron with prettily rounded, rather small leaves and orange-pink buds opening to lemon yellow, apricot-tinged bells and passing to pale yellow with a scarlet flare. The flower trusses are of the firmly-held yet open-shaded type of its parents. It is a neat but somewhat spreading plant.

*******'Goblin' (pink form) flowers at this time with us—but see medium-sized, late-flowering hybrids, as the scarlet form blooms later.

*******'Idealist' A.M. ('Naomi' × *wardii*) A–B. (9 ft. × 10 ft.) yellow.

With *wardii*-type flowers of soft creamy-yellow contrasting with a purple-brown calyx, broad soft-green leaves and a neat rounded habit, this is a good rhododendron and very hardy.

********'Lady Bessborough' F.C.C. (*campylocarpum* × *discolor*) A–B. (7 ft. × 8 ft.) cream.

Another really hardy, easy-to-grow creamy-yellow, 'Lady Bessborough' has flowers of tremendous quality borne in large, firm yet lax trusses. Pinky-yellow in bud, when open the flower colour is cream with a dark-red eye. The leaves, too, are good and of the 'discolor' type. In North Wales it does well in full sun.

'Lady Bessborough' var. 'Roberte' F.C.C. is salmon-pink in bloom, the flowers becoming suffused with straw-yellow as they age.

******'Letty Edwards' F.C.C. (*campylocarpum* × *fortunei*) A. (7 ft. × 8 ft.) cream.

There are so many good cream and pale-yellow coloured rhododendrons that it is difficult to choose between them. 'Letty Edwards' however is perhaps not quite as good in the truss as 'Lady Bessborough'. It is nevertheless a fine hybrid and one that is easy to grow in almost any garden.

*******'May Day' A.M. (*griersonianum* × *haematodes*) A. (5 ft. × 7 ft.) scarlet.

A very good hybrid—probably the best moderate-sized, completely hardy, red for the average garden. The foliage, too, is good, dark-green with a brown indumentum beneath. The truss is loose, composed of about eight bright-scarlet flowers.

*******'Margaret Dunn' A.M. (*discolor* × 'Fabia') A. (5 ft. × 7 ft.) salmon and yellow.

The A.M. form of this hybrid flowers now, in late May, but

there are later-blooming forms, notably one sold by Sunningdale, which flowers in July and is very useful at that season.

'Margaret Dunn' makes a compact bush with trusses of widely opened, salmon-pink and yellow bells.

\*\*\*\*\*\*\*'Winsome' A.M. (*griersonianum* × 'Humming Bird') B. (5 ft. × 6 ft.) rose.

A neat, handsome plant of compact growth, 'Winsome' has rich-rose, bell-shaped flowers borne in loose and graceful trusses. Very free in flower, after the blooms are over the young growth is coppery-bronze.

\*\*\*\*\*'Yvonne' grex. A group of lovely pearly-white flowered hybrids like small forms of 'Loderi' in type but too tender for many gardens.

## Mid to Late May-Flowering Hybrids (Small or very Lightly Built)

\*\*\*\*\*\*\*'Bow Bells' A.M. ('Corona' × *williamsianum*) A. (4 ft. × 4 ft.) pink.

Nearly all *williamsianum* hybrids are good and 'Bow Bells' is no exception. It has the pretty leaves and coppery young growth of its distinguished parent along with neat trusses of soft salmon-pink bells opening from rose-red buds.

\*\*\*\*\*\*\*'Carmen' A.M. (*didymum* × *forestii* var. *repens*) A. (1½ ft. × 3 ft.) ruby.

The species *forestii* var. *repens* is another fine parent and 'Carmen' is a worthy offspring. Low and neat in growth with glossy dark-green leaves and three-flowered trusses of waxy, deep ruby-red *repens*-shaped flowers, 'Carmen' is essentially a plant for a wall or high bank where its bells may be seen nearer eye-level. It should always be placed where they will catch the sun.

\*\*\*\*\*\*\*\*'Humming Bird' F.C.C. (*haematodes* × *williamsianum*) A–B. (3 ft. × 5 ft.) crimson-pink.

'Humming Bird' has even better foliage than most of the other *williamsianum* hybrids—dark green and substantial with a moderate indumentum, and beautifully rounded with red-tan petioles. The flower-bud scales, too, are reddish-tan and the flowers when open are a bright crimson-pink, waxen in texture, quite large, bell-shaped and carried in a lax cluster. I am told that it has proved very hardy at Harlow Car.

\*\*\*\*\*\*\*'Oreocinn' (*cinnabarinum* × *oreotrephes*) A. (5 ft. × 3 ft.) apricot.

When crossed, the Cinnabarinum and Triflorum series usually produce particularly charming offspring and 'Oreocinn' is no exception with soft-apricot Triflorum-shaped flowers and neat glaucous leaves. It is a lightly built, twiggy shrub, suitable for the large rock-garden or to be planted near a path in open wood-land.

\*\*–\*\*\*\*\*\*\*\*'Yunncinn' (*cinnabarinum* × *yunnanense*) A. (5 ft. × 3 ft.) lilac to rhodamine purple.

This hybrid has been made several times and the form and colour vary from the suberb Bodnant clone \*\*\*\*'Youthful Sin' with *yunnanense*-shaped flowers of a luscious rhodamine purple to the more tubular-flowered Sunningdale clone which is lilac-pink in colour. Neat and slender in growth with narrow, blue-green leaves, it is always an attractive plant and is very hardy.

## Late-Flowering Hybrids (June), Large Growing

\*\*\*\*\*\*\*'Albatross' A.M. ('Loderi' × *discolor*) B+. (12 ft. +) white.

A fine and very hardy member of the lovely group of tall, scented, late-flowering hybrids. 'Albatross' has good leaves of soft rich-green and flat-topped trusses of crystalline white flowers opening from pink buds. Green spotting and a green flush at the throat enhance its beauty. Very fragrant. There are several clones and all are lovely.

\*\*\*\*\*\*'Anglo' F.C.C. (*griffithianum* × *discolor*) C. (18 ft. +) white.

Not as hardy as 'Albatross' and an even bigger plant with huge trusses of pure-white flowers and a heavier scent. The clone 'Solent Queen' has a slight dark eye and is flushed pink at the petal margins with a central ray of green.

\*\*\*\*\*\*\*'Avocet' (*discolor* × *fortunei*) A. (15 ft. +) blush.

This, I think, is the hardiest of the group. We grow it in an exposed, east-facing position and it is quite happy. During bitter weather it rolls and hangs its leaves, looking as miserable as we all perhaps feel, but as soon as the wind changes to the south-west bringing warmth and moisture back to the air its leaves open and lift again, completely undamaged. Catalogues often refer to 'Avocet' as white but it is in fact blush with slightly frilly flowers of good substance and with a crystalline quality and a delightful scent. It is suitable for any garden but deserves a little wind-shelter and shade.

*******'Pilgrim' A.M. (*fortunei* × 'Gill's Triumph') B. (12 ft. +). pink.

Another of these beautiful, June-flowering fragrant hybrids, 'Pilgrim' has huge 'Loderi'-like trusses of soft rose. It has not, perhaps, so much scent as some of the others but is particularly notable as being with *yakushimanum* a parent of the compact-growing 'Lady Bowes Lyon' A.M., a lovely pinky-white fore-runner of the race of very hardy *yakushimanum* hybrids that it is hoped will find a place in the small gardens of today.

********'Lodauric' ('Loderi' × *auriculatum*) B. (12 ft. +) white.

'Iceberg' A.M. is a good clone of this cross with long, hand-some leaves and large trusses of green-centred, white, sweetly fragrant flowers. Later than the others, it flowers at the end of June and so makes possible a succession of these cool, fragrant, beautiful shrubs which give such pleasure in woodland and gardens large enough to accommodate them.

## Late-Flowering Hybrids (June), Medium-Sized

********'Fabia' grex (*dichroanthum* × *griersonianum*) A. (5–7 ft. × 7 ft.) shades of orange.

'Fabia' is the umbrella-name of the cross and includes some of the very best modern hybrids of moderate size.

Of the clones 'Exbury' is the tallest, making a compact plant of up to seven feet with typical sage-green leaves and lax trusses of orange-pink bells. 'Tangerine' A.M. has a slight double calyx and flowers of bright terra-cotta, flushed with crimson at the petal-tips. 'Tower Court' is the smallest grower with dark leaves and soft orange-pink flowers. 'Roman Pottery' has lighter leaves of sage-green with fine fawn indumentum beneath and most graceful trusses of soft warm-apricot flowers.

*******'Fastuosum Flore Pleno' A.G.M. A. (10 ft. +) Lavender blue.

An old hybrid with slightly double flowers that while muddling the individual bloom do not spoil the effect of the bush. Good dark-green, matt leaves and a splendid habit. One of the best large-flowered 'blues' and invaluable in woodland.

*****'Flamingo' (*griersonianum* × 'Loder's White') C. (7 ft. × 7 ft.) rose.

A useful plant for milder gardens with shapely trusses of rich-rose flowers.

******'Goblin' A.M. ('Break of Day' × *griersonianum*) B. (4½ ft. × 5 ft.) red and pink forms.

The soft-salmon form which I grow is not the Award of Merit form although it is an excellent plant. With us it flowers in mid-May and that is why I have listed it in that section, referring the reader to this page for the description. It is in commerce and is attractive with loose trusses of soft, luminous salmon-pink bells tinged with rich-salmon. In growth it is neat and compact with quite large *griersonianum*-type soft-green leaves.

The A.M. form is similar in growth, making a neat, low bush but has rather darker leaves and vivid orange-red flowers in similarly loose trusses.

'Goblin' does not like wind and the flowers keep their beauty longer in semi-shade.

*******'Golden Horn' A.M. (*dichroanthum* × *elliottii*) A–B. (5 ft. × 5 ft.) orange.

Another neat, compact grower, hardier than 'Goblin', with sage-green leaves and lax, flat-topped trusses of rich-salmon, orange-shaded, flowers spotted with brown and with double calyces. The colour of the flower, in garden effect, is orange. The clone 'Persimmon' is not double-calyxed and has rich-red, very waxy flowers.

********'Halcyone' ('Lady Bessborough' × *souliei*) B. (7 ft. × 7 ft.) cream.

Very useful as a late-flowering cream, 'Halcyone' has the attractive, open, shallow cup-shaped flowers of *souliei* carried in rounded trusses and cream in colour with a slight pinky-brown blotch. The leaves, too, are of the *souliei* type, oval and neat. The clone 'Perdita' A.M. has the same lovely flowers, pink in colour with a purple throat.

********'Hawk' ('Lady Bessborough' × *wardii*) A. (7 ft. × 7 ft.) yellow.

'Hawk' is the grex name of a family of very hardy, compact, beautiful hybrids in shades of true bright-yellow. They do not flower freely for the first few years but once mature are reliable and consistent flowerers. They are among the best of the really hardy yellow hybrids and are useful to prolong the season and contrast with late reds such as 'Persimmon' and 'Goblin' A.M. The original 'Hawk' A.M. is daffodil-yellow in flower colour with a slight red eye. The cross was made twice and perhaps the best clones are from the second cross and include:

'Crest', perhaps the finest clone, and a clear, vivid yellow.

'Jervis Bay' A.M. is taller-growing with large bright-yellow flowers and a bright scarlet eye.

******'Jalisco' ('Dido' × 'Lady Bessborough') A. (9 ft. × 7 ft.) pale yellow.

Another splendid late yellow. The flowers are waxy and large, straw-yellow in colour with a darker eye. It is, however, apt to be a little leggy and straggly in growth.

********'Lady Chamberlain' (*cinnabarinum* var. *roylei* × 'Royal Flush'—orange form) B+. (7 ft. × 5 ft.) Orange, yellow and salmon shades.

The grex name of another large family, all the members of which have the lovely glaucous or blue-green leaves of the Cinnabarinum series and dangling lapageria-like bells. They are all surprisingly hardy and Mr. Sigston Thompson reports that they stand up extremely well to exposed conditions in the Northern Horticultural Society's gardens at Harlow Car, Harrogate.

The F.C.C. form is flushed rich-orange and pink on a yellow ground.

'Gleam' is more pink and touched with more vivid colour at the petal tips.

The 'Exbury' form is predominantly orange.

'Golden Queen' F.C.C. is a deep golden-yellow marked with red.

'Salmon Trout' is the colour of a salmon trout, ready to eat.

*********'Lady Rosebery' (*cinnabarinum* var. *roylei* × 'Royal Flush'—pink form) B+. (7 ft. × 5 ft.) pink.

Similarly hardy and beautiful with glistening rose-pink bells.

'Pink Beauty' is white with a deep margin of rose at the edge.

'Pink Delight' is a fine pink form.

*******'Mahomet' A.M. (*dichroanthum* × 'Tally Ho') A–B. (7 ft. × 7 ft.) orange.

A deeper-coloured 'Golden Horn' with a heavier double calyx. This hybrid is good enough but not exciting. It is certainly not nearly as beautiful as 'Tally Ho'.

******'Purple Splendour' A.M. (*ponticum* × ?) A. (8 ft. × 6 ft.) purple.

Flowers of very rich, deep purple which one either likes or does not. It has its place amid greenery in woodlands or large gardens where it may be lightened by yellows such as 'Hawk' or 'Goldfort'.

Some people prefer the larger-growing and slightly later 'Royal Purple', the darkness of which is offset by a yellowish eye. This hybrid, however, is ugly in growth when young but improves with time to form a large, quite tidy mound of dark, pointed leaves.

******'Rosy Morn' A.M. ('Loderi' × *souliei*) B+. (7 ft. × 7 ft.) pink.

This is a pretty hybrid from Sunningdale with the perfect *souliei*-type of flower opening from rich-pink buds to pale salmon-pink with a darker eye rather similar to the 'Halcyone' clone 'Perdita'.

*********'Tally Ho' F.C.C. (*eriogynum* × *griersonianum*) B+. (8 ft. × 12 ft.) scarlet.

This is the *griersonianum* hybrid which seems to have inherited more of the authentic soft geranium-scarlet of its parent than any other. The flowers are the shape of *griersonianum* too, but borne in a better truss and the soft, dark-green leaves and well-furnished, spreading but neat habit are a great improvement upon the narrower leaves and thinner, more straggly habit of the parent.

'Tally Ho' has sometimes been listed as 'D' but it is definitely hardier than this and has survived below zero frosts in a frost-hollow at Bulkeley Mill for many years with absolutely no harm.

## Large Hybrids (July and August Flowering)

******'Aladdin' A.M. (*griersonianum* × *auriculatum*) B.
 (18 ft. +) rose.

Unique in its group for its colour. 'Aladdin' needs shelter and some shade because of its size and lateness in flowering. A fine plant for a woodland glade with large, flat-topped trusses of scented rose flowers with a deeper throat.

******'Azor' A.M. (*griersonianum* × *discolor*) A. (10 ft. × 8 ft.)
 pink.

Good, but not as good in colour as the more compact 'Vanessa'. There is a slight bluey tinge in the pink of the well-shaped flowers. Nevertheless 'Azor' is a useful plant. It is thrifty in poor woodland soil and very hardy.

*******'Bonito' A.M. (*discolor* × 'Luscombei') A–B. (15 ft. +)
 pink.

Completely hardy, 'Bonito' needs semi-shade only to protect its flowers from the July sun. Rather open in habit, it makes a large bush with bold, grey-green foliage and immense trusses of sweetly fragrant, soft rose-pink flowers. For me the rhododendron season can never be too long and I like especially these large late-flowering varieties with their delectable scent.

******'Bustard' (*auriculatum* × 'Penjerrick') B. (18 ft. +) cream.

Another large grower with handsome dull-green leaves and big trusses of dark-eyed creamy flowers.

*******'Grenadier' F.C.C. (*elliottii* × 'Moser's Maroon') B.
 (15 ft. +) red.

One of Mr. Lionel de Rothschild's fine late reds, 'Grenadier' quickly grows to tree-like size. With large dark-green leaves and great rounded trusses of waxy, rich-red, black-throated flowers it is a splendid July-flowering rhododendron for a large garden or for woodland.

\*\*\*\*\*\*\*\*'Polar Bear' F.C.C. (*auriculatum* × *diaprepes*) B.
    (25 ft. +) white.

Flowering into August, 'Polar Bear' is one of the latest and loveliest rhododendrons with handsome leaves and large trusses of *auriculatum*-type flowers with a yellow eye. A delicious scent is one of 'Polar Bear's' great attractions and like that of *auriculatum*, the scent has great carrying qualities and will pervade a whole area of woodland.

## July and August Medium-Growing Hybrids

\*\*\*\*\*\*'Beau Brummell' A.M. ('Essex Scarlet' × *eriogynum*) B.
    (5 ft. × 5 ft.) scarlet.

A good, moderately-sized, late red with round trusses of brilliant scarlet flowers, spotted with black. 'Beau Brummell' is a useful plant for the smaller garden.

\*\*\*\*\*\*'Coromandel' ('Roberte' × 'Vanessa') A. (5 ft. × 5 ft.)
    pale yellow.

Not quite of the quality of either parent, 'Coromandel' is nevertheless a useful garden plant, flowering at a season when its cool creamy-yellow blooms will be appreciated. At its best against a green background 'Coromandel' has quite large trusses of wide, shallow bells slightly frilled and spotted with red.

\*\*\*\*\*\*\*'Grosclaude' A.M. (*eriogynum* × *haematodes*) B+. (7 ft.
    × 7 ft.) red.

One of the best late reds, 'Grosclaude' is neat and compact with rich dark-green foliage with orange-indumentum beneath and loose but elegant flat trusses of unspotted scarlet bells. It will stand full sun although the flowers undoubtedly last better in some shade.

\*\*\*\*\*\*\*'Iviza' ('Bustard' × 'Fabia') B. (5 ft. × 5 ft.) yellow.

This is a hybrid that I like for the deep golden-yellow of its waxy, long-tubed flowers—a colour that is uncommon in rhododendrons at this season. 'Iviza' makes a neat, compact plant with attractive obovate glossy leaves.

'Philomel' is a clonal form with more pink in its colouring, giving an almost apricot effect.

\*\*\*\*\*\*\*'Margaret Dunn' A. (5 ft. × 7 ft.).
See Medium-sized mid to late May-flowering Hybrids.

\*\*\*\*\*\*\*'Romany Chai' A.M. ('Moser's Maroon' × *griersonianum*) B+. (8 ft. × 8 ft.) red.

In colour this hybrid is good, but not to my mind as good as 'Tally Ho'—nor do I think it as distinctive in flower-shape. It bears conventional trusses of up to fifteen flowers that are rosy-scarlet in colour, deepening at the throat and spotted with black on the upper petal. It is more reliable than 'Tally Ho' for cold midland gardens and its rather leggy habit improves as it gets older.

\*\*\*\*\*\*\*'Romany Chal' F.C.C. (*eriogynum* × 'Moser's Maroon') B–C. (12 ft. +) red.

Less hardy than 'Romany Chai', 'Romany Chal' is better in foliage and habit and deserves its F.C.C. with its large trusses of waxy blood-red flowers faintly spotted with brown.

\*\*\*\*\*\*\*\*'Vanessa' F.C.C. (*griersonianum* × 'Soulbut') A–B. (6 ft. × 7 ft.) pink.

This is probably the best of the late-flowering pink hybrids and should succeed in almost any garden where there is some shade for its open trusses of rich salmon-pink, crimson-eyed flowers. Its foliage, too, is good—of a rich, dark green and where there is room it is worth growing also the clone known as 'Pastel' for its rather different flower colour—pink on a yellow ground, becoming more yellow as the flower ages and giving an almost biscuit effect similar to that of some forms of the earlier-blooming 'Naomi'.

\*\*\*\*\*\*\*\*'Vesuvius' (*griersonianum* × 'Romany Chal') B+. (5 ft. × 5 ft.) red.

A Sunningdale hybrid that should be much more widely grown. 'Vesuvius' is similar to 'Tally Ho' in its superb, unspotted geranium-red flowers borne in a good yet not-too-tight truss. Being hardier than 'Tally Ho' it will thrive in gardens where growing that hybrid might be a risk.

## July-August Dwarf Hybrids

*****'Arthur Osborn' A.M. (*didymum* × *griersonianum*) C. (3 ft. × 3 ft.) red.

Rather dark in colour, this hybrid needs to be planted where the light will strike it. The foliage is neat, dark and shining, the habit good and the flower trusses compact deep-red. It is apt to be damaged by May frosts.

******'Lava Flow' (*repens*? × *griersonianum*) B–C. (2 ft. × 2 ft.) scarlet.

More vivid in colour than 'Arthur Osborn', 'Lava Flow' is much smaller in growth. Compact with dark-green, pointed leaves and quite large trusses of well-opened, bright-scarlet flowers spotted with crimson, it is the July-flowering equivalent of 'Elizabeth' but it seems to be less hardy. This may be due to the fact pointed out by Mr. James Russell of Sunningdale Nurseries, where the plant was raised, that the parent K.W.13225 referred to in the *Rhododendron Handbook* as *forrestii* var. *repens* seems nearer to *didymum* (which is very susceptible to spring frosts) but with bright scarlet flowers instead of the usual dark, blood-red. In fact, I am sure that Mr. Russell is right and that the parent was *didymum* as indicated by its very late flowering habit.

## Tender Hybrids

Hardy only in favoured gardens in Cornwall, western Scotland and Ireland or as wall plants in mild gardens elsewhere. Needing cold-house or conservatory conditions over the rest of the country.

***'Countess of Haddington' F.C.C. (*ciliatum* × *dalhousiae*) E. Pale pink. Early May.

With bright-green, hairy-margined leaves and neat trusses of large, long-tubed warm blush-pink flowers this is a most attractive plant. It is sweetly scented.

***'Fragrantissimum' F.C.C. (*edgworthii* × *formosum*) E. White. May.

If one has room for only one tender rhododendron against a

Hybrid Rhododendrons

wall or in a small greenhouse or conservatory, this is the one to choose. The large flowers open from pink-tinged buds to white flowers with a pale yellow flush at the throat. The scent is particularly strong and sweet.

****'Lady Alice Fitzwilliam' F.C.C. E. May. Blush.

Less leggy than most tender hybrids, 'Lady Alice' is an excellent plant for a sheltered warm garden in the milder counties and is a compact plant, too, for a large pot. Its flowers are blush-pink with a deeper pink stripe and its scent is delightful.

***'Princess Alice' F.C.C. (*ciliatum* × *edgworthii*) E. Early May. White.

More straggly but with good dark leaves and long tubed flowers that are pink-striped in bud but open to pure white with a slightly yellow eye. This hybrid is particularly free flowering and very sweetly scented.

****'Royal Flush' (*cinnabarinum* × *maddenii*) D. May. Yellow or pink.

Well known in its different forms as the parent of 'Lady Chamberlain' and 'Lady Rosebery' this is even more beautiful than its offspring and, unfortunately, more tender. The 'Orange' form has trusses of slightly scented, waxy tubular flowers that are more apricot than orange in effect, being champagne colour flushed with pink and fading to pale yellow. The 'Pink' form has wider-open, shorter flowers of deep, glistening rose-crimson.

****'Tyermannii' F.C.C. (*formosum* × *nuttallii*) E. June. White.

This is a magnificent hybrid growing more strongly than the others and so, unfortunately, becoming too big for the small greenhouse. With handsome bark, large glossy leaves and loose trusses of large, lily-like flowers, golden-throated and tinged on the outside with green and brown and fading to pure white, 'Tyermannii' is a beautiful plant. Its scent is strong and sweet.

***'White Wings' A.M. (*bullatum* × *ciliicalyx*) E. May. White.

'White Wings' is a good, small-growing, scented hybrid with the interesting corrugated leaves of *bullatum* and good trusses of four or five large, wide-open flowers with a yellow eye.

# Hybrid Rhododendrons

## Six Reliable Winter and Very-early Spring Flowering Hybrids

'Nobleanum', and varieties in crimson, pink and white.
'Jacksonii', pink with a deeper stripe.
'Praecox', lilac.
'Emasculum', to succeed 'Praecox', lilac.
'Racil', apple-blossom.
'Cilpinense', larger-flowered pink and white.

## Twelve Pretty and Very Hardy Hybrids for the Average Garden

'Emasculum', early, lilac.
'Yellow Hammer', yellow, April–May.
'Blue Diamond', to group with 'Yellow Hammer'.
'Elizabeth', small, large-flowered scarlet, April–May.
'Unique', compact, buff-yellow up to eight feet, mid-May.
'Susan', best medium-sized 'blue', good leaves, mid-May.
'Alison Johnstone', extremely pretty apricot, mid-May.
'Naomi', lilac and buff, slightly scented, compact, late May.
'May Day', fine scarlet, mid-May.
'Fabia', June flowering, orange-salmon or apricot.
'Hawk', best late yellow.
'Vesuvius', hardy, late scarlet.

## Twelve Tall Hybrids for Woodland, or Large Gardens with Shelter

'Shilsonii', hardiest of the early scarlets.
'Dr. Stocker', milky-white, April–May.
'Cornish Cross', slightly tender, large-flowered, distinctive, strawberry-pink.
'Penjerrick', early May, cream or pink.
'Sir Charles Lemon', handsome leaves, creamy flower, early May.
'Loderi', large-flowered, scented white or blush, mid-May.
'Carita', tall, champagne yellow *campylocarpum* hybrid, May.
'Avocet', very hardy, sweetly-scented blush, June.
'Lodauric Iceberg', cool, greeny-white, fragrant, June.
'Bonito', July, rose-pink, scented.
'Grenadier', superb late scarlet.
'Polar Bear', August-flowering, very fragrant white.

# Hybrid Rhododendrons

## Twelve Outstanding Reasonably Hardy Hybrids

'Joanita', yellow *lacteum* hybrid, early May.

'Mariloo', *wightii* hybrid, yellow, handsome foliage, early May.

*thomsonii* × *orbiculare*, tall, fine leaves, cherry-rose bells, May.

'Moonstone', extremely pretty cream and pink *williamsianum* hybrid, May.

'China', excellent leaves and good habit, buff-ivory, May.

'Loderi' clone 'Venus', a 'Loderi' with a more refined truss of soft-pink flowers, May.

'Lady Bessborough' clone 'Roberte', pink-and-buff flowers of great quality, late May.

'Humming Bird', extremely good foliage and cherry-crimson bells, mid-May.

'Fabia' clone 'Roman Pottery', good leaves felted with buff and with dangling apricot bells, June.

'Lady Chamberlain', wonderful salmon-orange, blue-green leaves, lapageria bells, June.

'Lady Rosebery', virtually a pink 'Lady Chamberlain', June.

'Grosclaude', fine late red with excellent foliage.

## Eight Beautiful Hybrids for Mild Gardens

'Cornubia', very early scarlet.

'Barclayi', magnificent April-flowering scarlet.

'Cornish Cross', strawberry-pink, good habit, May.

'Remo', small-leaved, medium-growing bright yellow, May.

'Electra', *augustinii*-like 'blue', mid-May.

'Angelo', white, scented, June.

'Flamingo', rose-pink, moderate-size, June.

'Tally Ho', geranium-scarlet, June.

## Twelve Hybrids for the Larger Rock-Garden

'Bric-a-Brac', early, apple-blossom.

'Tessa', 'Praecox' hybrid, lilac-pink to pink.

'Crossbill', *spinuliferum* hybrid with bright yellow and apricot tubular flowers.

'Fine Feathers', attractive early, slender-growing pale lemon.
'Intrifast', small 'blue' hybrid.
'Sapphire', larger than 'Intrifast' but neat and compact.
'Creeping Jenny', prostrate with large scarlet flowers.
'Temple Belle', rose-pink *orbiculare* bells and rounded leaves.
'Yellow Hammer', little yellow bells.
'Bow Bells', pretty pink *williamsianum* hybrid.
'Oreocinn', tall, slender apricot.
'Lava Flow', July flowering, low growing, scarlet.

The Colour Lists below are planned to include only reasonably easy hybrids.

*Six Good Reds for the Average Garden*

'Elizabeth'
'May Day'
'Matador'
'Ibex'
'Persimmon' 'Golden Horn' clone
'Vesuvius', late

*Six Good Pinks for the Average Garden*

'Naomi'
'Bow Bells'
'Temple Belle'
'Vanessa'
'Winsome'
'Lady Rosebery' (given light wind-shelter)

*Six Good Yellows for the Average Garden*

'Unique'
'Lady Bessborough'
'Hawk'
'Letty Edwards'
'Iviza'
'Goldfort'

# Hybrid Rhododendrons

*Three Good Whites for the Average Garden*

'Dr. Stocker' (not for frost pockets)
'Mrs. A. T. de la Mare'
'Albatross' (some wind shelter needed)

*Six Good Blues for the Average Garden*

'Augfast'
'Blue Diamond'  } small-leaved hybrids
'Sapphire'

'Susan'
'Blue Peter'  } hardy hybrid types
'Fastuosum Flore Pleno'

## Hybrids to watch for

Not yet available in commerce some of the new *yakushimanum* hybrids such as the apple-blossom 'Lady Bowes Lyon' ('Pilgrim' × *yakushimanum*) and the more rosy 'Renoir' ('Pauline' × *yakushimanum*) should prove splendid hardy plants for the smaller garden. With good foliage they make neat and floriferous mounds not exceeding three feet in height.

Also promising are some other new, Wisley-raised, hybrids— the yellow 'Moonshine' ('Adriaan Koster' × *litiense*) A.M. (in its various clonal forms 'Bright', 'Supreme', 'Crescent', etc.) which is very hardy and a fine yellow; 'Degas' (*elliottii* × *haematodes*) a fairly hardy, currant-red with a rather flat truss; 'Rosenkavalier' (*eriogynum* × 'Tally Ho') with round trusses of many scarlet flowers and 'Beefeater' (*elliottii* × 'Fusilier') A.M., with a large, rounded but flat-topped truss of about twenty-six rather small flowers of geranium-scarlet.

The R.H.S. gardens at Wisley have pioneered also the hybridizing of the compact but rather early-flowering yellow *chrysanthum* (like *yakushimanum*, a species of the Ponticum series) with later-blooming yellows in the hope of producing a race of deeper-coloured, hardy yellows with the excellent dwarf habit of *chrysanthum* but which should be easier to grow than this species.

## Hybrid Rhododendrons

One might mention, too, the *yakushimanum* × 'Fabia Tangerine' clones which appear very promising at Messrs. John Waterer, Sons and Crisp of Bagshot.

### Hybrids for Other Countries

In the most climatically favoured areas of the United States where the summer heat is tempered by moisture and the winters are mild—the San Francisco, coastal California and the Portland–Seattle area—most hybrids which succeed in British gardens can be grown. The next most favoured districts would seem to be the Washington and Maryland area and here Mr. David Leach in his monumental *Rhododendrons of the World* mentions that hybrids of the tough 'Britannia', 'Lady Eleanor Cathcart', 'Sappho', etc., succeed along with modern hybrids in which the blood of such tough species as *discolor*, *fortunei*, *dichroanthum* predominates, particularly the 'Naomi' and 'Azor' group and the *wightii* × *fortunei* hybrid 'China'.

The New York–Philadelphia area has more severe winters but even here 'Azor', 'Goldsworth Yellow', the 'Naomi' group and 'Nereid' succeed along with the older sorts.

For still more severe climates 'Doncaster', 'Countess of Athlone', 'Caucasicum Album', 'Nobleanum Venustum' and 'Old Port' are recommended along with some of Joseph Gable's scaly-leaved hybrids—specially bred to resist the cold—and the Dexter hybrids which the late C. O. Dexter raised at Cape Cod.

In the coldest regions of all, the old *catawbiense* hybrids prove the most reliable while in the drier, hotter areas of the south of the United States where sun-scorch is a problem, the hybrids of the native *carolinianum* offer the best chance of success.

In Europe, in Germany, at Linswege, between the Weser and the Ems, which at times experience very low temperatures when the cold east winds sweep from Scandinavia, Herr Dietrich Hobbie has raised several new sets of hybrids which have become popular in many extremely cold areas in Sweden, Finland and other European countries which have severe winter climates. As parents, Herr Hobbie has used *wardii, forrestii* var. *repens, haematodes, dichroanthum, souliei, discolor, williamsianum* and *chrysanthum*. Particularly successful are *wardii* × *discolor* (which we in Britain grow under the 'Inamorata' grex). 'Britannia' × *williamsianum,* 'Doncaster' × *williamsianum, discolor* × *williamsianum,* ('Cunningham's Sulphur' × *wightii*) × *williamsianum,* 'Britannia' × *forrestii* var. *repens* and 'Essex Scarlet' × *forrestii* var. *repens*. Some of these, frequently surviving temperatures of −20 degrees Centigrade, will surely answer those in the much milder British Isles who persist in the belief that few but the old *catawbiense* hybrid group are reliably hardy.

A selection of the Linswege hybrids was established at the Benmore Botanic Gardens in Argyll.\* I wish that propagating material from there might be made available to the more enterprising of our nurserymen so that these very tough and attractive clones might eventually become commercially available in this country and so join the good number of better hybrids and species which can be relied on in exposed and unpromising positions.

New Zealand is an area of the world which has no native rhododendrons, yet in many parts rhododendrons and azaleas do well and there are now a number of extremely keen growers of these lovely shrubs. On the whole the climate of the North Island is rather hot for rhododendrons. There they do well only near to the mountains and in the high country which, of course, is cooler and has more moisture in the air. At Pukeiti on the edge of the Mount Egmont range a band of enthusiasts have formed the Pukeiti Rhododendron Trust and planted out a trial ground.

Parts of South Island suit the genus very well—but the east coast from East Cape to Oamaru is too dry. While north of East Cape—from East Cape to North Cape—it is too hot. However, even in that area there are certain cooler, moister spots where rhododendrons do well. South of Oamaru, on the east and west of the Southern Alps the rainfall is adequate and the soil just

---

\* A few of these hybrids are now filtering into this country and one or two clones may be obtained from Messrs. Cox of Glendoick and from Frampton Plants Ltd.

right and there rhododendrons thrive. In this area the Exbury azaleas are popular along with the New Zealand raised Ilam strain which were raised by Mr. Edgar Stead from seed given him by Mr. Lionel de Rothschild.

Mr. Stead also hybridized the evergreen rhododendrons, and his hybrids, through the New Zealand Rhododendron Association, have been fairly widely distributed through the island as have those of Mr. L. E. Jury whose *griersonianum* hybrids are particularly noteworthy. Some which would be welcome in Britain are the deeper-pink forms of 'Loderi', 'Ilam Orange' and 'Ilam Apricot', both of which, carrying a large share of *dichroanthum* blood, should be hardy in this country. Also promising is the 'Scarlet King' grex raised from (Ilam *arboreum* × *griffithianum*) and ('Ilam Alarm' × *griersonianum*).

In favoured New Zealand climates the choice of rhododendrons that will do well is as wide as in Cornwall and coastal California. In the drier, hotter parts, the more sun-and-drought-resistant hybrids must be selected.

Azaleas of the dwarf evergreen type, especially, do well in South Africa in the province of Natal where the high atmospheric humidity offsets the summer heat. For instance in Pietermaritzburg, where November to February temperatures may reach 112 degrees Fahrenheit, one sees fine specimens four feet or more in height and as much in width. Hybrids of *malvatica* seem particularly to be grown, along with some of the older mollis hybrids. A visit to Natal in early September is worth while for these azaleas alone and there is no doubt that hybrids and varieties of *R. indicum* would also do well as most probably would the large-leaved rhododendron species and hybrids such as *R. sinogrande, falconeri, hodgsonii, rex, macabeanum* and *giganteum* which like a moist, peaty soil and high rainfall. They should however be grown in shade, particularly in the hotter areas. The often difficult *R. lacteum*, also, should be worth trying along with *griffithianum, auriculatum, barbatum* and hybrids such as 'Polar Bear'.

My husband and I visited South Africa, by Union-Castle mailship, in early September 1971 and found the wild flowers of Natal and the Cape, as well as the azaleas, most worth while.

# CHAPTER 17

# Azalea Species and Hybrids

⫸⫸⫸⫸⫸⫸⫸⫸⫸⫸⫸⫸⫷⫷⫷⫷⫷⫷⫷⫷⫷⫷⫷⫷⫷

Generally speaking the azaleas are less fussy as to soil than are many rhododendrons. They will also stand more wind. With the exception of some of the dwarf evergreen sections they are extremely hardy. Often brilliantly coloured and with interesting leaf patterns they are valuable in building up the garden scene. Moreover, the deciduous species and hybrids usually colour brilliantly in autumn and may therefore be counted dual-purpose shrubs. The evergreen azaleas on the other hand form valuable ground cover and some of their leaves in winter often assume colourful tints of crimson, scarlet and bronze which contrast well with the fresh-apple green that some, such as the pretty, pink-flowered 'Hinomayo', retain.

In general azaleas need the same conditions of cultivation as rhododendrons, viz.: an acid or neutral soil. If lime is present the deciduous species and hybrids should be grown in prepared beds of bracken peat while the dwarfs will do well on peat terraces or in raised beds of acid material overlying a layer of gravel. Azaleas do better in heavy soil than light. When grown in light soils, plenty of humus and moisture-holding material should be added. It helps also to place slabs of stone or large boulders over the roots. The North American species will do well even in very moist, near swampy, conditions and are particularly happy by a stream or pool. They will, however, grow perfectly well in ordinary loam in semi-shade. I have seen it stated that azaleas grow best in full sun. This is certainly not my experience. In

239

North Wales where nobody can say that the sun is particularly savage, the flowers of even long-established bushes of azaleas fade badly and wilt quickly in full sun. To get azaleas to last long in flower, semi-shade is necessary for all but the Kurume and some of the *indicum* evergreen types. Such light shade is to be found in most gardens on the west or north of hedges or large evergreens, or beneath the light shade of ornamental cherries, styraxes, sorbus species or maples.

Evergreen azaleas are usually propagated by cuttings and so are sold on their own roots. When buying deciduous azaleas it is essential to buy only plants that are on their own roots as grafted plants sucker badly and the sucker growths are not easy to detect.

## Deciduous Azalea Species

Most of the deciduous azaleas of the world come from North America and from Japan. At present they are themselves botanically regarded as a series of the genus Rhododendron and are divided into sub-series just as are many of the rhododendron series. Members of the same sub-series are sometimes to be found in both Japan and America—evidence of the pattern of their evolution and drift across the world via the no-longer-existent land bridge above the Bering Strait.

### SUB-SERIES CANADENSE

*********albrechtii* A. (5–6 ft. × 4 ft.) May. Japan. Bright pink.

This is one of the loveliest of all azaleas with fresh green leaves and waxy, 'butterfly' flowers that in a good form will be a really bright pink and in some clones may verge almost on to brilliant rose-magenta. It is very hardy and free flowering once established and is a lightly built shrub and when bearing its numerous rather small but very bright blooms before the leaves appear, gives an airy and delightful effect.

*******canadense* A. (2 ft. × 3 ft.) April. North America. Lilac.

A modest little species with grey-green leaves and small lilac-lavender flowers, *canadense* is an adorable species to combine with the smaller narcissi such as the informal *Narcissus pseudo-narcissus*, the wild 'Lent Lily'. It needs moister ground than most but while suitable for planting at the edge of a stream or pool it will do equally well in peaty soil in a shady spot that does not dry out. It suckers freely and so may be increased by rooted off-sets until worthwhile drifts are established.

*********vaseyi* A. (8 ft. × 6 ft.) North America. May. Soft pink.

Less brilliant in colour than those of *albrechtii*, the flowers of *vaseyi* are rather larger and of a soft pretty pink that makes them most attractive. They are widely open with reflexed petals and a white flare of upswept protruding stamens. The flowers vary a little in their shade of soft pink and are slightly spotted with greeny-brown on the upper petals. There is also a fine white form. The rather narrow leaves colour brilliantly in the autumn.

*****pentaphyllum* is a beautiful Japanese species with bright rose-pink flowers, but unfortunately it does not flower freely in all gardens. The warm, mild climate of the south-west suits it admirably and there it is the first deciduous azaleas of the season to flower.

Luteum Sub-species

*******arborescens* A. (8 ft. × 6 ft.) North America. July. White.

This is a beautiful late-flowering species for a green and shady place. It needs a certain amount of moisture to bloom freely. The flowers are white, long-tubed, beautifully shaped, of good texture and with a strong heliotrope scent.

******atlanticum* B. (3 ft. × 3 ft.) North America. June. White.

A freely-suckering shrub with arching sprays of soft green foliage which arch down to form an attractive mound-shaped bush. It is very free-flowering as long as it is grown where the shade is not too dense. On the other hand it needs shelter and a moist woodsy soil. Woodland or semi-woodland conditions suit it best. The long-tubed flowers open from pink-tinged buds to pure white and are light and airy in appearance. It is a delightful species.

*******calendulaceum* A. (6 ft. × 4 ft.) North America. June. Scarlet-orange.

Tough and strong growing with fine autumn colour and long-tubed flowers not unlike those of the Ghent hybrids of which it is an ancestor—in fact 'Coccinea Speciosa' is thought by many to be merely a form of this brilliant species. Its flowers range from deep-rich yellow to a brick-scarlet. The chromosome counts of this azalea show such variation that it is thought by some botanists to be a natural hybrid.

\*\*\*\*\*\*\**canescens* A. (6 ft. × 4 ft.) North America. May. Pink.

This species is not very often seen but is at least as attractive as many of the Ghents, with similar shaped flowers of warm clear pink with a richer tone in the tube and an exceptionally sweet scent. *Roseum* and *nudiflorum* are very near to this species.

\*\*\*\*\*\*\*\**japonicum* A. (3 ft. × 3 ft.) May. Japan. Yellow to flame and scarlet.

This species is thought to be the ancestor of the so-called 'mollis' azaleas. At one time it was thought that they were descended from the species *molle* but this seems so consistently tender that it seems more likely that they have sprung from *japonicum* and, in fact, a great many seem to be no more than colour forms of this brilliant species with its wide funnel-shaped flowers which range from yellow through salmon and flame to near-scarlet. It colours well in autumn.

\*\*\*\*\*\**lutem* A. (4–6 ft. × 5 ft.) Eastern Europe to the Caucasus. May. Yellow.

Indestructibly tough, this is the 'wild' yellow azalea which has made itself at home in many woodlands. Individually rather small, its honeysuckle-like flowers are rich in colour and sweetly-scented. It is a good azalea to blend with the colours of the brighter hybrids and is particularly effective drifting through the pink and flame-coloured azaleas where these are grown in a mass. Rich autumn colour adds to its usefulness and it is a plant that may be used anywhere in the woodland or the wild garden without fear of 'startling the nightingales'. Its scent, rising on the air of a warm May afternoon is particularly nostalgic and forever brings back to me a hillock overlooking the garden at Bettws-Garmon near Caernarvon where this azalea, the common purple *Rhododendron ponticum* and *Olearia macrodonta* make large mounds of yellow, purple and ash-white and the scent of the azalea mingles with that of the daisy bush in an indescribably heady mixture.

\*\*\*\*\*\*\*\**occidentale* A. (5 ft. × 5 ft.) North America. June. White or blush.

Parent of a number of hybrids famous for their scent, this species is itself one of my favourite azaleas. Its flowers are quite large and of good texture. They vary in colour from white with a yellow eye to blush-shaded-pink and are magnificently scented. Its autumn colour, too, is good. Flowering in June, it should be planted in shade as in sun its blooms quickly droop.

\*\*\*\*\*\**prunifolium* A. (8 ft. × 7 ft.) North America. July–August. Orange-scarlet.

This species is useful for its late flowering and should be grown in every garden where there is room for it. I have given it only two stars because it takes a long time to flower freely and because its long-tubed flowers though brilliant in warm weather are a dullish orange if they open during cold spells. They have not quite the quality of *occidentale* or *canescens*.

\*\*\*\*\*\**viscosum* A. (4 ft. × 3 ft.) North America. July. White.

Making large thickets of growth this species has usually only small flowers but with a very sweet scent. The pale pink *rhodanthum* and the blue-grey foliaged *glaucum* are apparently varieties of this species. *Nitidum* is later to flower. They are, I think, shrubs for an old-fashioned cottage garden where their quaint charm and sweet scent would be a delightful asset. The scent carries well and in woodland, too, it is worth planting a bush or two for this quality.

Schlippenbachii Sub-series

\*\*\*\*\*\*\*\**amagianum* A. (3 ft. × 3 ft.) Japan. Late July. Salmon-pink to brick.

This is a very distinct azalea with rosettes of substantial heart-shaped, pointed leaves and showy flowers of a rich bright salmon-pink ranging to brick. It needs shade to protect its flowers.

\*\*\*\*\*\*\*\**reticulatum* A. (5 ft. × 5 ft.) Japan. May. Purple.

Not everyone would agree with the four stars I have given

this species and I have read the opinion of at least one expert that it is not easy growing. However, I think that its bright purple 'butterfly' flowers are delightful and all the plants that I have known have done very well indeed in normal rhododendron conditions of moist, woodsy soil. Like many of the azalea species I think the flowers last longer and colour better in part shade. At Bulkeley Mill there is a plant of *reticulatum* over eight feet high but I think it has been drawn up by too much shade. It is a striking sight, however, grouped with the ruby-bells of *Rhododendron thomsonii* and the buff-ochre of *R.* 'Unique'.

*******schlippenbachii* B. (3 ft. × 3 ft.) Korea and Manchuria
　　　Early May. Pink.

This is a beautiful species with large, open flowers, varying from a warm blush to a deep rose-pink. It has good leaves which colour very well in autumn. It does well in full sun and in cold districts will benefit from wall protection though care must be taken not to let it become dry at the roots when grown in such a situation. In fact it is an azalea which needs a reasonably moist soil to flower freely.

*******quinquefolium* B. (8 ft. × 5 ft.) Japan. April–May. White.

This is a species which needs shade and a moist soil, Its flowers are charming—icy white with cool, green spots. Unfortunately it is apt to be shy-flowering.

*****weyrichii* B. (3 ft. × 3 ft.) Japan. June. Salmon-red to
　　　brick.

In colour, like a deep *amagianum* which species it resembles in leaf. Its flowers, however, are smaller and have a deep mauve flare.

### Mostly Evergreen Japanese Species

SUB-SERIES OBTUSUM

******indicum* (macrantha) B. (2–3 ft. × 3 ft.) Japan. June–
　　　July. White, orange, pink, red, purple.

The type species of a very useful, late-flowering group of dwarf evergreen azaleas which vary in height from two to three feet. Its evergreen foliage is neat, dark, and slightly hairy when young. Much hardier than was originally thought it needs some shade to prolong the length of its flowering period and to prevent the richer-coloured forms from fading. In cold districts it may occasionally be cut back by severe frost but will usually grow strongly again from the root. It is the parent of the lovely Satsuki hybrids.

## Kurume Group

\*\*\*\*\*\*\*\**kaempferi* A. (7 ft. × 3 ft.) May–June. Japan. Orangy-salmon.

This species is only semi-evergreen and the flowers show up well against the rather open, and upright, pattern of the branches. Taller than the other members of the group, it may reach seven feet or more in height. It is very hardy but needs light shade if the flowers are to last well. Its leaves usually colour well in autumn. One of the parents of the garden Kurumes, it is a useful species in its own right. It has two very useful late-flowering forms 'Mikado' and 'Daimio' which are dealt with later in the hybrid and garden forms section.

\*\*\*\*\*\*\**kiusianum* (*obtusum* var. *japonicum*) A. (1½ ft. × 2 ft.) May. Japan. Lilac.

Thought to be the wild type of some of the Kurume azaleas, some of which have interbred with *kaempferi*, this is a pleasant little azalea. Small and dense in habit, it is slow-growing and makes a dark mound of small, nearly deciduous leaves and covered with flowers about the size of those of 'Kirin' but not of hose-in-hose formation. They may be white, pink, lilac or purple, although most that I have seen have been near the last two shades.

*obtusum*. April. Japan.

To describe this species is difficult as nobody knows whether the true plant is in cultivation in this country or not. The variety *amoenum* is often regarded as near the type with small dark leaves, attractively tiered branches and masses of small magenta flowers. The clone 'Amoenum Coccineum' has bright red flowers. The magenta form has been decried by purists on grounds of its strident colour but in my opinion both are attractive plants. The late-flowering 'Macrostemon' is thought to be a form of the species and is perhaps better known in the garden form 'Kokinshita'.

> ***linearifolium* (*macrosepalum*) B. (3 ft. × 3 ft.) May. Rose-lavender.

A botanical curiosity, this species has long, narrow, soft-green, hairy leaves and looks when out of flower more like some form of cut-leaf maple rather than an azalea. The flowers are mere strips of rose-lavender. In my experience it is not a good 'doer' out of doors, but is an interesting and attractive plant for a cold greenhouse.

> ********** *mucronatum* (ledifolium) A. (2 ft. × 4 ft.) May. Japan.

This is a beautiful species, low-growing and spreading with very large, well-shaped white flowers with faint green or brown markings and deep-emerald, softly hairy leaves. It is very hardy as is the soft lavender form *mucronatum* var. *ripense* which is thought by some to be the wild form of the species. 'Bulstrode' is taller and stronger growing with silkily-furred leaves. Its white flowers are tinged and edged with lavender. A plant listed as a 'Malvaticum' × *kaempferi* hybrid 'Atalanta' resembles this species very closely and has large soft-purple flowers. Its leaves, however, though similar to those of the species in some respects, are hairless. The loveliest variety of all has its large white flowers softly striped with pink. This was grown at Bulkeley Mill under the name 'Noordtianum' and is low and spreading in habit. In their book, *Modern Rhododendrons*, Messrs. E. H. M. and P. A. Cox describe the pink-striped plant under this name. Some nurseries, however, describe 'Noordtianum' as pure white but I think the pink-striped variety is the true plant and I should like to hear from any nurseryman who has it.

> *****simsii* D. (Eventually 5 ft. × 5 ft.) May. China.

This very tender azalea is the parent of many of the greenhouse hybrids. It has a hardier form, var. *eriocarpum*, which flowers in June and July and is the forerunner of the useful Gumpo group of late-flowering hybrids. The Gumpos are under a foot in height, neat and spreading with single or double flowers in various colours. They are reasonably hardy and will be discussed later in this chapter under the hybrid and garden form section of late-flowering evergreen azaleas.

*******yedoense* A. (3 ft. × 3 ft.) early May.

This is one of those plants of which a long cultivated form has been taken for the type. It is a compact, neat shrub with double pale mauve flowers that are quite pretty in shade. The wild variety *poukhanense* is a very attractive plant for woodland or to grow beside a stream and has pale lilac, fragrant flowers about two inches across.

## HYBRID AZALEAS

**Deciduous—Early Flowering**

(As with all azaleas it is essential that they are grown on their own roots.) Some of this group can be 'miffy' and all need a mulch.

MOLLIS GROUP. A. (4–6 ft. × 8 ft.). Little Scent. Early May.

There are so many of these azaleas, descended mainly from *japonicum*, which have now largely been superseded by the Exbury–Knap Hill group that I have picked out only a few of the best and more vigorous.

******'Adriaan Koster'.

Large, rich flowers of mid-yellow with orange spots on upper petal.

******'Babeuff'.

Medium-sized flowers of bright salmon with an orange flare. Vigorous. This is actually a seedling strain which breeds true to the parent.

*******'Christopher Wren'.

Very large trusses of large deep-yellow flowers opening from orange buds. One of the best of the group and a strong grower.

*******'Comte de Gomer'.

A very good pink hybrid.

****'Koster's Brilliant Red'.

Under this name are many examples of a seedling strain that

always came approximately true to colour. In fact, they vary slightly but one can usually be sure of a good bright red for garden purposes if one buys a plant under this description.

\*\*\*\*\*\*'Lemonora'.

Apricot with pink shading.

\*\*\*\*\*\*'Mrs. Peter Koster'.

A good 'red' mollis. The flowers are actually a vivid orange-red.

\*\*\*\*\*\*\*'Queen Emma'.

Equal to the Knap Hill and Exbury strains in size of flower though less vigorous. In colour this hybrid is a soft-apricot with richer tones on the upper petals.

\*\*\*\*\*'Salmon Queen'.

A large-flowered good pink with an orange flare.

\*\*\*\*\*\*'Spek's Brilliant'.

Large orange-scarlet flowers with a green flare.

\*\*\*\*\*'Yellow Prince'.

Large rich-yellow flowers.

## RUSTICA FLORE-PLENO GROUP

These hybrids have large, double flowers and are the result of crossing the Mollis with the Ghent hybrids. The flowers last long in semi-shade and are most attractive.

\*\*\*\*\*\*\*'Freya'. A.

Sweetly scented with orange-pink buds opening to bright rose double flowers which quickly fade to an apricot-tinted yellow. This is a good hybrid.

\*\*\*\*\*\*'Il Tasso'. A.

Double rose-red, tinted salmon flowers.

\*\*\*\*\*\*\*'Norma'. A.

Larger flowered than 'Freya' and more vigorous in habit. It is rather more aggressive in the brightness of its rose-pink double flowers but is none the less a good azalea.

\*\*\*\*\*\*\*'Phebe'. A.

A pretty hybrid with sweetly scented, pale-yellow double flowers.

# Azalea Species and Hybrids

## GHENT HYBRIDS

These hybrids have smaller flowers than the Mollis and Rustica Flore Pleno group and flower late in May and at the beginning of June. They are hardy and vigorous. Most have excellent autumn colour.

*******'Altaclarense'.

Very strong growing and earlier in bloom than the rest of the group with good trusses of deep yellow flowers opening from red-tipped orange buds. Especially good autumn leaf colour. 'Altaclarense Sunbeam' is more apricot in colour with larger flowers.

*******'Amabilis'.

A pretty variety that is not often seen with cream flowers flushed with pink, edged and tipped deep-rose and with a yellow flare.

*******'Aurore de Royghem'.

Excellent in habit and growth with beautifully shaped pale rose flowers of which the top petal is yellow.

*******'Bouquet de Flore'.

June-flowering and one of the finest of all azaleas, strong growing with bright salmon flowers with a pale central stripe down each petal and an orange-yellow flare. This hybrid has a most attractive leaf pattern and excellent autumn colour. Blooming late I find it needs shade which will often delay its flowering until late June when it is particularly useful to lend a warmer note to the mock-oranges and other midsummer shrubs.

*******'Coccinea Grandiflora'.

This particularly brilliant azalea is probably a form of *calendulaceum,* itself thought to be a natural hybrid. It is larger in flower and brighter in its glowing orange-red than the popular 'Coccinea Speciosa' which it should replace whenever it can be obtained.

*******'Emma'.

A showy plant with warm salmon-pink flowers with an orange flare. As it flowers earlier than 'Bouquet de Flore' both may well be used.

249

******'Guelder Rose'.

Good yellow flowers with a flush of apricot quickly passing to ivory and yellow. A good azalea to place between quarrelsome colours.

******'Joseph Baumann'.

Bright coral-red.

*******'Nancy Waterer'.

Vigorous with good rich-yellow flowers. A splendid azalea.

*******'Prince Henri de Pays Bas'.

A good late hybrid to extend the season with large salmon-pink flowers that are shaded with vermilion and a dark orange top petal.

******'Rembrandt'.

An uncommon, small-growing hybrid with large trusses of tiny bright raspberry-pink flowers. Good garden value and an interesting plant to associate with old *spinosissima* roses.

********'Unique'.

A strong growing azalea that is good enough and bright enough to stand alone. 'Unique' will make a shrub up to eight feet high with vivid orange-flame buds opening to yellow with an orange-gold upper petal. It is quite brilliant in its effect in the garden.

DOUBLE-FLOWERED GHENT HYBRIDS. A.

These hybrids are smaller and later in flower than the Rustica Flore-Pleno group.

*******'Corneille'.

A pretty, old-fashioned azalea with double flowers of soft rich pink which pale as they age.

********'Fanny'.

This is a fine hybrid with large trusses of deep strawberry-rose flowers suffused with orange and fading to soft rose. It quarrels with other pinks and reds and should either be planted alone or with the soft buff-yellow double 'Narcissiflorum' or with the uncommon single Ghent 'Guelder Rose' (see the previous list). A compact, neat habit coupled to robust growth and the fine autumn colour makes this a first-class azalea.

*******'La Surprise'.

A useful late variety with salmon-pink flowers flushed with deep yellow.

\*\*\*\*\*\*\*'Narcissiflorum'.

A pretty hybrid with starry flowers of soft buff-yellow and a very sweet scent.

\*\*\*\*\*\*\*'Raphael de Smet'.

One of the most pleasing of these hybrids with pale salmon-pink flowers fading to buff-pink. It has a good leaf pattern and fine autumn colour.

OCCIDENTALE HYBRIDS. A.

This group contains some very attractive hybrids bred mainly for their scent. They are very hardy and make bushes that are in time six to eight feet high. Their flowers last better in semi-shade.

\*\*\*\*\*\*\*'Delicatissimum'.

This hybrid has large slightly frilly creamy flowers flushed with rose and with an orange flare. Sweetly scented.

\*\*\*\*\*\*\*'Exquisitum'.

Large trusses of soft apricot-pink scented flowers.

\*\*\*\*\*\*'Graciosa'.

Rather similar with large, slightly frilled flowers of pale yellow flushed with rose.

\*\*\*\*\*\*'Irene Koster'.

Late, flowering well into June and needing shade, with long tubed blush flowers marked with yellow and rose. Very sweetly scented.

\*\*\*\*\*\*\*'Roseum'.

This hybrid is like a blush-pink *occidentale* with a yellow eye and rose-pink stripes down the outside of each petal. Excellent scent. Good autumn colour.

\*\*\*\*\*\*\*'Superbum'.

Frilly rich pink flowers tinged with yellow. Very sweet scent and fine autumn colour.

\*\*\*\*\*\*\*'Viscosepalum'.

Greeny buds opening to pure white flowers with a faint yellow flare. Fine carnation scent and good autumn colour. 'Viscosepalum

Daviesii' has creamy flowers slightly flushed with rose and with a deep yellow flare. It is late flowering, equally finely scented and has good autumn colour.

Various nurseries offer seedling strains of these scented hybrids which are excellent for drift-planting, notable among which are Sunningdale's 'Harry White's' hybrids and the *prunifolia* × *occidentalis* hybrids offered by Knap Hill which flower in July and are of varying shades of pink and apricot. They are extremely useful for their late flowering but need shade and have not as much scent as the Harry White hybrids and the named varieties just listed.

## KNAP HILL AND EXBURY HYBRIDS

The breeding of these hybrids was begun by Anthony Waterer about 1870 and developed by Waterer's of Knap Hill, Slocock's of Goldsworth Old Nursery and Lionel de Rothschild at Exbury. They are developments of the mollis azaleas crossed with *calendulaceum*, *occidentale* (for large flowers and scent) and *arborescens* (also for scent).

With a few exceptions they flower in late May and June— all are very hardy and have brilliant autumn colour. They are vigorous growing up to six or eight feet and often are deliciously scented.

*******'Avocet'. Late May. Pinky-white.

This is a fine vigorous hybrid with very fragrant, large white-flushed-pink flowers.

*******'Brazil' (Exbury). Late May. Tangerine.

A brilliant large-flowered tangerine that is apt to fade in full sun but lasts long in semi-shade.

*******'Basilisk' (Exbury). Late May. Pale yellow.

Large pale yellow flowers with a deeper flare and bronze young growth.

*******'Berry Rose' (Exbury). June. Salmon.

A good salmon with a tinge of orange. The flowers are shaded at the throat with yellow and the young growth is bronze. It is a very strong grower.

********'Buzzard'. Late May. Pale yellow and pink.

A very sweetly-scented hybrid with large pale yellow and pink flowers. Excellent in shade.

\*\*\*\*\*\*\*\*'Cecile' (Exbury). June. Pink and yellow.

This hybrid is one of the best of the group with satin-pink and yellow flowers that sometimes measures as much as four inches across and are carried on a neat, compact plant.

\*\*\*\*\*\*\*'Devon'. Mid-June. Red.

A hybrid with particularly good scent. Bluish young foliage and deep-red flowers. This is the azalea that used to be known as 'Satan'.

\*\*\*\*\*\*\*'Farall Yellow'. Late May. Yellow.

A good yellow with well-shaped flowers. The petals are slightly crimped at the edges and it has a compact habit.

\*\*\*\*\*\*\*'Firefly' (Exbury). Mid-June. Rose-red.

A large-flowered, deep rose-red with a faint orange flare.

\*\*\*\*\*\*\*\*'Gannet'. Late May. Pale pink.

Large, scented, pale pink with an orange-yellow flare and a sweet scent—one of my favourite azaleas.

\*\*\*\*\*\*\*\*'George Reynolds'. Mid-May. Yellow.

This, perhaps the first of the original Knap Hills, was the azalea from which Mr. Lionel de Rothschild bred the Exbury group. It is exceptionally large-flowered and a fine parent with deep butter-yellow flowers that are green at the throat and spotted with deeper yellow.

\*\*\*\*\*\*\*\*'Gold Crest'. Late May. Yellow.

This is a low-growing azalea with a dense habit and rich yellow flowers. It is fine to group in front of later or earlier-flowering rhododendrons as it shows up so well against their dark green foliage.

\*\*\*\*\*\*\*\*'Golden Eye'. Mid-June. Red.

A particularly good Knap Hill with large rich red flowers blotched with gold, and bronzy foliage.

\*\*\*\*\*\*\*\*'Golden Oriole'. Early May. Yellow.

Similar to 'Gold Crest' but earlier to flower and very sweetly scented.

\*\*\*\*\*\*'Harvest Moon'. Mid-June. Pale yellow.

A fine pale yellow that looks well in shade. Not as good a

grower as some and needs mulching and feeding to do itself justice.

\*\*\*\*\*\*\*\*'Hotspur' (Exbury). June. Orange.

Very large brilliant trusses of 'hot' orange-vermilion with a greeny-yellow flare and bronzy foliage.

\*\*\*\*\*\*\*\*'Klondyke' (Exbury). Mid-May. Orange-yellow.

Wide-open orange-yellow flowers tinged with green. Bronzy foliage. A brilliant azalea.

\*\*\*\*\*\*\*'Lapwing'. Early to mid-May. Pale yellow.

The first of the very sweetly-scented azaleas to bloom. Vigorous and good with full trusses of pale yellow and pink-tinted flowers.

\*\*\*\*\*\*\*\*'Marion Merriman'. Mid-May. Yellow.

Another fine early yellow. Rich and bold in colour with a spreading habit. Able to stand alone in the garden.

\*\*\*\*\*\*\*'Rosella'. Mid-June. Pink.

A vigorous plant with large, scented, clear pink flowers.

\*\*\*\*\*\*\*'Sandpiper'. Mid-May. Pink and yellow.

Another exquisitely scented hybrid with pale pink and yellow flowers.

\*\*\*\*\*\*\*\*'Strawberry Ice' (Exbury). Early June. Pink.

Pink, edged with deeper pink and with a yellow flare. Light green foliage and a fine bushy habit.

\*\*\*\*\*\*\*\*'Whitethroat'. Early June. Double white.

An unusual hybrid. A white, double-flowered hybrid with light green foliage. Cool and lovely in shade.

\*\*\*\*\*\*\*'Wryneck'. Early June. Sulphur yellow.

Rich sulphur yellow just tinged with pink and very sweetly scented. Vigorous in habit. In effect a finer and more satisfactory 'Harvest Moon'.

## Evergreen Hybrids and Garden Forms

Early-flowering Kurume and *obtusum* 'Amoenum' groups.

Small-leaved and neat growing to four or five feet and doing well in full sun where their flowers show little tendency to fade.

\*\*\*\*\*\*\*\*'Agamujin'. B. White.

Neat and compact in habit and very pretty with frilly white hose-in-hose flowers spotted with green.

\*\*\*\*\*'Aioi' (Fairy Queen). C. Rose-lavender.

One of the Wilson Fifty but unfortunately not very hardy; it is nevertheless delightful for warm gardens with bright rose-lavender hose-in-hose flowers.

\*\*\*\*\*\*'Asagasumi'. B. Magenta.

Another Wilson plant with near-magenta flowers that are, as always, forgivable in these gay little azaleas, especially when associated with the whites, pinks and reds in an all-colour group.

\*\*\*\*\*\*\*'Aya Kammuri' (Pinkie). B. Salmon-red.

Another of the 'Fifty' with warm salmon flowers set off by white anthers.

\*\*\*\*\*\*'Azuma Kagami' (Pink Pearl). C. Pink.

A Wilson plant that is not too hardy, especially when young. It is extremely pretty with pink hose-in-hose flowers with chestnut spotting.

\*\*\*\*\*\*'Benegiri'. A. Rose-crimson.

Bright rose-crimson. Slow growing but a tough little plant.

\*\*\*\*\*\*\*'Choraku'. B. Lavender-pink.

Pretty, lavender-pink flowers with white anthers.

\*\*\*\*\*\*\*\*'Fude Tsuka'. B. Rose and cream.

Rose and cream hose-in-hose flowers.

\*\*\*\*\*\*'Gaeshi'. A. Salmon-pink.

Starry, striped flowers of deep salmon-pink with white anthers.

\*\*\*\*\*\*\*'Gosho Zakura' (Vanity). Rose.

One of Wilson's Fifty with large, deep rose flowers.

\*\*\*\*\*\*\*'Hana Asobi' (Sultan). Rose-carmine.

Another of the 'Fifty' with pretty rose-carmine flowers.

\*\*\*\*\*\*\*'Hatsugiri'. A. Magenta.

A vigorous and hardy plant. Its quite large, brilliant flowers and tiered habit make it a pleasing garden subject.

\*\*\*\*\*\*\*\*'Hinodegiri' (Red Hussar). B. Crimson.

Another easy, vigorous dwarf, eventually making a tiered bush of up to four feet or more. One of the Wilson Fifty.

\*\*\*\*\*\*\*\*'Hinomayo'. A–B. Pink.

A very good, hardy, and easy plant with fresh, lettuce-green leaves and large rose-pink flowers. One of the best of the early-blooming dwarfs.

\*\*\*\*\*\*\*'Ima Shojo' (Christmas Cheer). A. Scarlet-crimson.

The English name of this hybrid is misleading as it flowers with the other members of this section in April. It is slow growing but very hardy and free-blooming with small bright scarlet-crimson flowers.

\*\*\*\*\*\*\*'Kasane Kagaribi' (Rosita). B. Rose.

One of the more hardy of Wilson's Kurumes with deep rose-pink flowers.

\*\*\*\*\*\*\*'Kasumi Gaseki' (Elf). B. Pale pink.

An extremely pretty Wilson azalea. Hardy but not very strong growing with small flowers of soft pink.

\*\*\*\*\*\*\*'Katsura No Hana' (Ruth). C. Lilac-pink.

Like too many of the original Wilson Fifty this hybrid is tender when young but it is most attractive with white-anthered flowers of bright lilac-pink.

\*\*\*\*\*\*\*\*'Kirin' (Coral Bells). B–. Rose-pink.

Another of Wilson's fifty best Kurumes, chosen for the beauty of their flowers and habit rather than for any great degree of hardiness. 'Kirin' is apt to be slightly tender when young. I think, though, that it is the prettiest of the section with warm rose-pink, hose-in-hose flowers. It is also one of the first to flower. We group it with 'Hinode-giri', 'Hatsugiri' and 'Hinomayo' and the effect of their strong, clear colour with the white of 'Kure-no-yuki' is very pleasing.

\*\*\*\*\*\*\*'Kokinran'. B. Pale pink.

A starry-flowered little hybrid—pink with white at the throat —with a most attractive tiered habit of growth.

\*\*\*\*\*\*\*\*'Kure-no-yuki' (Snowflake). B+. White.

Very hardy and a good 'doer' with large, white, hose-in-hose flowers. A beautiful plant in its own right and useful to soften the more strident colours and to enable them to 'mix'.

*******'Rashomon' (Meteor). B.

Wilson's Number 37 and a very good, bright salmon-red with large flowers.

'Tamafuyo' (Fancy). B.

A Wilson plant. Reasonably hardy with small, starry white flowers set off by brown stamens.

## Dwarf Evergreen Mid-Season Hybrids—reaching to four or five feet when fully grown. Most need shade to prevent the flowers from bleaching in the sun.

********'Addy Wery'. A. Dark scarlet.

A hardy, strong-growing plant with rather narrow flowers of a very deep, and slightly darker, scarlet than most.

********'Eddy' (*kaempferi* × *oldhamii*). B. Rose-red.

Exbury-bred with large bright rose-red flowers that fade badly in the sun.

*******'Favorita'. B. Crimson-pink.

Smaller but attractive flowers of crimson-pink.

********'Jeannette'. A. Rose.

Very large rose-pink flowers on a vigorous, easy plant.

********'John Cairns' ('Hinodegiri' × 'Orange Beauty'). A. Indian red.

A little later than most to flower. Very hardy and not so apt to fade in the sun as are most of the orange-reds.

********'Leo' (*kaempferi* × *oldhamii*). B. Orange-pink.

One of the latest of the group to flower, with a low spreading habit, and orange-pink flowers, this is a useful and vivid azalea for shade.

*******'Oberon' ('Malvaticum' × *kaempferi*). A. Pink.

This is a fine azalea, very hardy and free flowering with medium-sized flowers of soft pink.

*******'Orange Beauty' ('Hinodegiri' × *kaempferi*). B. Orange.

Worth three stars when grown in semi-shade but fades hideously in sun. Good habit and vigorous growth.

********'Pink Treasure' ('Malvaticum' × *kaempferi*). B. Pink.

Very like 'Hinomayo' but taller and slightly later to bloom.

\*\*\*\*\*\*\*'Princess Beatrice'. B. Orange.

A good orange-flowered hybrid that needs shade, 'Princess Irene' is very similar and 'Princess Juliana' is more of an orange-red. All are vivid when kept out of the sun. These are nearer the Vuykiana group in type and are, I believe, derived from crosses of a Vuyk hybrid and *indicum*.

\*\*\*\*\*\*\*\*'Sir William Lawrence' (*kaempferi* × *oldhamii*). B. Orchid-pink.

A good Exbury evergreen hybrid, tall growing and attractive, with orchid-pink flowers.

\*\*\*\*\*\*\*'Willy' ('Malvaticum' × *kaempferi*). A.

Appallingly named but one of the most useful with a spreading habit and pretty rose-pink flowers that do not fade.

*Late-Flowering Evergreen Azaleas*—all are best in semi-shade.

\*\*\*\*\*\*\*'Akatsuki'. B. Late June. Rose.

Belonging to the reasonably hardy *indicum* group this is a sturdy, spreading clone with large, deep rose-coloured flowers. 'Asagi' is similar but, to my mind, not quite so good.

\*\*\*\*\*\*\*'Bungo-nishiki'. B. Late June. Terra-cotta.

A double-flowered *indicum* clone with semi-double terra-cotta flowers.

\*\*\*\*\*\*\*'Caldwellii'. B. July. Rose-pink.

An *indicum* hybrid making a vigorously spreading low bush with light green leaves and bright rose-pink flowers.

\*\*\*\*\*\*\*\*'Daimio'. B. Late June. Tomato red.

A seedling of *kaempferi*. Semi-evergreen, reaching four feet, with open branching and 'Orange Beauty' type flowers. Needs shade.

\*\*\*\*\*\*'Hexe'. B. June. Magenta.

Absolutely hardy and a useful late-flowering azalea with large, semi-double magenta flowers. Taller than the others in this group this hybrid will eventually reach four feet high. It is very similar to 'Forsteranum' which it should entirely replace as that hybrid is not fully hardy.

\*\*\*\*\*\*\*'Balsaminiflorum'. B. June. Salmon.

Very low growing with dark, silkily-haired leaves and double, rosette-like, salmon-pink flowers.

\*\*\*\*\*\*\*'Crispiflorum'. B. June.

Taller, reaching to four feet or more with wavy-petalled, semi-double flowers of rich carmine-pink.

****'Kokinshita'. B. June. Salmon-orange.

Like a single-flowered variety 'Balsaminiflorum' with rather thin-textured salmon-orange flowers. Fades badly in sun and is a weak grower. The plants offered under the type *indicum* are usually much better and more effective azaleas. They range in colour from orange-pink to rose and lilac-pink and are well worth a place in the garden, particularly as they do not easily fade and will stand sun and wind provided they have a moist root-run or are well-mulched.

***'Mikado'. B. June. Pale salmon.

Flowering at the same time as *indicum*, this clone of *kaempferi* is useful to give height to the group. It needs shade.

********'Satsuki'. A–B. June–July. Crimson-pink.

Probably the finest of the *indicum* group with neat, dark leaves, a good habit and long-lasting flowers that do not easily fade. It is also extremely hardy. Probably this should be included under the Satsuki hybrids at the end of this chapter and no doubt it will later receive a more distinctive clonal name. As it is, it was probably the first of the Satsuki group to reach us and so was given, probably quite wrongly, the name of the group.

********'Gumpo'. B. June–July. Pale colours.

Hardy members of a tender species, these are the 'Gumpo' azaleas and make very low bushes only six or nine inches high. Very neat and dark in appearance they bear large, long-lasting flowers that make them invaluable in the summer garden. 'Gumpo' is a lovely green-tinged white. 'Gumpo Fancy' is frilly blush with deep pink splashes and markings. 'Jitsugetsu' is a soft lavender-pink and 'Pink Gumpo' is white tinged with blush.

AZALEODENDRONS

This group consists of hybrids between the deciduous azaleas and evergreen rhododendrons. There are, in this section, one or two plants of exceptional beauty and garden worth. As a whole the group is apt to be sparsely foliaged or even semi-deciduous but the flowers are most attractive and in some cases have a strong, sweet scent. The azaleodendrons need a moist but well-drained, humus-rich soil and shelter from sun and wind.

\*\*\*'Azaleoides' (*ponticum* × *nudiflorum*). B. (3 ft. × 3 ft.). June–July. White, edged lilac.

Interesting because it is the first recorded rhododendron hybrid this plant has a quiet charm with its rounded trusses of white, azalea-like flowers edged with lilac and a delicious scent. 'Fragrans' and 'Odoratum' are both rather similar to it.

\*\*\*\*\*\*\*'Broughtonii Aureum' F.C.C. B. (*maximum* × *ponticum* × *sinensis*). June. (4 ft. × 3 ft.) Yellow.

Also, and perhaps more correctly, known as 'Norbitonense Broughtonense' this is, to my mind, the finest of the group, its only fault being the characteristic sparseness of its rich green leaves which, when young, have almost a violet tinge. The flowers are pale yellow, richly marked with a deeper colour and borne in compact trusses.

\*\*\*\*\*'Dr. Masters' (*japonicum* × 'Prince Camille de Rohan'). B. (5 ft. × 4 ft.) June. Salmon.

This is an azaleodendron with good foliage and it is also a vigorous, healthy grower. The flowers, opening from pretty pink buds, are salmon flushed with yellow.

\*\*\*\*\*\*'Galloper Light'A.M. B.(3 ft. × 3 ft.) May.Apricot-pink.

Another good hybrid with reasonably generous foliage and large trusses of rose-pink flowers that gradually turn to apricot-yellow.

\*\*\*'Glory of Littleworth' A.M. B. (3 ft. × 3 ft.) June. Cream with an orange blotch.

Many people think that this hybrid with its flowers of old ivory boldly splotched with orange is one of the most beautiful but for some reason I dislike it. The blotch to my mind is over-bold and although the long blue-green leaves are handsome enough; it is not a good grower.

, \*\*\*\*\*'Govenianum'. B. (5 ft. × 4 ft.) June–July. Lavender.

This old hybrid is like a deeper-coloured 'Azaleoides' in appearance and is attractive with its soft-green leaves and green-tinged lavender flowers. Planted with 'Azaleoides' or 'Fragrans' it offers a pleasant contrast. It would look delightful with 'Broughtonii Aureum' and if the latter were planted in deeper shade it might be possible to make the flowering coincide. It is certainly worth trying to achieve this combination.

\*\*\*\*\*\*\*\*'Norbitonense Aureum' ('Smithii Aureum') is equally good with slightly bullate, rich-green leaves and good trusses of soft-yellow flowers. Both hybrids spring from the same cross but 'Smithii Aureum' is more vigorous, reaching six feet or more in time and is rather more prolific in foliage. The flowers have a distinctive old-world look.

### FERNDOWN HYBRIDS

A June–July group of dwarf evergreen hybrids. Very free flowering and hardy. This useful race was introduced by Messrs. Stewarts Nurseries of Ferndown, Dorset. Most of these hybrids need to be planted in light shade to prevent the flowers fading.

\*\*\*\*\*\*'Andrew Elphinstone'. (4 ft. × 3½ ft.) Mid-July. Orange.

Much taller than the others of this group and so making a strong colour effect with its vivid orange, single flowers that show to their best against a green background. Needs some shade.

\*\*\*\*\*\*\*'Armada'. (1½ ft. × 1½ ft.) June. Rose.

A useful dwarf, delightful to make an edging to a shady path or to group on the shady side of a peat-garden. The flowers are single, small and dainty and rose-pink in colour.

\*\*\*\*\*\*\*\*'Beatrice Stewart'. (2½ ft. × 2½ ft.) June. Silver-pink.

This hybrid is fade-proof and will stand even full sun providing the soil does not dry out too much. Clear pretty pink flowers with a wavy edge to the petals.

\*\*\*\*\*\*\*'Cerita'. (3 ft. × 3 ft.) Mid-June. Mandarin red.

Needing shade but sizeable enough to be a notable feature in a shady border or to place at the base of a north wall.

\*\*\*\*\*\*\*'Clarissa'. (2½ ft. × 2½ ft.) Mid-June. Salmon.

One of the prettiest of the late-flowering dwarfs with frilly-petalled, pale orange-salmon hose-in-hose flowers. Needs shade to prevent fading.

\*\*\*\*\*\*\*'Crown Jewel'. (1 ft. × 1½ ft.) Mid-June. Scarlet.

Another hybrid with the very attractive type of hose-in-hose flower, this time in scarlet, 'Crown Jewel' is a neat foreground plant with dark evergreen leaves and a low spreading habit.

*******'Fenella'. (1½ ft. × 1½ ft.) June. White.

Very useful with its shapely white flowers to place between other colours. It makes an effective group with 'Beatrice Stewart' or 'Armada' and the lilac-coloured 'Ferndown Beauty'.

*******'Ferndown Beauty'. (2 ft. × 3 ft.) June. Lilac.

Taller, but spreading and most attractive with its large lilac-mauve flowers. Like the other hybrids of spreading habit, it is easily increased by layering. Shade.

*******'Ferndown Mandarin'. (3 ft. × 3 ft.) July. Red.

Useful to extend the season this is a fine hybrid with flowers of light mandarin-red.

*******'Ida'. (1¼ ft. × 1¼ ft.) June. Rose-pink.

This is a splendidly compact hybrid for the shady side of a rock-garden or peat-terrace or to plant in a mixed bed of dwarf rhododendrons and azaleas. Its rose-pink flowers are vivid and deep in colour.

********'Kilimanjaro'. (3 ft. × 4 ft.) June. White.

A particularly good taller white with a most effective greenish eye.

********'Lady Elphinstone'. (3 ft. × 2½ ft.) June. Salmon-pink.

Upright in habit and practically fade-proof, this is a useful and attractive plant with extremely pretty salmon-pink flowers. One of the best of the group.

********obtusum* 'Macrostemon Improved'. (1 ft. × 3 ft.) July. Deep orange.

Useful and good with a prostrate, spreading habit and vivid deep orange-coloured flowers that do, however, need shade to preserve their colour.

*******'Stewart's Treasure'. (2 ft. × 3 ft.) June. Pink.

Large, warm pink, single flowers make this an exceptionally pleasing clone. Its habit is neat and inclined to mound and spread.

*******'Vida Brown'. (1¼ ft. × 1¼ ft.) Mid–June. Rose-pink.

## Azalea Species and Hybrids

Neat and compact with deep rose-pink, hose-in-hose flowers. This is a favourite plant for peat-terraces and even window-boxes. Its flowers last longer in semi-shade.

### VUYKIANA GROUP

This group of hybrids was introduced by the Vuyk van Nes Nursery of Boskoop, Holland, and are bred from the mollis azalea 'J. C. van Tol' crossed either with a kaempferi hybrid, the Maxwell azalea (a form of *phoeniceum*, a species allied to *mucronatum*) or *mucronatum* in an attempt to produce hardier evergreen azaleas with larger flowers. In appearance they resemble the evergreen parents and one wonders whether the crosses in fact really came off or whether the plants are not the result of apomoxis—that is, a form of self-reproduction triggered off by the hybridizing without fertilization having occurred. At any rate little evidence of mollis blood is apparent. All the same the hybrids are a useful group, flowering in mid-to-late May, reasonably hardy and with large, well-shaped flowers. They are tall in habit but rather slow growing.

\*\*\*\*\*\*\*\*'Beethoven'. (2–3 ft. × 2–3 ft.) Orchid-purple.

This is a good hybrid of which the Maxwell azalea was the seed-parent. It bears large and showy single flowers of clear orchid-purple that measure nearly three inches across.

\*\*\*\*\*\*\*'Chopin'. (3 ft. × 3 ft.) Deep rose.

This plant offers a useful contrast to 'Beethoven' with flowers of deep rose with a deeper blotch.

\*\*\*\*\*\*\*'Joseph Haydn'. (3 ft. × 3 ft.). Lavender.

Another pleasant hybrid with large rosy-lavender flowers with a brownish blotch.

\*\*\*\*\*\*\*\*'Mozart'. (3 ft. × 3 ft.). Rosy-lilac.

Almost as large in flower as Beethoven—many of its blooms are quite two and a half inches across and are of a luminous rosy-lilac.

\*\*\*\*\*\*\*\*'Palestrina'. (3 ft. × 2 ft.) White.

One of the best white azaleas and a truly lovely plant with large white flowers blotched at the throat with chartreuse.

\*\*\*\*\*\*\*\*'Schubert'. (3 ft. × 3 ft.) Phlox-pink.

Attractive on its own or useful to group with the others as it has in its make-up the faintly purple tone common to most of the group. 'Schubert' has two-inch flowers of phlox-rose. In habit it strongly resembles *kaempferi* which was the seed-parent.

\*\*\*\*\*\*\*\*'Sibelius'. (1½ ft. × 2 ft.) Orange-red.

Quite different in tone and without any blue in its red, 'Sibelius' is lower in growth than most others in the group and has two-inch flowers of orange-red with a chocolate-purple blotch.

\*\*\*\*\*\*\*\*\*\*'Vuyk's Rosy Red' (3. ft. × 3 ft.) Rose-red.

Another good hybrid, adequately described by its name.

## GALE HYBRIDS

This is a group of evergreen hybrids bred by an American nurseryman, Joseph B. Gable of Stewartstown, Pennsylvania with hardiness as a primary aim. To this end the very hardy *yedoense* var. *poukhanense* was crossed with *kaempferi*. Secondary crosses and re-crosses were made, involving 'Hexe', *mucronatum*, *macrosepalum* and various Kurume hybrids. Only a few of these are at present in commerce in Britain but I hope more will eventually be introduced and for this reason I am listing some of the best below. Many are iron-hardy. Most flower in late April or May and in time make quite large spreading bushes up to four or five feet high and as much as eight feet wide.

\*\*\*\*\*\*\*'Apricot'. Apricot-pink.

One of the hardiest, with pretty apricot-pink flowers that do, alas, fade unless grown in shade.

\*\*\*\*\*\*\*\*'Carol'. Late May. Red.

Another extra-hardy hybrid with attractive hose-in-hose flowers of spiraea-red.

\*\*\*\*\*\*\*\*'Caroline Gable'. Rose-red.

Very hardy, with flowers almost two inches across and rose-red in colour.

\*\*\*\*\*\*'Claret'. Dark, wine red.

This is one of the few at present available in Britain but unfortunately it is not one of the most vigorous. Hardy enough, it is rather a poor grower. For a rock-garden or small peat-bed, however, it is ideal.

\*\*\*\*\*\*\*'Kathleen'. Pink.

One of the original *poukhanense* × *kaempferi* hybrids this is a reliably hardy plant with flowers of a pretty clear pink.

\*\*\*\*\*\*\*\*'Louise Gable'.

Spreading and low in growth with large semi-double flowers of bright purple-pink with a darker blotch this is a useful foreground azalea. Available in Britain.

\*\*\*\*\*\*\*\*'Rosebud'. June. Pink.

This hybrid is now available from at least one British nursery and is an excellent plant. Dense and low in habit with double hose-in-hose flowers of soft pink that resemble the rosebud after which it is named.

\*\*\*\*\*\*\*'Viola'. Petunia-purple.

In time this hybrid makes a very large plant. It is fascinating with large single flowers of reddish violet. It is said to be bred from *poukhanense* × *mucronatum* and is very hardy.

GLENN DALE HYBRIDS

These were developed by Mr. B. Y. Morrison, former director of the Plant Introduction Section of the U.S.A. Department of Agriculture and former director of the United States National Arboretum. The plan behind their breeding was to raise plants with flowers as large and varied as those of the greenhouse azaleas but to be hardy enough for the middle Atlantic seaboard of the U.S.A. Plants that fulfil this specification will be hardy almost anywhere in Britain. There are many fine hybrids among them but unfortunately only a few are as yet available in Britain.

\*\*\*\*\*\*\*'Advance'. (4 ft. × 5 ft.) May. Tyrian rose.

This hybrid has a dense, bushy habit, good dark-green leaves and two-inch flowers of Tyrian rose borne in trusses of two to four. Reliably hardy.

\*\*\*\*\*\*\*'Angela Place'. (3 ft. × 5 ft.) Early May. White.

Good and rather spreading in habit with three-inch wide-open flowers of pure white this is a handsome but rather formal plant.

\*\*\*\*\*\*\*'Bettina'. (5 ft. × 3 ft.) Late April. Carmine.

Rather like a tall Kurume in habit with trusses of carmine flowers.

*******'Colleen'. (6 ft. × 4 ft.) Bright pink.

Bred from *kaempferi*, this is a splendid plant for garden effect with almost lettuce-green leaves and trusses of two-inch, bright-pink flowers. It is exceptionally free flowering.

*******'Coquette' (5 ft. × 3 ft.) Early May. Salmon-pink.

With soft salmon-pink, hose-in-hose flowers this is one of the few Glenn Dales at present available in commerce in Britain.

******'Dimity'. (5 ft. × 3 ft.) Late April. White, flaked red.

Pretty and unusual in effect, this hybrid has the *kaempferi* habit and lighter green leaves with one-and-a-half-inch flowers of white, flaked and striped with red.

********'Robin Hood'. (5 ft. × 3 ft.) Late April. Rose-red.

Very large-rose red flowers up to four inches across. This hybrid can be bought in Britain.

*******'Souvenir'. (5 ft. × 3 ft.) Early May. Salmon-rose.

Now in Britain, this is an effective azalea. Arching in growth when fully grown, it has hose-in-hose flowers of salmon-pink with a deep rose blotch.

*******'Tanager'. (5 ft. × 5 ft.) May. Red.

A very good azalea with brilliant red, dark-blotched flowers and narrow, dark-green leaves. It is now available in Britain.

### SATSUKI HYBRIDS

These are late-flowering hybrids, mainly bred from the hardy *indicum* and the *indicum* var. *eriocarpum* group. Some, however, contain the blood of Belgian greenhouse azaleas. Very hardy, it is a pity that more are not available in Britain. Apart from the wrongly-named 'Satsuki' already mentioned, introductions to watch for are the spreading, frilly red striped white 'Gunrei'; the orange-red 'Keisetsu' and the Delft-rose form of 'Tamagiku'. There are many other Satsukis awaiting introduction from Japan. All are lovely in shape and many are white, flushed, margined, or striped, with rose, violet, pink, wistaria-purple, or red. Often the petals are frilled.

# Useful Addresses

꙳꙳꙳꙳꙳꙳꙳꙳꙳꙳꙳꙳꙳꙳

*Nurseries specializing in rhododendrons and azaleas (specify plants on own roots and selected clonal forms when ordering).*

Messrs. E. H. M. and P. A. Cox, Glendoick Gardens, Glendoick, Perthshire (species and some first class hybrids).

Mr. Michael Haworth-Booth, Farall Nurseries, Roundhurst, Haslemere, Surrey (also specializes in camellias and hydrangeas).

Messrs. Hydon Nurseries Ltd., Hydon Heath, near Godalming, Surrey (able to supply 'St. Tudy' and the new 'blues').

Messrs. Knap Hill Nursery, Knap Hill, Woking, Surrey (azaleas and older hybrids, shrubs and trees).

Messrs. Hillier and Sons, Winchester, Hampshire (species, hybrids, also shrubs and trees).

Messrs. G. Reuthe Ltd., Keston, Kent (species, hybrids, azaleas; plants exported).

Messrs. Sunningdale Nurseries, Woking, Surrey (species, newer hybrids, azaleas, shrubs, trees and underplanting).

Messrs. John Waterer, Sons and Crisp Ltd., Bagshot, Surrey.

*Rhododendron Peat*

Eclipse Peat Co., Ashcott P.O. Box 12, Bridgwater, Somerset.

267

# Useful Addresses

*Oak and Teak Tubs for alpine rhododendrons and azaleas*
> Thos. Trevis Smith Ltd., Hollybush Street, Cradley Heath, Staffordshire.

*Mist Equipment and Propagators*
> Roberts Electrical Company (Humex), 11–13 High Road, Byfleet, Surrey.

*Rhododendron Group of the R.H.S., and R.H.S.*
The Secretary, the Royal Horticulture Society, Vincent Square, London. S.W.1.

*The American Rhododendron Society*
> The Secretary, 3514 N. Russet Street, Portland 17, Oregon, U.S.A.

*Rhododendon Handbooks published by:*
> The Royal Horticultural Society, Vincent Square, S.W.1.

# General Index

269

# Index of Species and Hybrids

⟫⟫⟫⟫⟫⟫⟫⟫⟫⟫⟫⟫⟫⟫⟫⟫⟫⟪⟪⟪⟪⟪⟪⟪⟪⟪⟪⟪⟪⟪⟪

# Index of Species and Hybrids

## Index of Species and Hybrids

# Index of Species and Hybrids

# Index of Species and Hybrids

# Index of Species and Hybrids